Praise for Satisfaction Selling

"*Satisfaction Selling* is an absolute must-read! If you're looking to transcend competition and cultivate a fiercely loyal customer base, this book holds the key. At Hästens, we've embraced these strategies wholeheartedly, and the impact has been nothing short of remarkable. Our customers have transformed into passionate ambassadors, eagerly sharing their love for our exceptional brand and products. From established businesses to ambitious startups, *Satisfaction Selling* has the power to ignite business success worldwide."

Jan Ryde, 5th Generation CEO/Owner, Hästens Sängar AB & Author of "When Business Is Love"

"*Satisfaction Selling* is a must-read for anyone who wants to improve their B2B sales skills and results. The book offers practical and proven strategies for listening to what customers truly want, reading the signals of the other person by listening and seeing what's being communicated, and establishing good cooperation with the other person to create the right solution together. *Satisfaction Selling* is not only a book about sales; it's also a book about personal growth and development. By following the principles and practices in this book, you will not only increase your sales performance but also your satisfaction and fulfillment in your work and life."

Sascha Häuser, VP Sales, NKT Photonics

"Since 2008, when I was first introduced to the *Satisfaction Cycle*, it has been a great inspiration to me, and I have worked intensively with the model. I sincerely appreciate the ethics behind the model, and it has changed the way I operate my business - from a product-oriented approach to creating value in the sales process by aiding the customer in truly understanding their needs. If you work in sales, I would strongly recommend you read the book to understand the value of the model."

Rasmus Kriegel, Market Director, NIRAS

"The *Satisfaction Cycle* model supports both sales and coaching for managers. The defined steps make it a simple approach that provides structure in the way we communicate. Quality of communication is key towards customers and incredibly important internally. Based on our experience, I'd recommend anyone applying this model in sales to also apply it internally, as it supports the success of the company."

Maarten van den Burg, Director Global Commercial Excellence, Radiometer Medical Aps

"The *Satisfaction Cycle* has been my secret key to unlocking hidden potentials, both in management roles and as a growth advisor. In my role as a growth advisor for over 400 companies in the past three years, I have witnessed how this method creates a natural and effective approach to customer engagement and international success - often far more efficient, cost-effective, and sustainable than traditional approaches. It is a pleasure to see that this approach is now available in an easy-to-understand book."

Anna Marie Damgaard Kristensen, Internationalization Specialist, Erhvervshus Sydjylland & Former Managing Director, Bitzer Electronics

"The *Satisfaction Cycle* has a major impact on my ability to sell myself, my ideas, and the products/services that we represent. It is not just another model; it is a different way of thinking and acting."

Henrik Mørch, Chairman of the Board and Director

Not only does it convert customers into Positive Activists, but it also boosts marketing and leadership effectiveness, fostering a virtuous cycle. When applied with commitment and consistency, it creates a competitive advantage grounded in customer centricity."

Patrick Hofer, Managing Director, Neuroth

"In sales, "Customer Value Adding" is often seen as the philosopher's stone. While true and relatively easy for unique and simple products, real value creation usually involves understanding each customer's unique situation and driving sales from there. The *Satisfaction Cycle* and the communication tools that support it have shown me how to create true value for individual customers."

Niels From, Head of Animal Health Nordics, Boehringer Ingelheim

"*Satisfaction Selling* is a hugely satisfying read. Riggio, Varjonen and Wenøe address one of the most urgent challenges facing business leaders today: How to succeed with selling complex solutions within complex business environments. Drawing on their vast experience, powerful case examples, and proven approach, they demonstrate how ambitious sales professionals can bring their performance to the next level. Warmly recommended!"

Christian Bason, Ph.D., Co-Founder, Transition Collective, and Co-Author of Expand - Stretching the Future by Design

"I have found the model presented in *Satisfaction Selling* to be profoundly enlightening. It resonates differently with individuals based on their understanding of the NLP approach, making it accessible and valuable regardless of one's prior experience. The *Satisfaction Cycle* is a game-changer in customer communication.

Implementing even the subtlest changes inspired by this model has significantly deepened relationships with customers. The framework encourages an approach where customers feel genuinely appreciated and understood, fostering a profound level of trust and understanding. It effectively helps to unleash customers' desires and directed thoughts, creating a more meaningful and satisfying purchase experience.

While mastery of the model is rare, the journey toward it is immensely rewarding. Every incremental improvement in applying these techniques translates to a deeper, more impactful connection with clients. "Satisfaction Selling" is not just about making sales; it's about building lasting relationships and becoming a trusted advisor in the process.

I wholeheartedly endorse *Satisfaction Selling* and the *Satisfaction Cycle* for anyone involved in high-value complex sales. It has the power to transform not only your sales approach but also the very nature of your client relationships, ultimately leading to a movement of positive activists who believe in and advocate for your solutions."

Gitte Sjørslev, Commercial Director, Asiros

"I had my first Satisfaction Cycle training with Joseph back in 1995 in Singapore while working at Maersk. It was the best training I have ever attended. It's fantastic that these ideas are now available to a broader audience. Reading Satisfaction Selling has been a pleasure, reminding me of the powerful tools and effective strategies for creating value with customers. Read it and take your sales work to the next level."

Steffen Schiottz-Christensen, Managing Director, China/Hong Kong, NTG Nordic Transport Group A/S

"The Satisfaction Cycle has been nothing short of life-changing for me. After having had the pleasure of training people in the model for several years alongside Henrik, I decided 15 years ago to return to the food and biotech industry and apply what I had learned. It has completely transformed how I manage people, organizations, and the art of selling.

Everything starts with the individual, both within and outside the company, and how we can create a shared vision of the future and build it together.

'Satisfaction Selling' is a must-read, and learning to apply the model will change how you manage your organization and sales process.

The model has been a key ingredient in the transformation and growth success of the companies and teams I have led over the past 15 years."

Per Rehné – CEO, Clasado Biosciences Ltd. (UK)

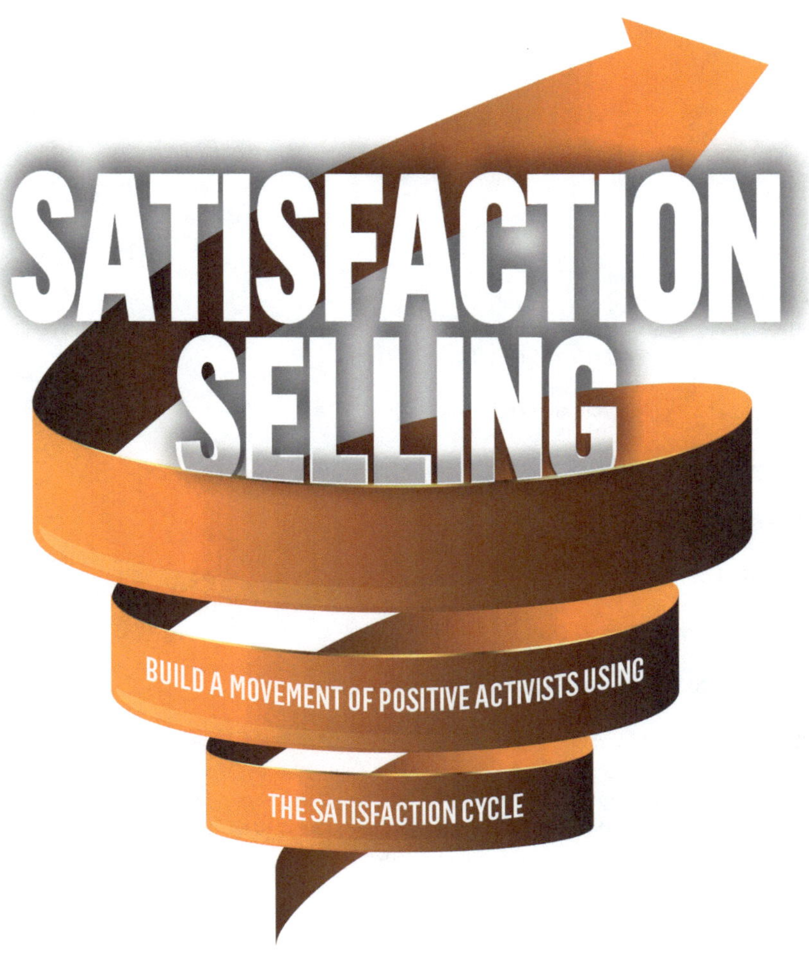

RIGGIO, VARJONEN, WENØE

Title: Satisfaction Selling: How to become a Trusted Advisor in high-value complex sales and build a movement of Positive Activists using the Satisfaction Cycle

Author: Joseph Riggio, Virpi Varjonen, Henrik Wenøe

Publisher: Acuity World Press

Publication Date: August 2024

ISBN (eBook): 978-87-973281-6-3

ISBN (Paperback): 978-87-973281-5-6

Acuity World Press

Dalsø Park 67, DK-3500 Værløse, Denmark

info@acuityworld.com

First Edition: August 2024

Disclaimer: The information in this book is provided "as is" without any representations or warranties, express or implied. The authors and publisher will not be held liable for any damages arising from the use of this book.

TABLE OF CONTENTS

FOREWORD: SATISFACTION SELLING

Hello, I'm Joseph Riggio, the architect and designer behind *Satisfaction Selling* and the *Satisfaction Cycle* model, and I'm thrilled to guide you through an enlightening exploration of sales and selling. This journey draws upon decades of experience and my research in cognitive science, neurolinguistic programming, and particularly, modeling extraordinary success in high-value, complex sales environments.

From the dynamic floors of tech startups to the high-stakes world of medical equipment sales, I've seen many traditional sales strategies fail to fully satisfy the deeper desires and needs of customers. It was during a particularly revealing conversation in the early 1990s, amid the ambition of burgeoning tech companies, that the concept of the *Satisfaction Selling* began to take shape. I realized the most effective salespeople were not just selling; they were engaging in a dance of discovery with their customers, tuning into their desires rather than simply addressing needs.

The *Satisfaction Cycle* model emerged from the belief that selling isn't about convincing someone to buy what you have; it's about helping them discover that what you offer is exactly what they've been seeking. This book is designed not just to explain this model but to integrate it into your approach so deeply that it becomes a part of your instinctive way of interacting and engaging with others in every sales conversation.

The Sales Process Unveiled

We'll start by delving into the nuances of the *Satisfaction Cycle* itself. The model is straightforward yet incredibly powerful, composed of five key stages: *Present State Positive (PS⁺⁺)*, *Desired State Positive (DS⁺⁺)*, *Process* and *Solution Experience,* and *Action*. Each stage takes you deeper into the psyche and aspirations of your customer, revealing their decision-making strategies and seamlessly moving from understanding their current state to aligning their desires with your offerings.

A Deeper Distinction

As I often say,

"All selling is the selling of certainty - the certainty that the future will be as good as or better than the present."

This insight forms the basis of the content here as we reveal the process customers go through when making a purchase decision. We'll demonstrate how to align your actions with their internal processes by mastering *Satisfaction Selling* and the skills needed to interpret their responses meaningfully.

Satisfaction Selling is fundamentally about uncovering each person's unique decision-making process. The tools and techniques embedded in this model will enhance your effectiveness as a sales professional. What I find particularly compelling about developing and applying the *Satisfaction Cycle* model is its universal applicability.

Revealing What's in the Black Box

To effectively use the *Satisfaction Cycle* model to achieve outstanding results, you'll need to appreciate that it offers a way to see how others think, respond, and communicate. Remember, you are never simply talking to a version of yourself but to someone who may perceive situations quite differently from you. This is particularly true for decision-making processes.

It's important to recognize that the deeper thinking processes of others are often hidden - like a "black box." However, as you delve into this book, you will learn to decipher the patterns others use to make decisions and align your interactions to match their natural decision-making styles.

Applying the Model

Understanding the *Satisfaction Cycle* model is just the beginning; the real magic lies in its application. Throughout this book, my co-authors and I will guide you through various scenarios - from straightforward to complex sales challenges. You'll learn how to adapt the *Satisfaction Cycle* to fit different contexts, making necessary adjustments as each unique situation requires.

Expect to find playful anecdotes, challenging exercises, and real-life case studies that not only demonstrate the model's effectiveness but also inspire you to think creatively and act strategically. Whether you're a novice eager to make your mark or a seasoned professional aiming to refine your skills, this journey will transform how you view sales and, more importantly, how you practice it.

So, buckle up and prepare for an engaging and instructional ride. By the end of this book, you won't just be selling; you'll be creating lasting partnerships and satisfying customers alike. Let's start this adventure together and transform every sale into a story worth telling.

Dr. Joseph Riggio

PREFACE

This book is dedicated to all those who believe that business is more than just business - that all business is personal and human.

We are writing this book with a very particular point of view for you dear reader. Since you've picked up this book you understand and agree that sales are a vital function for any thriving business. Sales leaders dedicate themselves every day to improving their company's activities to sell what they have to offer - tangible or intangible goods, services, or assets. They have developed sales strategies, plans, and even training programs to continuously enhance their performance. Despite being a well-understood discipline with established strategies and methods, sales remain an area where businesses constantly seek improvements.

Sales and the skill and science of selling have generated - and continue to generate - so much interest that thousands of books have been written on the subject. And not only books. There are also plenty of consultants, trainings, and experts offering you their supposedly powerful selling techniques. Each method claims to be the best, most powerful, unique, proven, and so much more. As you are holding this book on sales in your hands, you might wonder what sets it apart and what you will gain from reading it. What could possibly become different after you have read this book?

We wrote this book because we believe something essential is missing, hindering companies from becoming even more successful. A particular sales strategy and approach that one of our co-authors, Dr. Joseph Riggio, began developing and presenting over three decades ago - a unique take and approach to professional sales that continues to be taught through exclusive training sessions and programs by him and our other co-author, Henrik Wenøe.

While thousands of sales professionals are familiar with The *Satisfaction Cycle*, as this sales model is called, and its methods due to their attendance in the programs led by Joseph and Henrik and their teams, these individuals constitute only a select few globally who have had the opportunity to access this invaluable insight. Similar to the Jedi Archives in the Star Wars saga, it has remained accessible to a privileged few. However, there is no reason why this unique sales strategy and method should not be accessible to anyone interested in achieving exquisite sales performance.

This book is for individuals who recognize that sales entails more than simply closing the next transaction.

For you, who want to work in a more customer-centric than product-focused manner.

This book is a guide for those who aspire to move beyond selling and genuinely assist customers in buying what they truly want.

For you, whose aim is to focus more on true value creation than on price discussions.

This book is for those who comprehend that business is an infinite game and that adopting this mindset is the key to fostering success for their company.

For you, who desire to work more strategically with your customers.

For you, who wish to inspire and challenge your customers in a positive way.

This book is for individuals who acknowledge that their company and offerings are not meant for everyone, but are perfect for some.

For you, who want to spend more time with the right customers and thereby create greater value.

This book is for those who embrace the ideal of practicing good ethics and recognize that a business deal can only be deemed ethical when both parties achieve their desired outcomes.

For you, who wish to stop having to convince others of the value of your products and instead focus on helping your customers buy from you more quickly.

This book is for those who are willing to and want to be capable of saying "no" to a customer when that's appropriate or necessary.

This book is for those who grasp that the ultimate metric of success in business lies in long-term profitability, not just short-term revenue.

This book speaks to those who realize that what made them successful in the past is not going to get them where they want to be in the future.

This book is a compass for those who actively seek high-performing structures and systemic processes within an increasingly complex and unpredictable business landscape.

This book is for those who firmly believe that their organization possesses the potential to achieve exceptional outcomes and more outstanding successes than they have experienced thus far.

This book is a beacon for dreamers.

This book is a guide for doers.

Whether you are a dreamer or a doer or both ...

This book is for you!

So how will you know that *Satisfaction Selling* is the truly most effective way to achieve exquisite sales performance? That is exactly what we intend to present and share with you in detail here in this book, along with the evidence you need to make sense of why this approach will revolutionize how you think about selling, the successes you create, and the impact this will have on your business.

We do not only believe that many companies lack crucial elements in their sales strategies, but we also know and understand the transformative impact when the missing pieces become available and what kind of success they can bring. In this book, we aim to describe the *Satisfaction Cycle* comprehensively for the first time, shedding light on its depth. We also claim that "our way" is the most powerful in the context of high-value complex selling. Of course, we don't just say it; we truly mean it. Sounds familiar, right?

As you will find this book is different from either of the two approaches normally used by authors of sales training books who are speaking exclusively from either personal experience or models built from controlled experimental research.

As both a highly qualified researcher and a professional with decades of high-ticket B2B sales experience Joseph's approach to building the *Satisfaction Cycle* model that you will discover as you continue reading this book, stands outside of those limitations. Joseph's approach to selling based on the *Satisfaction Cycle* model was originally developed in the early 1990s based on three unique and intersecting pieces:

1. His experience working with a Master of transformational change that led him to realize the value of starting purely from positive expectation.

2. His own experience in luxury consumer sales and high-ticket B2B selling.

3. His work with a small group of exemplary sales professionals modeling the exacts in the process they used to create extraordinary results.

Joseph decided to name his sales model the *Satisfaction Cycle*. Here, the term "*Satisfaction*" refers to the fulfillment of one's wishes and desires and the pleasure derived from it, and "*Cycle*" denotes something recurring, regularly repeating without an end. Thus, the *Satisfaction Cycle* is literally an approach that cultivates virtuous recursive sales cycles wherein things get better each time the customer goes through the process with you. With each cycle, you collaboratively enhance what has already been accomplished, progressing from good to better to better. The whole idea is that there is no endpoint, and at every stage of a cycle, the customer experiences a profound sense of satisfaction.

In the early 1990s, the prevailing sales models primarily emphasized creating motivation to purchase by highlighting pain and fear, commonly referred to as a *Burning Platform*. Customer satisfaction was often only achieved at the end when a solution to the problem was presented. Still, looking into their processes and techniques, it became evident that only a tiny part at the end of the process centered on building satisfaction. The remainder of the process carried a considerable risk of turning the customer off by leading and keeping them in a negative state. The primary distinction of the sales model Joseph created lies in its purpose of ensuring customer satisfaction at all times, which is why he incorporated it into the name of the model.

The focus of this book centers around the *Satisfaction Cycle* as a high-value complex sales technology, or more precisely, how to apply the model in high-value complex B2B and B2C sales. We are aware that what we will present may not be universally applicable to all sales scenarios. For example, other strategies may be more useful for purely transactional businesses, where the product is self-explanatory and does not need expert support. This same criterion also applies to selling commodities.

In more complex business settings, there are also situations where our sales strategy simply doesn't apply. For example, when you receive *Requests for Proposal (RFPs)* or *Requests for Quotes* (RFQs), the only appropriate action is to respond with a proposal or quote. This does not involve selling; you are merely ensuring a transaction.

Thus, the content within the book revolves around high-value complex selling, which pertains to selling complex solutions within potentially complex business environments. The complexity arises when solutions are wholly or partially intangible in nature. They may require customization of a product or service. Even in the case of tangible products, the overall solution may contain service or support structures beyond the physical product, which increase complexity. Complex sales typically also entail significant investment from the customer's side, both in terms of time and money.

In a complex business environment, multiple components in the system are dynamic and changing fast. These factors can be internal or external such as political environment, technology, suppliers, customers, competitors, and more. Things are not only changing fast, but the rate of change is often accelerating. The speed at which technology develops and old technologies become obsolete is a prime example. Changes within a complex business environment are also unpredictable and uncertain. No one can know or predict what is going to happen. The factors are interconnected and interdependent, so a change in one aspect affects other factors in a highly complex manner.

Sales in a complex business environment require an adaptive strategy and high-level skills. Any approach that resembles a scripted or rigid process is bound to fail because of low predictability. The certainty lies in the fact that all situations are going to be different from each other. You need an approach and a strategy that enables you to navigate the complexity efficiently.

In this book, we present precisely this type of strategy. It is like an operating system for selling in complex situations. How to acquire sales leads is a separate matter from what we're presenting here about sales and falls outside the scope of this book. When we refer to sales within the context of this book, we mean the process of converting a sales lead into a committed customer who agrees and complies by taking the action to finalize the deal.

We are now opening the Jedi Archives of exquisite sales performance to a wider public, but this is about reaching a level of skill that ultimately requires more than just reading a book. Like with anything else, where you want to perform at a high level, reading will help you become more knowledgeable, but you are certainly going to need to train and practice as well. Mastering *Satisfaction Selling*, as presented in this book, is akin to mastering a martial art. Starting with the basic techniques is easy; anyone can follow the fundamentals. However, achieving true mastery and performing the art in its whole form may take a lifetime. Joseph has been training people for nearly 30 years, and Henrik has dedicated over 20 years to the same pursuit. Even after all these years, both Joseph and Henrik continue learning and enhancing their skills.

Over the years, thousands of sales and business professionals have trained with Joseph and Henrik and their teams. I (Virpi) am one of them. I have the privilege of co-authoring this book with them, but it doesn't really matter to you. I could be any one of the many individuals who Joseph and Henrik have trained. In my current work, I am involved in both sales and sales leadership. My perspective offers reflections from both angles, but none of the ideas in this book are originally mine. What I know and can share is my journey (so far) to learn this approach.

My journey with Joseph and Henrik began in late 2017. The first years I was mostly focusing on learning and practicing the different elements of the *Satisfaction Cycle* model. Since then, it has gone beyond mere techniques; at its core, it has involved a transformation in how I experience and perceive myself and the world. Techniques alone hold little significance. While practicing a single technique is a valuable training exercise, it does not directly translate to high performance in real-life situations. It takes time to learn the deeper things that allow you to perform in a real-life dynamic situation where you must constantly adapt to what is happening. Mastery of the concepts described in this book demands time and dedication.

All that said, you do not need to be a black belt in *Satisfaction Selling* or a master sales professional to begin utilizing the *Satisfaction Cycle*. I began training with Joseph and Henrik two years after I began my martial arts training and just like in martial arts, beginners and black belts can be trained in the same things. They simply learn different aspects at different levels. Now a few years later I can say with confidence that I have begun to develop some of the mastery I experienced the first time I was in the room with Joseph and Henrik at the front teaching us the basic principles of the *Satisfaction Cycle* model.

So, just like I've learned how to use and apply this sales model successfully, anyone who wants to can do so too. Nothing is holding you back from implementing the basics right away. The rest is just about how good you want to become and where you want to focus. As Joseph always reminds us:

"Where you put your attention is where you get your results."

We have decided to divide this book into two parts. First, there is Part 1, which basically describes what the *Satisfaction Cycle* model is. *What* makes this sales model work? *Why* does it work so well and prove its worth over time?

Part 2 is meant much more like a playbook - your recipes for success in high-level complex selling and your preferred cookbook, so to speak. Here, we go through *Satisfaction Selling* step by step, and you will get specific ideas on how to implement each part of the model successfully in your own sales activities. In Part 2, we will also include some sections describing the kind of skills and communication strategies you need to master to really access the full value of the model.

So, the first part of the book covers the *What* and the *Why*, and the second part focuses on the *How* - how to do *Satisfaction Selling* by applying the *Satisfaction Cycle* in your sales world.

Now, let's jump in ...

PART 1

UNDERSTANDING SATISFACTION SELLING

THE WHAT AND WHY

1

BEYOND THE ZERO-SUM GAME

Exceeding the Limits of Competition

In May 2000, during a global strategic meeting at DAKO, a marketplace leader specializing in diagnostic solutions for hospitals and research laboratories based in Denmark, the company management struggled with an urgent and pressing question: how could they stop the competitor from stealing their customers? One by one, DAKO's customers had begun opting for the competitor's product - an automated solution which was in fact easier to use and saved laboratory employees several hours of work each day. In contrast, DAKO had a traditional open system, allowing pathologists and their staff to create and optimize their own protocols as they desired, but at a slower pace than the automated system, the competitor offered.

The purpose of the meeting, dubbed Warfare 2000, was to develop a catalog of ideas to counter the attacks from the competitor and regain DAKO's lost customers. One of the participants in this meeting was Henrik Wenøe. At that time, he worked as the Area Sales and Marketing Manager for DAKO in the Nordic area in Europe.

During the meeting, Henrik noticed that the discussions revolved around products, products, and more products. However, the mood in the room was not good; there was tension and a sense of the severity of the situation. It was a fight for survival. Although DAKO still retained some of its best customers, the competitor and their new product deeply impacted DAKO's sales and - just as importantly - what the sales team believed was possible to achieve as a result of competing with what they thought might be a better solution. The prevailing sentiment was:

"If only DAKO had an automated instrument too, we could counterstrike and outpace the competition."

At one point during the meeting, Henrik asked a question:

"I understand that everyone thinks it would be a good idea for us to have an automated instrument like our competitors. When will we be able to have such an instrument ready for launch?"

The development director, who was present at the meeting, answered that developing such an instrument was a complex task that could take up to 3 to 4 years if everything went according to plan. Henrik then followed up with another question:

"What should we live on until then?"

At that moment, he could sense the mood in the room shifting from bad to even worse. Panic and fear were evident in everyone's eyes. Eventually, the managers who were in that meeting had to confront the truth; they would need several years to develop and bring to the market an automated solution similar to the one that the competitor already had and was selling. There was simply no defensive move that could have stopped the competitor. They needed to do something else. Facing this reality, Henrik proposed a shift in perspective:

"What if we train our people to sell the products we already have, emphasizing quality and precision over automation? With our solution, the customer spends more time but ends up with a more precise result. Let's focus on making the right diagnoses, aligning with what's crucial for the customer."

The global strategic meeting ended with an agreement to update the company's sales strategy and implement a comprehensive sales training program to train 350 salespeople multiple times over the next 2-3 years. Henrik was appointed to lead a task force, comprising a few other sales managers who were selected to design and develop the new strategy and a sales training program to support it. This marked the beginning of their search for potential consultants and collaboration partners - a process that eventually led them to Sun Valley in Idaho to meet Dr. Joseph Riggio a few months later that year.

When the Game Changes

A marketplace is a dynamic and complex landscape where companies have limited control over external changes. It is a complex system with various components that are rapidly evolving. Competition is just one aspect among many factors that contribute to this complexity. Political environments, technological advancements, suppliers and supply chains, and shifting customer landscapes are some of the external elements that add to the intricate nature of the business environment. The pace of change is not only swift but often accelerating, especially when it comes to technological advancements rendering old technologies obsolete. Just consider the recent developments within artificial intelligence (AI) and its accessibility to the general public.

In a complex business environment, changes are not only intricate but also unpredictable and uncertain. It becomes impossible to foresee what lies ahead. Factors within the system are interconnected and interdependent, resulting in a highly complex web of cause and effect. Even when you have followed previously successful strategies, the desired outcomes may elude you. New products and technologies might fail to gain traction, and business growth can stagnate despite overall market expansion. This happens because something has shifted - a new competitor has emerged, or unfamiliar buyers have entered the scene. The business faces the recognition that it is under threat due to these new forces in the market.

You may have noticed similar dynamics within your industry, perhaps even encountering challenges to succeed when launching new products. Take a moment to consider the most successful companies in your industry. Who holds the dominant market shares? Who leads in technology? Maybe even your company has maintained a superior position over a longer period of time. In many industries, the market leaders have in the past often held a superior and steady position with their technology, products, and service that nobody could compete with until something changed the market dynamic. We have witnessed the downfall and even disappearance of significant corporations and market leaders. In today's marketplace, everything can change in an instant.

In the mobile phone industry, Apple's story provides an excellent example of this kind of market dynamics because many are familiar with their story. In 2006, Apple was preparing to launch a new mobile phone product which the industry regarded as having little chance of success. At that time, Nokia was significantly leading the mobile phone market. However, Nokia's fall was quick, as was the rise of Apple, and it's new *iPhone*. Suddenly, the dynamics of the marketplace were not only changing but changed at an astonishing pace.

Beyond Apple's entry into the mobile phone marketplace, new content platforms for the mobile phone industry were emerging. The software giant Google acquired a company called Android that was another player in the mobile phone content market too. At the same time as this was happening, Nokia decided to transform their original proprietary mobile operating system, Symbian, into an open-source platform. However, their attempt at keeping Symbian vital failed, leading Nokia to explore a new operating system, and they chose Windows. Nokia introduced new mobile phone models and ventured into apps and content platforms, first based on Symbian and then on Windows.

Unfortunately, the release of these new products and services did not yield the same level of success as before in part because the new competitors and emerging players posed challenges that disrupted the traditional operations of the mobile phone industry. In this increasingly complex marketplace, Nokia failed to find its footing to continue their previous success.

Let's travel back in time to understand the reasons behind Apple succeeding, where Nokia was failing. In 1979, Steve Jobs paid a visit to Xerox Palo Alto Research Center – a trip that would shape the future. Among the many things he encountered there, the graphical user interface (GUI) that Xerox Labs had developed captured his imagination. At the time, when everyone else was still relying on command-based interactions with computers, Jobs saw the immense potential of a GUI. To him, it was evident that the GUI represented a path to the future in using computers beyond the specialists who managed mainframe-based systems, or the slow and cumbersome command driven operating systems used on personal computers, including Apple's own operating system, at that time.

The future was there; it just had not been realized yet. Jobs returned to Apple, determined to change everything, and redirect their work to create what we now know of as the *Macintosh* personal computer and the *Macintosh* point-and-click GUI-based operating system.

The experts at IBM dismissed GUI operating systems as a passing fad. They believed that mainstream computing was confined to dumb terminals managed solely by the IT department. However, within a few years, Apple ventured into the business sector, expanding beyond their stronghold in education. Suddenly, executives and professionals wanted *Macintosh* computers on their desks. What set Steve Jobs apart from IBM was his willingness to dismantle a successful business model to tap into something even greater. Apple was already making significant sales at the time, just not yet in the business marketplace or with an executive or professional audience.

Playing a Losing Game

Steven Jobs then made the fateful decision to recruit John Sculley who came from PepsiCo to Apple based on his belief that he could implement a successful marketing strategy for them and expand their customer base into the proliferating business market for personal computers. After a while, tensions arose between Sculley and Jobs. Sculley likely saw Jobs as an ignorant individual detached from the realities of the business world. Their conflicting visions and beliefs on developing Apple's business model eventually led Sculley to rally the board and strip Jobs of his managerial duties. He then forced him to resign from Apple in a very public way with his tail figuratively between his legs.

Undeterred, Jobs founded NeXT, a company that set out to develop a highly sophisticated computer driven by a graphical user interface. Meanwhile, IBM clung to their mainframe computer strategy, resisting change, and Microsoft built the MS-DOS for their personal computers. Eventually, Microsoft licensed their software to become the operating system for IBM Personal Computers (*PCs*). Initially, Microsoft's operating system was primarily code-driven. However, Microsoft's MS Windows operating system gradually made its way into the market that *Macintosh* had pioneered. Sculley disapproved of this development and desired Microsoft's downfall, leading him to take three significant actions.

First, Sculley opened Apple's software to external companies, similar to Microsoft's strategy and approach to the personal computer market. The largest company to license this software was Orange. As a result of losing control of the hardware that their operating system ran on, Apple's profits significantly dropped. Rather than showcasing computers with superior software and operating systems, they shifted to merely licensing the operating system, following in the footsteps of IBM and Microsoft.

The second consequence was Sculley's pursuit of market share. He believed that acquiring market share was paramount. His thinking went: we need market share, we need market share, we need market share, a holdover from his time spent promoting soft drinks to consumers. Consequently, Apple reduced the prices of *Macintosh* computers to appear competitive. From an external perspective, John Sculley had built his own competition by licensing Apple's software to a company selling computers for less than Apple was selling them. Now Sculley had to sell Apple computers at the price the competitor was selling them at to compete in the market and that meant spending a lot of money on advertising. This double blow of lower revenues and higher expenses devastated Apple's previous profit margins.

Last, Sculley succumbed to the demands of Wall Street analysts, focusing on quarterly numbers to meet stock analysts' estimates. Consequently, despite having a solid cash position, Apple's market value - reflecting the total value of the company's shares - fell below their cash reserves. Now, Apple was in a dire situation where Wall Street refused to extend any loans due to its low market value. Sculley had played the classic business game, bringing Apple perilously close to bankruptcy.

Sculley's approach to business, learned from his tenure at PepsiCo, is known as a zero-sum game. In this game, companies relentlessly pursue sales, often at the expense of profitability, with a singular focus on immediate sales and capturing a larger market share. A sense of urgency drives the prevailing mindset: we must secure sales today, attain a higher market share, and increase sales volume at any cost. The belief is that pushing harder and selling more will compensate for any losses incurred.

However, the absurdity of this approach becomes evident because losses multiply along with increased sales volume. For instance, if a company reduces prices, resulting in a $1 per unit loss, and then proceeds to sell a million computers instead of 100,000, some may mistakenly assume that it will make a substantial positive difference. Yet, the underlying absurdity should be evident - instead of losing $100,000 in profits, the company now faces a staggering ten times greater loss! Now extend this to an even greater discounting of the sale price and the effect is exaggerated in direct proportion to the discounted percentage.

Resetting and Playing a New Winning Game

Meanwhile, Steve Jobs engineered getting rehired by Apple through his previous acquisition of NeXT. He had already made a mark with Pixar, skillfully integrating the NeXT GUI system and the NeXT computer operating system to cater to Pixar's high intensity graphical needs. The result was the wildly successful movie Toy Story - the first digitally produced animated film with realistic animation that everybody wanted to watch.

With his return to Apple, Jobs shifted the company's focus away from market share, declaring the need for a loyal customer base to drive profitability. He reintroduced the *iMac*, raised its price, and terminated all licensing contracts. Apple's sales volume declined, but their profit per unit soared. Within a decade, Apple became the most valuable company on Wall Street. They were the largest market share-valued company in the entirety of Wall Street. Steve Jobs had broken free from the zero-sum game with a new winning game which later led and created the conditions for Apple to disrupt the mobile phone market with *iPhone*.

This is an example of complexity in play within the market where multiple smaller events cascade to create a massive terminal effect, sometimes referred to as the *Butterfly Effect*. The sales department typically plays a central role in implementing company strategies within a marketplace. Sales has the game-changing power to shift challenging situations for the better. More correctly would be perhaps to say that the sales team could have this power when they are properly trained and managed and are allowed to engage at world-class levels of performance. For example, a sufficiently organized sales process should be adaptable enough to account for and operate in relation to the complexity in the system.

However, ever too often the orientation to sales is placed on just the immediate future revenue results. How do we secure this sale? At the sales management level the focus is on pushing the sales team and the salespeople within it to increase their pace and fight for (and often with) their customers. This mindset prioritizes only short-term monetary gains.

When sales strategy is operated like this, emphasizing solely short-term thinking and results, it is all about playing a zero-sum game. In the zero-sum game mentality, the belief is that there is a limited pool of customers. The objective then becomes capturing as many of them as possible, regardless of the means employed. Sales teams enter aggressive selling modes, doing whatever it takes to secure the next deal, even if it means reducing prices and cutting back on quality and service to do so. The focus is on numbers: market share and short-term sales revenue.

This could be an acceptable strategy in a world where everything would be predictable and certain. The sales pitch highlighting *Unique Selling Points (USPs)* would work fine in a world where customers' choices are clear and stable over time. But in a dynamic and rapidly changing business landscape, playing the zero-sum game in sales is like driving blindfolded on an unknown road that's still in the process of being built.

When a company faces external threats, the common response is often to pursue volume, increase market share, and boost sales to offset losses, and many choose the path:

"We need to get volume, we need to increase market share, we need to increase sales to make up the losses!"

The focus often shifts to the competition and what it is doing in the marketplace, and to how it's affecting market share, revenue, and profitability. When focusing on competition, the typical approach is to consider how to position the company's offering in relation to the competitor and identify more and better *Unique Selling Points (USPs)*.

When a company presents its new products and services to the customers this way, the competition often has a chance to learn about them and maybe even copy certain things. The typical loop in a company is then to consider the next iteration: what the next solution could be that would give them the edge in the marketplace again, regardless of how short-lived. One solution within this scenario maybe be shifting the focus to the next move to "push" the sales up again for the next quarter, a cycle that repeats quarter after quarter at great cost to profitability and placing a great drain on the sales force. So many companies adopt such business and sales strategies because they deliver results in the short term. It works to get bonuses that are based on short-term numbers. However, it takes courage to pause and reconsider what else might be possible.

In the zero-sum game, the premise is that if someone wins, someone else must lose. While sports operate on the principle of a zero-sum game, real businesses do not. Business does not have to be a finite game with winners and losers. Yet the idea that business is a zero-sum game is deeply rooted in many organizations. Since competition exists for companies, it may seem like business is a zero-sum game. This idea that a company would need to fight for a limited number of customers is very persistent. However, business is fundamentally different, as it lacks limits. There is no specific pie to be divided, and if there were, it would be at least continuously expanding when the proper strategies and techniques to drive growth are present.

Business can be played as an ever-evolving, infinite game - a positive-sum game. Thus, Steve Jobs approached Apple's business with a different mindset. He believed there were infinite customers for everything the company produced if they chose to make what those customers wanted. His focus was first on existing customers who wanted what they had. Then, his objective was to identify the products or services they could develop to cater to the desires and needs of potential customers who were not yet part of their existing customer base but were likely to become valuable additions.

This approach led to the creation of groundbreaking products like the *iPod*, *iPhone*, and *iPad*. Apple's value, profits, and revenue skyrocketed. We then began to see the series of things, first *iPod* and then *iPhone* and *iPad*. All of this happened because Steve Jobs played a different game beyond the confines of the zero-sum mindset.

But is it merely a utopian dream to envision a robust and sustainable business that thrives regardless of what is happening in the external business environment? We say it is not. Such a reality *is* possible, and there are companies out there that thrive, show resilience, and operate sustainably. Both Apple and DAKO, the laboratory diagnostic company, where Henrik Wenøe worked, experienced a significant transformation in becoming more robust. Instead of selling to everyone, they shifted their focus to selling their exceptional products to those who wanted what the company had to offer them. This shift in focus serves as the starting point to transcend the zero-sum game and enter a positive-sum game.

In a positive-sum game, the notion of one's winning does not mean another's losing. All parties involved can experience gains simultaneously. It becomes a win-win-win scenario for the company, its customers, and even its competitors. The underlying mindset is that there is an infinite number of potential customers, eliminating the need for fierce competition for the same customers. As a result, a company engaged in a positive-sum game can simultaneously increase sales *and* profits. Thus, to truly succeed over time, it is essential to transcend the zero-sum game and embrace the infinite mindset.

Shifting Time Perspective - A Game Winning Strategy

Another distinction between the positive-sum and zero-sum games lies in their respective perspectives on time. For decades, sales strategies, tactics, and methods have primarily revolved around the near future. The focus has been on securing immediate sales and involving the right people in the process to achieve that objective:

"How do we get this sale?"

"How do we get the people we have to be part of the process to get it?"

While the zero-sum game prioritizes short-term gains, focusing on and securing the next win, the positive-sum game adopts a long-term perspective, ensuring future business vitality and emphasizing customers' lifetime value rather than a single transaction.

In this book, we explore a different timescale. We explore, how organizations and salespeople can attain results that linger. Viewing sales as a cyclic and iterative process, we will look into how relationships can grow stronger, better, and healthier with each interaction with the customer in a way, where each interaction yields improved outcomes for all parties involved.

The *Satisfaction Cycle* helps reorient salespeople and customers to a through-time orientation:

"What will happen in this particular sale?"

"How does it influence all future sales?"

"How does it impact the future relationship?"

"How does this purchase affect your business, your people, yourself, and the entire system?"

This approach fosters a sustainable business that thrives not only in the present moment but also in the long term. The key distinction between *Satisfaction Selling* and other existing sales models to date is that the other sales models are trying to play the game that IBM and Microsoft played. The *Satisfaction Cycle*, as Joseph designed and developed it and how Henrik teaches it, aligns with the game that Steve Jobs and Apple played. That is the crucial difference.

Satisfaction Selling revolves around different metrics, focusing on real customer value, lifetime value, and profitability per customer rather than market volume and an obsession with selling as many units as possible at any cost. Rather than lowering prices and subjecting oneself to the whims of the marketplace, the goal is to build a devoted tribe and fan base - a movement of *Positive Activists* who actively engage in promoting the business simply because they are thrilled by what they get from it and their interactions with it over time. This only happens by serving customers in a way that ensures they get what they truly want and need, and then some, every time they buy from you.

To do that, you must know the customer better than anybody else who's trying to sell to them. *Satisfaction Selling* focuses on the customer and what the customer wants. It is a sales model which gives you access to information and knowledge about your customers that no other sales model will ever give you. Thus, *Satisfaction Selling* is beneficial to have as a strategy for selling and as a strategy in developing more success in sales: it lets the organization define its future without the limitations of the past. It provides a means to change the game from a zero-sum game to a positive-sum game.

The Power of *Positive Activists*

The *Satisfaction Cycle* operates on the foundation of positive expectations, paving the way for the initiation of new cycles of satisfaction. Each cycle serves as evidence that improvement is possible, fueling the belief that things will continue to get better. Over time, customers can evolve into loyal patrons, making recurring purchases, and as discussed above, some customers become exceptionally satisfied with the value provided by the seller and the established relationship, transforming into *Positive Activists*.

Positive Activists are enthusiastic advocates who willingly and happily pro-mote the company and its offerings, actively persuading others to share in their excitement. They not only generate recurring revenue and high profitability but also serve as a powerful and dependable marketing channel, reaching out to new customers in the spirit of the positive-sum game.

The journey towards gaining a *Positive Activist* commences with a potential customer who may be unfamiliar with the company and its offerings. The path from initial engagement to the ultimate goal of acquiring a *Positive Activist* can span years, encompassing numerous sales cycles. But it doesn't have to. Applying the *Satisfaction Cycle* approach will speed up the process considerably. You may even in rare cases encounter a *Positive Activist* after the first meeting. After the first purchase, the customer returns, driven not only by the company's tangible offerings but, more importantly, by the desired outcomes they seek to achieve. With each subsequent cycle, the *Satisfaction Cycle* consistently improves the customer experience, building trust and satisfaction until they transform into a *Positive Activist*. Although this journey may be lengthy, the result is a robust marketing channel that brings recurring revenue and high profitability.

When a customer reaches *Positive Activist* status or is on the verge of becoming one, they view the salesperson as their *Trusted Advisor*. Establishing a relationship with such a customer makes the sales process smoother and more intimate. As customers realize that the company can provide them with what they desire, the buying decision becomes effortless. In Chapter 3, we will discuss the concept of becoming a *Trusted Advisor* for the customer in more detail. This is a central part of succeeding with *Satisfaction Selling*.

On the other hand, new customers often require more time to make a decision as they are still unfamiliar with the company, its personnel, and the potential outcomes they could achieve. The sales process takes on a slightly different nature depending on whether one is selling to new or existing customers, with both types of sales playing integral roles in long-term business development.

The term, *Positive Activist*, has its origin in the *Customer Development Strategy* model, developed by Henrik back in 2015. The *Customer Development Strategy* model (shown in Fig 1.1) comprises two integral components: *Customer Acquisition* and *Customer Development*, with the ultimate objective of fostering *Positive Activists*.

Customer Development Strategy™

Figure 1.1 The Customer Development Strategy

The process of acquiring new customers is a collaborative effort between marketing and sales. The company's marketing initiatives play a pivotal role in generating *Awareness* and *Interest*, attracting qualified sales leads. Once genuine interest is established, the sales process commences. The salesperson establishes rapport with the potential customer, converting general *Awareness* and *Interest* into a specific *Interest* in the company's offerings.

When the specific *Interest* is established by the *Desire to Action* step, the salesperson achieves their first successful sale to a new customer, often referred to as a *Shopper* - someone who has bought once. This phase, encompassing marketing efforts and the completion of the initial purchase, is known as *Customer Acquisition*.

Following the first purchase, the dynamics of sales undergo a transformation, transitioning into the *Customer Development* phase. This phase focuses on nurturing existing relationships and identifying opportunities within the current customer base. Subsequent sales to existing customers are typically easier, as trust in the company and its offerings has already been established. As the customer continues to experience desired outcomes being created, the relationship deepens, requiring less effort in subsequent sales.

The customer progresses through various stages, evolving from a *Shopper* to a *Client* (someone who has bought more than once), *Member, Ambassador*, and eventually a *Positive Activist*. Selling to existing customers becomes more streamlined, resulting in lower sales costs. Throughout the *Customer Development* phase and recurring buying cycles, the customer perceives a continual improvement and progress in their interactions with the seller, transitioning from good to better and better.

The principles of the *Satisfaction Cycle* have been instrumental in shaping the *Customer Development Strategy* model. Thus, the model depicted in the center of the *Customer Development Strategy* in Figure 1.1, called the *Personal Leadership Spiral*, is essentially a simplified version of the *Satisfaction Cycle*. This indicates that the dynamics of the *Satisfaction Cycle* fuel the actions within the *Customer Development Strategy*, moving from *Customer Acquisition* to *Customer Development* - turning *Shoppers* into *Clients* - and eventually into *Positive Activists*.

The Essence of Complex Sales

When playing the positive-sum game and viewing the marketplace as an infinite pool of potential customers, your focus will be directed toward those who genuinely want what you have to offer. However, it is important to recognize that these potential customers are not operating in isolation. Most likely, they are already engaged with a similar product or service from one of your competitors. This holds particularly true in most selling-buying scenarios that are complex. Most of the time, complex sales are about convincing customers to change from their existing solution to yours.

But aren't we now back to where we started - competing fiercely and trying to win over the competition? Do we need to have sharper *Unique Selling Points* (*USPs*) to outshine our competitors? The answer is no. You can still choose to play the positive-sum game. You can still define your success on different metrics, such as lifetime value and profitability per customer.

Given that potential customers would have to make a change to adopt your solution, you want to have a clear understanding within your organization of the following points:

"Why would a customer choose to make that change?"

"What motivates them to purchase your offering when they already use a similar product or service?"

These questions are essential in high-value complex B2B and B2C sales. Whatever you offer your customers comes at a cost to them. Therefore, it becomes imperative to identify what they gain from investing their time and money, i.e.:

"What is it that the customers get from spending the money?"

"Why would they buy from you?"

"What is the value to them as they perceive it?"

The only reason for buying what you have to offer is that your solution allows them to have a better future than with somebody else's solution. This notion is paramount. Take a moment to think about it...

Selling Certainty

The idea of certainty is central in all selling. Joseph puts it this way:

"All selling is about the selling of certainty - the certainty that the customer's future will be at least as good as or better than the current situation."

Your task as a professional salesperson is to instill certainty in a potential customer that their future will be improved by choosing you. Convincing someone in a selling-buying scenario entails selling the benefits, often referred to as the "value" of your solution. In any high-value complex B2B or B2C purchase, the customer buys either increased value, lower risk, or both.

In a B2B selling environment, the concept of value creation is straightforward, and successful businesses and salespeople are constantly building on the value the customer is seeking. Ultimately, the value in B2B always relates to the ultimate value measure in business: profitability through time. In B2B selling, the dynamics are distinct. The sole reason a customer makes a purchase in the B2B context is the expectation that it will positively impact their business and profitability. The purchase should enable them to generate more revenue, reduce costs, or minimize the risk of increased expenses over time - any one of these alone or in combination equates to value in B2B selling.

In a B2C setting the perception of value is different. For example, when buying a new shirt or car, the customer often seeks a value associated with looking good in the eyes of others, elevating their status, or desiring to be admired by others. There are any number of subjective as well as objective distinctions that enter into the perception of value in B2C selling demanding that discerning the particular and specific ways that a B2C customer perceives value becomes part of the sales process.

These ideas are not groundbreaking for any professionals in sales. Skilled salespeople possess the ability to find out a customer's perspective on the value they seek. They also know how to sell certainty and convince customers to believe that the solution will give them the value and benefits they seek.

The greater one's strategies and skills regarding these essential aspects of selling, the higher the sales performance. It is as simple as that, although simple should not be confused with easy. In this book, everything we share boils down to these two fundamental elements in any purchase within the B2B or B2C sales context: i.e. value and certainty.

What Makes High-Value Selling Complex?

Not all sales face the same level of complexity. When the product you are selling is self-explanatory and does not need expert support, other strategies may prove more effective than the ones we are about to present. Selling a commodity differs significantly from selling a knowledge-based service. If you are involved in commodity trading, your approach to achieving success will likely differ from what is described in this book. Also, when you receive *Requests for Proposals (RFPs)*, decide to bid for a tender, or participate in an online auction, your options may be limited to meeting customer requirements rather than selling. These scenarios focus on transactional fulfillment, distinct from sales, as already mentioned in the Preface.

One factor contributing to the complexity of high-value sales is the nature of the product being sold. The selling situation is relatively straightforward if the product is widely known, and its usage is self-evident. However, complexity often arises in sales, especially in high-value selling, when intangible aspects are involved. Customers may require service or support together with a tangible product. They might seek advice, knowledge, software, or user rights. In cases where the sale revolves around intangible solutions, we refer to it as a complex sale.

Another source of complexity arises when customers require customized solutions. The selling process gets more complicated and complex whenever there is a demand for customization, whether it be the product, service, or sales/purchase agreement. This complexity stems from the need to gather extensive information from the customer and various stakeholders to tailor a solution that specifically meets their needs. And even though the product or service is non-customized, there might be customized elements of how the customer wants them to be delivered or other aspects in the agreement that increase complexity.

Complex sales also arise in team interactions, in both one-to-many and many-to-many scenarios. These situations tend to be more complex due to the involvement of multiple stakeholders from both the customer's side and/or your own side. You have the whole *Buying Center* on the customer side which may include *Influencers*, *Users*, *Decision-makers*, *Buyers*, and *Gatekeepers*, and they may also often require collaboration with multiple experts and colleagues within your organization to coordinate the sales effort. Suddenly, a considerable team is involved in the buying and selling processes, and it becomes crucial to gather the right information and maintain momentum throughout the sales journey. We will discuss this more in detail in Chapter 7.

Similar complexity can also emerge when customers make significant purchases requiring budget allocation or specific budgeting. An example of increased complexity arises when your offering means that the customer and their organization need to make changes in their systems to integrate their purchase. Large investments with substantial impacts make many if not most high-value sales more complex. For instance, when customers consider switching from an existing vendor to a new one, they must give up doing business with a known entity and, they might need to modify their systems and documentation to adapt to new terms and conditions that requires. Software purchases often present an example of these kinds of challenges to an extreme as customers may need to change their IT systems significantly and retrain staff to use the new system.

Sometimes it happens that customers may resist sales approaches altogether. This resistance can stem from preexisting, unbreakable vendor relationships or negative past experiences with your company. Regardless of the underlying reasons for resistance, any attempts to engage in creating this change in the sales relationship can potentially worsen the situation. So suddenly, the situation can become even more complex than a typical sales scenario would be.

Beyond the complexities of the external business environment, the nature of the sales situation can make high-value sales complex. High-value complex sales typically involve one or more of the following factors:

- Selling services, support, knowledge, ideas, or user rights.

- Customization of offers or sales processes.

- Engagement with multiple stakeholders.

- Significant purchases with a substantial impact on the customer.

- Resistance from customers towards adopting new solutions.

These criteria often apply to many high-end service-based industries, such as strategic consulting, where consulting projects can be multi-million-dollar investments for the customer. Additionally, the banking and finance sector, the software industry, and other industries associated with digital platforms and technologies frequently experience high sales complexity. Similarly, high-technology solutions and manufacturing, whether related to equipment, chemicals, or bioengineered compounds, require ongoing support and service to facilitate solution adoption.

New Metrics of Success

The marketplace introduces complexity with its unknown, uncertain, and unpredictable factors. Within the sales environment, intangible solutions, multiple stakeholders, and high investment purchases further contribute to this complexity. To achieve optimal outcomes, companies must effectively navigate these challenges.

Companies that have been dominant in the market often possess strengths such as advanced technology, quality products, and an existing customer base. They have gained money that can be spent on rebuilding the basis for long-term success. These strengths enable business continuity and provide a foundation for long-term success. However, if the sales department continues employing outdated selling approaches to customers, who are no longer interested in what was previously offered, the competition has an easy game. Failure to adapt to the changing marketplace can lead to real threats to the growth and even survival of the business.

When salespeople are asked about the key to successful selling, many emphasize the importance of building relationships. While relationship-building plays a role, relying solely on it is insufficient, as depicted in Figure 1.2 below. Engaging in meetings, sharing coffee or lunch, and maintaining a friendly demeanor may create positive impressions, but they may not secure long-term loyalty if your product or service fails to provide the desired value.

The surprise is significant when a customer informs the salesperson that a competitor has made a better offer. This could involve similar products at a lower price or products offering additional features. Despite maintaining a friendly relationship, the customer declines to make a purchase, resulting in a polite rejection. You will get a "no" with a smile, as indicated in Figure 1.2

Personal Relationship vs. Value Creation

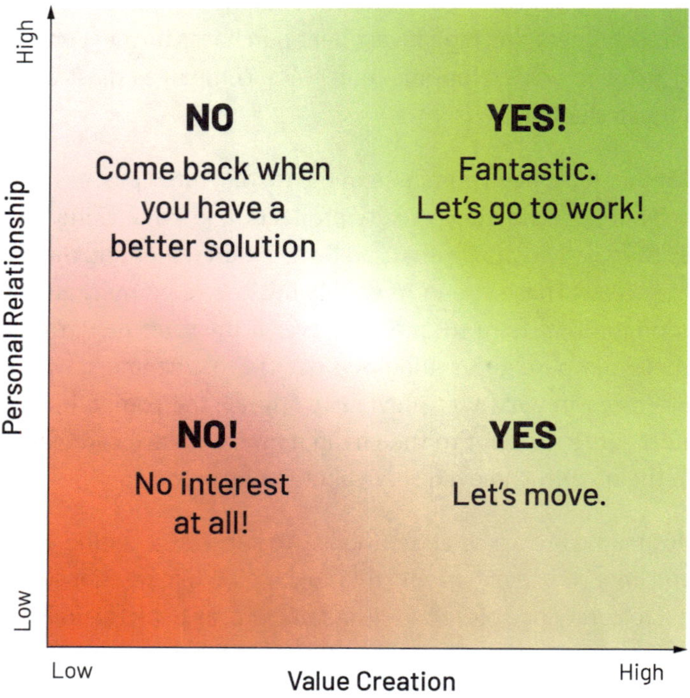

Figure 1.2 Personal Relationship versus Value Creation

While relationship-focused sales strategies may have worked in the past, the current marketplace demands more than mere social interactions. The evolving business environment requires sales professionals to offer tangible value beyond fostering relationships.

At times, marketing might intervene and reassure the sales team, suggesting that strengthening the brand will ensure ongoing customer loyalty. They might argue that even in high-value complex sales scenarios, people prefer to purchase a brand rather than a generic product. But the customer is going to see a brand with a price premium next to the generic product. When both are perceived to be providing the same thing, despite the reality of the distinctions they may offer, guess what the customer is going to buy?

Put your hand on your heart; what would you buy if you perceived both to offer equal value? If you are like the most people, it's likely to be the less expensive one.

Salespeople might still feel assured that they can fix the situation, believing they do not need help. They will work harder with the customer. Then the customer might experience a salesperson that is getting desperate. As desperation sets in, the customer relationship may deteriorate further.

You cannot force or push sales in simple ways or continue doing what you did in the past and hope you will magically succeed. To have a thriving business, you must deal with the complexity connected to sales. We will focus in this book on high-value complex sales and how to effectively deal with external complexity and the complexity within the sales process. In all fairness, many things are already working in sales, and many skilled salespeople exist. However, the questions remain:

"Is your sales strategy and performance as good as it can get?"

"What could become even better in your sales performance?"

For all those who believe that their sales can become even better than it is today, this book presents the same sales strategy and model that Henrik's company, DAKO, implemented - the *Satisfaction Cycle*. DAKO chose to work with Joseph's team because they believed it would give them the results they wanted.

One of the key metrics they focused on was customer satisfaction. This is a crucial measure, as satisfied customers are more likely to remain loyal, and loyal customers generate higher returns on sales compared to what it takes to win entirely new customers. But the implementation of the *Satisfaction Cycle* led to notable improvements in other areas at DAKO as well - similar to what Joseph and Henrik have observed in other companies, where they have trained thousands of sales professionals to employ the *Satisfaction Cycle* strategy over the years.

So, what does success look like in high-value complex selling based on *Satisfaction Selling*? Here are a few metrics that stand out:

1. ***Greater customer satisfaction and loyalty.*** Probably the most re-markable outcome of using the *Satisfaction Cycle* is that it consis-tently leads to higher customer satisfaction and loyalty. We have

seen it repeatedly. Once you have a satisfied customer, it is highly likely that they will come back again. And again. And again. This approach fosters a natural loop of satisfaction that gets stronger over time.

2. ***Increased revenue and profitability.*** All businesses aim to improve their profitability, and the *Satisfaction Cycle* has been shown to improve profitability by focusing on providing greater value to customers. Creating value is not a new idea, so what is the difference here? We have seen how this sales strategy has helped salespeople get the customer's purchase decision before negotiating pricing and other commercial terms. Focusing on the customer value until they have made the decision increases the chance that the customer is also willing to pay for the value. We have therefore also seen that the revenue grows after adopting the strategy of the *Satisfaction Cycle.*

3. ***Enhanced return on sales.*** Salespeople have limited hours in a day, and the *Satisfaction Cycle* has been shown to help them allocate their time more effectively. It enables salespeople to assess early on whether a customer is a good fit for their products, services, and organization. This clarity ensures that salespeople avoid wasting their time on wrong and unproductive projects, allowing them to focus on customers and cases with the highest probability of success. The derived effect of this approach is an increase in the energy levels of salespeople as well. When time is invested inefficiently, it not only hampers productivity but also drains everybody's energy levels. Conversely, when salespeople are confident that their time is being spent effectively, generating tangible value for both customers and their company, their positive energy levels soar. This heightened energy translates into improved efficiency and a greater sense of fulfillment in their work.

4. ***A more effective process by reducing friction in aligning the customer Buying Center, your internal sales team, and the available resources.*** The *Satisfaction Cycle* enables enhanced collaboration with customers and yields significant benefits. Notably, it facilitates the alignment of the entire *Buying Center* on the customer's side, ensuring a shared vision and avoiding conflicting agendas. Moreover, when engaging in team selling either many-to-many

or one-to-many, the *Satisfaction Cycle* provides salespeople with a clearer understanding of when to involve others and leverage additional resources and expertise. This higher-level opportunity-based thinking, combined with a deep understanding of the customer's desired solution, enables easier alignment, and ensures that the necessary resources are provided to meet the customer's needs. Ultimately, these aspects contribute to a smoother and more effective selling process overall.

"What does success look like for you - the kind of success you desire but haven't yet experienced?"

If you recognize that the strategies that brought your business to its current position won't propel it to where you want it to be in the future, then this book is worth your attention. You don't have to get stuck and remain confined by external factors, including competition. Instead, you can continue to aspire to maintain and strengthen your leading market position. You want to be in charge and drive your business toward continuous growth and success.

However, this book is not meant for everyone. It is specifically applicable to high-value complex sales, and it targets experienced and skilled sales professionals. It is intended for those who are eager to embrace the positive-sum game. Keep in mind that this book is not intended to apply to every sales situation. Some other strategies might be more helpful in securing short-term value creation. Yet, for those who believe that customer satisfaction and loyalty are the most valuable assets for long-term business success, this book offers something unparalleled.

For those who want to focus on lifetime customer value, *Satisfaction Selling* provides something that very few or maybe no other sales strategy can provide - delivering customer satisfaction all the time. It ensures the delivery of customer satisfaction at every stage of each sales cycle, not just at the end. Every encounter deepens customer satisfaction, fostering the potential for longest-term close customer relations.

Now, imagine when all of this will have come true for your business...

"What would that get you?"

"What new possibilities have you now unlocked?"

2

MODELING SALES EXCELLENCE

Applying the Lessons of Extraordinarily Successful Sales Professionals

When Dr. Joseph Riggio and Henrik Wenøe met for the first time in Sun Valley, Idaho, they had no idea at the time that they would become partners, collaborating on various endeavors, including running sales training programs for international companies. Henrik and the task force he led were on a mission to develop a new sales strategy for DAKO, supported by a training program.

The meeting with Joseph was just one of many they held with potential service providers for training programs. These previous encounters involved PowerPoint presentations and people talking about their solutions. Henrik later recalled that there were two consultants who stood out during these early meetings. One emphasized the importance of listening as a key skill for salespeople, but ironically, all he did was talk and talk without truly listening. The other consultant highlighted the significance of asking good questions for successful sales, but the only question he asked was,

"Can I have 15 minutes to finish my presentation?"

Henrik realized that these two consultants weren't the right fit. Salespeople don't learn as much from what the trainer is saying. They learn much more from observing, what the trainer is doing. Monkey see, Monkey do! These conventional presentations were focused on saying all the right things, but in the wrong way. However, the meeting with Joseph turned out to be far from a conventional sales meeting for Henrik and his colleagues...

Although they had received positive references about Joseph's company before-hand, they anticipated nothing more than another PowerPoint presentation. But to their surprise, there was none. In that sales meeting, there were six people from DAKO, including Henrik. Joseph simply walked in, looked at everyone, and asked:

"What do you want?"

At first, the participants were surprised and a little confused. However, they quickly began telling Joseph about the entire situation, the aggressive competitors, and their desire to make their salespeople less product-focused, more customer-focused, and effective in selling. After asking numerous questions and listening curiously for about 20 minutes, Joseph stood up, went to the flip chart, and began sketching and explaining how he could help them turn the situation around and move toward a successful future.

As Henrik reflected on what had transpired, he realized that approximately seven minutes into Joseph's presentation, he was sold. Henrik realized that Joseph was practicing what he preached—he used his own sales model to sell to them. It was convincing, and it meant at the very least that Joseph believed in his own model.

Towards the end of the meeting, Joseph spoke about the Satisfaction Cycle - the sales model he had been developing:

"Almost every sales model you have been introduced to has been produced in one of two ways. The first common way is that a salesperson who has been extremely good at selling has packaged their way of selling and presented it to others. And that is a fine way if you are that salesperson. It will work if you have their charisma, knowledge, and skills and work with their customer on their market and have their network. When all these things are in place for you, using their model will absolutely work for you. But I guess you are not that salesperson."

"The second type of sales model you surely have been introduced to is a sales model produced by a professor sitting at an office in a university - someone

who went out and studied sales but has never sat in front of a customer or sold a thing in his life. He is going to tell an academic truth about what makes a perfect sales situation work, which is going to work fine if you are selling in a laboratory-like environment. If you can control all the conditions in sales, their sales model will work."

"Neither of these approaches is what we did when we put the Satisfaction Cycle together. What we did instead was that we went to look at salespeople who were actually selling and doing it extraordinarily well. We paid attention to what is common with those salespeople, not what is unique. Because what is going to be unique for a salesperson is unique for them but not for anyone else."

"When you can identify a few things that all those highly successful salespeople are doing well, you can eliminate those 30 things they do uniquely differently. Then, when you teach new salespeople these things that the successful sales-people always do that work, you start getting great results. And that is what we are going to talk about today."

Generative Exemplar Modeling

In the early 1990s, Joseph pioneered the development of *Satisfaction Selling* and the sales model now recognized as the *Satisfaction Cycle*. His approach differed from conventional methods for creating sales models, which have traditionally followed two primary routes - both in the 1990s and today.

The first approach involves accomplished sales professionals packaging and presenting their successful selling methods to others. For instance, Solution Selling emerged from the experiences of a few successful sales professionals in the late 1970s and early 1980s. The second method involves research-based models. Some models based on research and publications, were released in the late 1980s and remain well-known today. SPIN Selling is an example of one of those models.

However, as Joseph stated at the meeting in Sun Valley, Idaho, where he and Henrik met for the first time, there are dangers in generalizing the sales models derived from these two distinct approaches. Copying successful individuals' selling method only works if you share their attributes and operate within their environment. Similarly, research-based models will only work optimally in a controlled, theoretical laboratory-like setting, not reflective of real-life sales processes.

Instead of following the traditional approaches, Joseph created the *Satisfaction Cycle* by studying and modeling the practices of high-performing sales professionals in high-value complex sales using *Generative Exemplar Modeling* - a method that differs from traditional qualitative research methods and does not require extensive projects or large numbers of study subjects. It is a faster and less complex approach compared to building models based on mediocrity.

Most models center around the average, extending a bit beyond. For instance, let's contemplate a scenario with 300 salespeople, with nearly all, approximately 294, falling within the standard deviation curve concerning their skills and performance. Among these 300 individuals, two perform inadequately, while four surpass what the curve signifies. In proximity to the top four individuals, around 40-50 perform above average. A conventional study would concentrate on this group, excluding the four from being research subjects due to their extreme nature.

Generative Exemplar Modeling, however, examines these extremes, specifically the top 0.1% on the standard deviation curve. Quantitative researchers argue against using exceptional examples, claiming they are markedly different from those who will use the model and that these extremes will distort it. Nevertheless, Joseph intentionally sought to distort the model to create outcomes surpassing anything an average model could produce.

To achieve this, he sought examples of individuals at the extreme ends of the curve with outstanding sales performance. He observed these exceptional salespeople in real-life situations, focusing on commonalities rather than uniqueness. Joseph's approach then involved identifying patterns and isolating the five or six strategies consistently employed by these highly successful salespeople, disregarding all the things they did uniquely differently. The resulting model comprised those five or six strategies, consistently producing positive outcomes and could be taught to salespeople, leading to exceptional results.

During the *Generative Exemplar Modeling* process, Joseph explored the gap between a great salesperson and an extraordinary one. Achieving a tenfold difference in sales results may seem exceptional, prompting him to investigate whether these individuals possessed superhuman qualities or unique charisma. Were they tall, attractive, and charming enough to make people just say "YES"? Because ultimately, he aimed to create a model usable by regular individuals, not just outstanding specimens of humanity.

Therefore, he found additional exemplars – "normal" people without particular charisma but who achieved extraordinary results. These exemplars shared commonalities with other top performers, indicating that charisma alone was not the determining factor. Joseph also discovered that skills alone were insufficient for exceptional results; a well-functioning strategy, comprising a process and an approach, made the difference.

The foundation of the *Satisfaction Cycle* was formed by codifying the common practices of the top 0.1% of salespeople consistently producing extraordinary results. Over time, the *Satisfaction Cycle* model was refined and validated using cutting-edge neuroscience and linguistics research on persuasion and influence. Thus, Joseph's two doctoral studies, conducted ten years apart in two different doctoral programs, significantly influenced the development of the *Satisfaction Cycle*.

From 2001 to 2005, his research focused on transpersonal decision-making with senior leaders and professionals operating within data-limited human systems, resulting in his dissertation: *Towards A Theory of Transpersonal Decision-Making in Human Systems*. In 2013, Joseph pursued another doctoral program in organizational change, studying action research, designing a generative consulting research methodology, and developing a thesis on: *The Ontology of Change and the Exertion of Power as Influence and Persuasion*.

These studies contributed to Joseph's deep understanding of high-quality decision-making, which has been incorporated into the *Satisfaction Cycle* as a model to assist salespeople in guiding their customers toward making high-quality decisions. Ultimately, the *Satisfaction Cycle* revolves around the concept of facilitating high-quality decision-making with others, including but not limited to co-workers and customers.

The Link to Neuro-Linguistic Programming

It wasn't a coincidence that Joseph used *Generative Exemplar Modeling* to create the *Satisfaction Cycle*. Already at that time in the early 1990s, Joseph was a Trainer in the field of Neuro-Linguistic Programming, NLP. The history of NLP goes back to the early 1970s, when its founders Richard Bandler and John Grinder modeled the patterns of outstanding influential figures in the therapeutic community such as Virginia Satir, Fritz Perls, and Milton H. Erickson.

Through their modeling efforts, they replicated some selected behaviors and demonstrated similar outcomes with people in therapeutic encounter groups. Richard and John refined the modeling process until they could identify exemplars of behavioral patterns they wanted to model and replicate. They employed this modeling approach to elicit, extract, and encode the patterns that made the difference in creating the extraordinary results they had identified. Alongside Virginia Satir, Fritz Perls, and Milton H. Erickson, they modeled various other wizards of transformational change, such as Moshe Feldenkrais, Gregory Bateson, Frank Pucelik, and others.

Even today, NLP remains an important human communication technology and a model to uncover, map, and codify how individuals create their personal experiences. One of the fundamental ideas of this technology is that all experiences are sensory based. Another notion highlights that experience is almost immediately translated into semantic forms, in other words, labeling and assigning words and phrases to activities, information, people, places, and things as language constructs. A third central premise is that each person responds to an experience in a subjective manner unique to themselves, while the fourth premise posits that all experiences are simultaneously held with the body and mind.

The Four Fundamental Ideas of NLP are the following:

1. All experiences are sensory based.

2. Experience is translated in semantic forms as language constructs.

3. All experience is subjective to the person experiencing it.

4. Experience is simultaneously held in body and mind.

NLP emerged from these and other discoveries. It embodies an attitude regarding the nature of experience and provides a toolkit to choose and create desirable and useful experiences, especially those leading to behaviors that support the individual's desired outcomes. It is about curiosity and mindset, noticing data and what is actually happening in the present moment.

In essence, NLP is about modeling the behaviors and thinking of exemplars who perform with excellence. What made the discovery of the unique *Exemplar Modeling* process of NLP so profound was that the results of the codification process led to NLP applications that could be directly transferred to others without the years of training, practice, and development it took the models to develop their behavioral and cognitive mastery. Joseph employed this same approach in creating the *Satisfaction Cycle*.

However, even though Joseph utilized the basic modeling approach of NLP to create the *Satisfaction Cycle* which incorporated NLP techniques in its application in practice, it is important to note that the *Satisfaction Cycle* is *not* an NLP model. There are a few significant distinctions in Joseph's work compared to NLP.

Joseph deviated from the standard NLP *Exemplar Modeling* process and created a *Generative Exemplar Modeling* process to identify the deep onto-logical basis of the exemplars he was modeling that went beyond just their behaviors and thinking to the commonalities in the way they perceived and responded from a deep identity-based position. In developing his unique *Generative Exemplar Modeling* process Joseph incorporated the fundamental principles of phenomenographic research that seeks to understand the idea of the *Outcome Space* that a group of exemplars use to create outstanding performances.

The phenomenographic model was originally developed by Ference Marton at Göteborg University in Sweden as an educational research model that has been used now for decades to explore how groups of people operate to perceive what they are experiencing, make sense of it, understand, and learn from it, and then translate what they've learned to create their performances.

Because the phenomenographic approach emerged from an empirical orientation versus the standard theoretical or philosophical approach to research it allows researchers to explore context as part of how the exem-plars construct both their subjective and shared experience of reality. Based on what he uncovered using a phenomenographical *Generative Exemplar Modeling*-based approach Joseph incorporates the idea of context as part of the process of human interaction in the *Satisfaction Cycle* model in a unique way that insists on starting from a position that is positively oriented and grounded in relation to possibilities, not problems.

NLP has traditionally been applied successfully in curing fears and phobias, but this success has created a double-edged sword, so to speak, where many NLP Practitioners intentionally use fear as a starting point in their work with individuals to tap into deep survival responses related to safety and security.

One of the most renowned NLP Practitioners, Tony Robbins, uses this exact approach when working with clients. He elicits a fear response by creating and utilizing an avoidance sequence, beginning with thoughts about what the individual does not want – whether it is not to be alone or be poor or weak or something else. Then, he reinforces the potential negative outcomes if they were to remain in that state: they would not be able to obtain what they need to survive, and ultimately, they would face the possibility of demise. This might sound dramatic, but that is the pattern.

The Starting Point Counts!

Joseph thinks the opposite. He does not believe that a fear-based, inhibitory response should be used as a starting point when working with people. There is no necessity to rely on fear and pain to initiate change, as a significantly more positive and potent approach exists. So, the starting point counts. As we shall discuss in the following chapters, this is actually one of the key points that distinguishes the *Satisfaction Cycle* from other sales models.

Another element that was ingrained into the origins of NLP is the premise that the past organizes the present. Joseph holds a different view. You don't need to get caught in the psychological trap of trying to resolve problems from the past that have already happened. Neither do you need to get stuck in the present when trying to create futures that haven't yet happened. Joseph's approach focuses on creating a future that is independent of the past and thereby creating a *Future Memory*, so to speak. These distinct perspectives which will be discussed much more in Chapter 6 can be traced back to the time when Joseph was apprenticing and studying under Roye Fraser.

Now, delving deeper into the theoretical underpinnings of *Satisfaction Selling* and the development of the *Satisfaction Cycle* model, we cater to those seeking a comprehensive understanding of the subject matter. Alternatively, readers may opt to skip ahead to the section on *Modelling Excellence* without sacrificing comprehension of the *Satisfaction Cycle*.

A notable aspect of NLP is its design as an epistemological model aimed at facilitating behavioral change and performance enhancement. It was specifically crafted to dissect the cognitive framework underlying subjective experiences, as conveyed through language, and internally processed in the form of mental representations such as pictures, sounds, feelings, smells, and tastes. Thus, NLP primarily deals with the *Transforms of Experience*, a term coined by one of its developers, John Grinder, focusing on the subjective interpretation rather than the immediate sensory perception.

NLP utilizes language as a means of modeling reality, recognizing that language merely represents reality rather than directly mirroring it. This concept, elucidated by Grinder, underscores the distinction between language's symbolic representation and the actual sensory experience it references. In developing the NLP model, Richard Bandler and John Grinder concentrated on understanding and manipulating the processes by which individuals internally represent reality, rather than directly engaging with the external sensory input. This emphasis on internally constructed representations, expressed through language structures, characterizes NLP as an epistemological model.

Joseph's studies with Roye Fraser of NLP™ America/Blue Dell Systems served as a guiding force, steering him towards an ontological modeling approach. This approach diverges from traditional NLP by focusing on the direct, pre-representational sensory form, which is generative and predates the cognitive representation process.

Unlike NLP, the ontological approach involves working directly with sensations as they unfold in real-time, without relying on shifting cognitive processes between the brain's hemispheres. Instead, it seeks to fully integrate the processing capacities of both hemispheres, as well as the front and rear regions of the brain, in what Joseph terms as "whole-form," learned through studying the *Generative Imprint Model™* with Roye Fraser.

The foundation of this approach lies in facilitating individuals to enter an open and receptive excitatory bias in their neurological state, referred to in this book as the *Green State*. Further elaboration on this mental bias will be provided in Chapter 4.

Joseph later refined this approach to include the intention of accessing and balancing the *Autonomic Nervous System (ANS)* to stabilize the *Parasympathetic Vagal Response*. This enables quicker access to the excitatory bias -

the *Green State* - and enhances the ability to sustain a generative internal position.

The *MythoSelf Process*™

Roye Fraser developed his *Generative Imprint Model*™ based on a deep personal association with combat and many years of specialized training and study in how the best military special operatives were able to access extraordinary states of being that in turn allowed them to perform at elite levels of performance on demand and consistently. Besides his personal experience including training in NLP, this model was based on other brilliant ideas such as Konrad Lorenz's *Imprinting* and Joseph Campbell's *Hero's Journey*. Combining the essence of these models with the technology of NLP, Roye began asking a different set of questions.

The original NLP model asks:

"How does a person create an experience that leads to a particular set of behaviors, and how could they modify this perception and thinking to alter the behavior in ways that are more useful to them?"

However, Roye delved deeper into self-awareness and the structure of personal identity and asked:

"How does the person know who they are and how do they develop this understanding?"

The Generative Imprint Model™ was the result of this inquiry. Simply put, the *Generative Imprint Model*™ uses the technology of NLP to access and model the internal configuration of the iconic, symbolic representation of beliefs and their resultant behavioral manifestations. To get to this level of calibration and sensory acuity – which Roye refers to as *Adumbration* – the most elegant and subtle perception must be employed. What is calibrated are the characteristic behaviors, idiomatic phrases, and the structural forms of language used by the individual.

In the early 1990s, before developing the *Satisfaction Cycle*, Joseph began to design his own models, the *MythoSelf Process*™ and the underlying *SomaSemantic*™ *Modeling* process. These models were initially based on the *Generative Imprint Model*™.

SomaSemantic™ Modeling asks:

"*Who does a person know themselves to be in relation to that which is Greater than Self, and how do they configure and manifest this in terms of the integration of their semantic and somatic experience?*"

The *MythoSelf Process*™ then explores in a broader sense how individuals know themselves in relation to something greater than themselves and how they manifest this understanding. It leads to a transpersonal, transconscious state where personal realization and its manifestations reside.

Since the early days when the original model was designed, it has undergone many updates, revisions, and refinements, especially those involving mythic form and metaphorical language in relation to autobiographical narrative, symbolic representation and semantic modeling, precision somatic modeling and intervention, cerebellar processing, implicit intelligence, developmental-evolutionary-socio-cognitive modeling, symbolic representational logic, and propositional modeling.

The *MythoSelf Process*™ finds its application in various areas, facilitating the development of a broader array of choices and enhancing clarity in attaining high-quality outcomes and results. It strives to enhance transformational performance by guiding individuals through a progressive series of steps:

- Sensory acuity

- Situational awareness

- Self-awareness

- State control

- Strategic thinking

- Behavioral flexibility

- Communication performance

While this book does not delve into the specifics of these details, the key takeaway remains: the *Satisfaction Cycle* is a technology and practical application rooted in the *MythoSelf Process™*, crafted through the *Generative Exemplar Modeling* of exceptionally talented salespeople.

Modeling Excellence

The modeling process that eventually led to the development of the *Satisfaction Cycle* started partially by coincidence when one of Joseph's customers asked him to train their high-level major account salespeople. This company sold IT services, which back in the 1990s, was very different from IT in the 2020s. However, at its core, the company sold an intangible concept for enhancing organizational performance.

The solution revolved around database management, quick data access, and database efficiency. Although the company was an upstart compared to IBM, which dominated the corporate IT market at the time, they were already a multi-billion-dollar company selling software systems for database management.

Joseph agreed with the company to initially examine the practices of their most successful salespeople and then teach those strategies to the rest of the sales team. So, Joseph started exploring. They identified a select group of three individuals who demonstrated exceptional proficiency in selling the software, achieving remarkable levels of profitability, revenue, and overall effectiveness that surpassed the capabilities of the majority of the salespeople. These individuals were true exemplars.

After modeling three exemplary IT salespeople, Joseph and his team aimed to broaden their research beyond the IT industry, exploring other sectors to determine if their findings were unique. They continued modeling with three diverse salespeople: one selling Mercedes cars, one selling private timeshares for jet airplanes, and one selling power plants globally. The exemplar group eventually comprised six individuals.

Joseph conducted the actual modeling with his business partner, who was primarily involved in selling financial services. During the modeling process, they observed exemplars in real-life sales situations and looked into what those six people did differently compared to all their colleagues. Additionally, their training sessions with other salespeople allowed them to participate in customer meetings, providing firsthand insights into how the interactions with the customers were unfolding.

Their qualitative research approach was unconventional. Instead of starting with the typical research question:

"What are these people doing?"

they chose to enter the process with preconceptions. Joseph's initial hypothesis was that exemplary salespeople were doing something different, and the second presumption was that they weren't merely selling. Joseph assumed they would build uniquely organized relationships to better understand customer wants and needs. Thus, the research question became:

"How do they do what we expect them to do?"

While this approach may be deemed unscientific, defining the outcome first and then seeking evidence to support it, they confirmed their expectations and initial assumptions regarding exceptional sales performance.

The salespeople didn't just conduct consultative-like sales they fully embraced a consultative role, acknowledging that their solution might not align with the customer's desires or needs. They were upfront about this notion, grounded in the belief that customers' businesses were already functional - an almost "do no harm" approach.

Their mindset seemed to say:

"Let's not disrupt the customers' business or make it more difficult by incorporating our solution."

Their premise was clear: if customers were to buy their solution, it should genuinely enhance their overall situation. Adapting this mindset of a *Trusted Advisor*, they started by asking what worked well for the customers and understanding how their businesses operated.

During this time, Joseph continued to study with Roye Fraser, developing his *MythoSelf Process*™ and the underlying *SomaSemantic*™ Modeling process, as discussed above. The focus was always on working from an excitatory bias - the *Green State* - as introduced above. Coincidentally, the exemplar salespeople also held the *Green State* themselves and approached sales from this perspective. When asking the customers:

"What is working well for you today?"

the salespeople unintentionally applied their *Green State* perspective without conscious awareness of their process. This lack of awareness led to inconsistency in their sales approach across different customers. What Joseph did was to isolate and codify how these exemplar salespeople were working at their best: starting from a positive standpoint and leading to an even more positive point of view when discussing the customer's desired future state. These features will be discussed in Chapter 5.

Joseph further refined the model by intentionally including non-charismatic individuals in the modeling process. He sought to determine if outstanding sales skills were exclusive to charismatic individuals capable of charming others with elaborate storytelling or if more ordinary people could also excel in sales. After observing additional exemplars confirming his hypothesis, Joseph knew he had everything to isolate the components in the model and train other people to use them.

From 1994 to 1997, Joseph significantly refined the model, now known as the *Satisfaction Cycle*, with each training session. He evolved the structure itself and eventually integrated the idea of the *Evidence Strategy* into the *Solution Experience* step of the model (see Chapter 8 in Part 2 of the book, where we go through the *Satisfaction Cycle* model step-by-step). The training methods also evolved to ensure that participants could learn and implement the model more effectively.

One thing that later became a part of the training were selected communication tools from the NLP model because advanced communication skills are essential in implementing the *Satisfaction Cycle*. Beyond NLP tools, Joseph later also included the specific use of metaphor and storytelling to how salespeople could use stories both in their examples as well as throughout the sales cycle.

The *Satisfaction Cycle* as a sales model is functionally a practical application of the *MythoSelf Process* in a sales context. One could even say that it is a fabrication of Joseph's imagination. He approached the *Generative Exemplar Modeling* with the fundamental belief that the excitatory neurological bias - the *Green State* - formed the foundation of extraordinary sales performance. He believed that if he could train salespeople to first lead themselves into the *Green State* and then guide potential customers there, that alone would dramatically improve sales performance.

After completing the initial modeling, Joseph returned to the IT company, training and working with their sales team to implement the findings. In the first six months, they witnessed a substantial increase in sales, almost 30%, for high-level customers, translating to tens of millions of dollars in revenue.

That is how the *Satisfaction Cycle* came about. Instead of being tailored to a specific company, the model was generalized to function in any high-value complex sales situation. Proving effective with diverse salespeople in various companies and cultures, the *Satisfaction Cycle* emerged as a strategy delivering extraordinary results.

A comprehensive description of The *Satisfaction Cycle* model will be provided in Part 2 of the book, along with a detailed guide on effectively applying the model within your own company. This guidance aims to help you attract and develop a larger base of *Positive Activists* - loyal and satisfied customers, who will actively promote your company, your products, and your services.

In the next chapter, we will delve deeper into the concept of adapting the mindset of a *Trusted Advisor* as a means to achieving a true partnership with customers. As discussed above, this ability to embrace the *Trusted Advisor* mindset is a fundamental prerequisite of working effectively with *Satisfaction Selling*.

3

THE MINDSET OF A TRUSTED ADVISOR

Achieving True Partnership with Customers

The meeting in Sun Valley, Idaho marked the beginning of a highly success-ful collaboration between Joseph and DAKO, putting the company back on track. However, while Henrik and his task force colleagues whose job it was to design and develop the new sales strategy for DAKO and identify a sales training program to support it, were on board with Joseph and the Satisfaction Cycle, there were of course other stakeholders within DAKO who also had their say.

Making purchase decisions for intangible services is a complex process. Nothing was agreed upon during the meeting with Joseph in Sun Valley itself. After the meeting, the six participants engaged in discussions among themselves, and it was only later that they collectively decided to schedule a follow-up meeting with Joseph a month later. They agreed to have Joseph conduct a short demo training and present the case and ideas for the sales training.

The following month, a big group gathered in Frederiksdal, Denmark, includ-ing the directors who held the economic decision-making authority. Midway through the day, the US Sales Director said to Henrik:

'It's interesting. I began the day skeptical about this idea, but now I believe it's excellent.'"

Following this day, internal discussions arose regarding the training program's purpose and necessity. The directors expressed concerns about the associated costs. Eventually, they approved the budget on the condition that they wanted to be able to measure the direct effect of the sales training as it was rolled out.

There are many ways to measure the effect of sales training. One of the most frequent suggestions is measuring the development in sales revenue, but the recommendation DAKO got from Joseph was to measure the development in customer satisfaction directly in relation to the sales encounter with the DAKO sales team and organization, because – as he explained – this would be the best way to obtain a direct measure of the improvement of the skills held by the sales force.

One month later, the training program, featuring Joseph and the Satisfaction Cycle, commenced. Initially, the C-suite directors underwent a two-day training in Denmark, followed by Henrik and his sales manager colleagues in Santa Barbara, California. Subsequently, the program expanded to encompass all salespeople, undergoing five days of annual training for three years, while sales managers also engaged in biannual two-day sales leadership sessions.

Interestingly, the global strategy meeting that eventually led to this sales training program was called Warfare 2000. DAKO started their transformation from the perspective that the company was now at war with its competitor. The competitor was the enemy, and somehow, they were supposed to find tactics to win and disarm the competitor. Yet, the strategy employed prioritized customer satisfaction as the ultimate measure, aiming to transform their salespeople, who in most cases had a background as technically skilled product specialists, into Trusted Advisors for their customers. The semantic shift away from "warfare" and "competition" to "customer satisfaction" was massive.

The collaboration with Joseph and his team had a profound impact not only on DAKO's sales but also on the future of the company. The journey from desperation to regaining lost customers demonstrated the transformative power of the Satisfaction Cycle, bringing positive change to the organization. After three years, DAKO had reclaimed the majority of the market in Henrik's Nordic region, leaving only a few major hospitals for the competitor. On top of that, DAKO managed to increase prices by up to 40% in some markets utilizing existing products and technology, signaling a shift from a product focus to a value focus. The price adjustment wasn't driven by introducing new products or features but rather by the actual value delivered to the customer.

There were also other consequences beyond excellent business outcomes. The "product specialists" began to thrive as salespeople and eventually became highly efficient Account Managers acting as truly Trusted Advisors for the customers. There was higher enthusiasm in the sales teams. The impact of the approach on individuals was significant – they also became much more satisfied. In all situations, the salespeople and their managers began to shift away from problem-thinking and reorient toward seeing which things were working for them. From this positive view into the present, the individuals started to think about the world in terms of possibilities.

The most significant shift for individuals who participated in the Satisfaction Cycle training was the profound shift in self-perception and their customer relationships. The relentless pressure to "SELL SELL SELL" was replaced, and the customer no longer held control over the salesperson. Salespeople realized their purpose was not to sell but to gather information, with two key responsibilities: first, to prompt the customer to share information openly, and second, to collect information for their own decision on whether they could assist them or not.

This empowered the salespeople to say "no" to a customer, a pivotal factor in achieving economic outcomes. This was the difference that made the difference in getting the economic outcomes for DAKO. And this also remained the difference that made the difference for those who became true Trusted Advisors for their customers.

As predicted by Joseph, DAKO witnessed a substantial rise in customer satisfaction. Recurring sales is in itself a success and tells something about customer satisfaction. However, one aspect stood out above all that made DAKO notice when the customers were satisfied: When the customers started acting as Positive Activists who actively told others about their good experience with DAKO. That was the ultimate success for the salespersons that had learned how to use the Satisfaction Cycle in their sales.

As Henrik incorporated the Satisfaction Cycle into his daily work as a sales manager at DAKO, he realized its significance beyond a mere sales model. He found it applicable to the leadership of his team and himself. He eventually left the company to start his own leadership and sales training business in 2005 and began working as a partner with Joseph. Since then, they have trained thousands of sales and business professionals around the world. In 2017, I (Virpi) became one of those when I participated in my first training with Henrik.

What is a Good Buying Experience?

Whether in our professional or personal lives most of us have made substantial purchases, like buying a house or a car, requiring significant consideration. We've all encountered instances where a skilled salesperson played a crucial role in guiding us toward the right purchase.

If you're a homeowner, there was a point when you contemplated the idea of acquiring a new property. From the initial idea to the final decision, you encountered numerous possibilities, considering various houses, locations, and maybe even the option of keeping your old house. Your buying process might have been lengthy, but in the end, you chose a specific house, rejecting all other possibilities.

Along the way, you made several decisions that ultimately led to the final purchase decision. This decision involved commitment and proactive steps - going through paperwork, transferring the required funds, and finally, getting the keys. Most likely, you engaged with a salesperson at some point, progressing through various steps together with that person. If your buying experience was positive, the salesperson certainly played a role in it.

Take a moment to recall one of your most positive buying experiences – specifically one where you bought something substantial that you are still happy to own. Is there a specific instance that stands out, where the person who sold it to you behaved in a way that made it a remarkable buying experience? Think about that experience and what the salesperson did to contribute to it. Consider their behavior and actions that positively impacted your experience.

There may be multiple ways the salesperson acted that made it a good experience for you. What specifically did they do, and how did they do it? It could be something related to the structure of the process that worked well for you. Perhaps in that positive experience of buying something the salesperson helped you achieve more than you initially expected. You might have felt genuinely heard and understood, with the salesperson assisting you in finding the best solution. It's possible that they treated you as an individual and provided a unique solution tailored to your needs. Whatever it was, you can begin to identify the factors that made the experience positive for you.

Reflecting on your experiences as a buyer helps shape an understanding of the qualities a salesperson needs to create a great buying experience for their customers. Drawing from our extensive experience working with salespeople worldwide, we have discovered that customers describe a salesperson who provides a positive buying experience as someone who:

- Demonstrates professional competence and expertise in their field.

- Exhibits passion and authenticity in their approach.

- Listens deeply and curiously and shows a genuine interest in the customer.

- Asks high-quality questions to better understand the customer's situation, wants, and needs.

- Assists the customer in making an informed decision that suits them.

- Challenges the customer to consider alternative options and helps them find something even better than their initial choice.

- Acts with honesty and transparency throughout the process.

- Facilitates the buying experience without resorting to pushy or aggressive sales tactics.

- Makes the buying process easy for the customer.

- Demonstrates good business acumen and understands the importance of creating value for the customer.

- Has the ambition to give the customer a little more than they would expect.

Adopting the customer's perspective during the buying process prompts a crucial question:

"Who do we need to be to become the salesperson we would want to engage with ourselves?"

Certain qualities and approaches must be inherent in the salesperson to create a sense of security, attentiveness, and enthusiasm for progressing through the buying process. These factors collectively contribute to a positive and satisfying buying experience. Our experience shows that the better you become as a professional salesperson in creating positive buying experiences for your customers, the faster and more frequently they will buy from you!

Beyond Selling

Salespeople typically present their offers to potential customers, highlighting the features and benefits they provide, aiming to solve essential issues for the customer. While this approach appears obvious, does it truly lead to the best buying experience? Let's shift our perspective back to the buyer's side and consider how effective it is when someone talks about their offer and its benefits. How genuinely are they listening to our thoughts?

As discussed in the previous chapter, Joseph envisioned that exemplary salespeople would do something different. His hypothesis was that they wouldn't simply be selling; he sought to understand their approach and how they achieved it. He presumed that these salespeople connected with customers on a deeper level to uncover their true desires and not only their needs.

These exceptional salespeople differed significantly from average ones in their self-perception and how they related to customers. They appeared distinct in their feelings about themselves and their customer relationships. it appeared that they shifted away from the belief that customers were obligated to make a purchase. Instead, they approached meetings with the understanding that the decision to pursue a business deal was in their hands - the salespeople. This control over the decision-making process, whether to proceed, pause, abandon, or conclude a sale at any point, significantly boosted their self-confidence and proficiency. This empowerment directly translated to more effective sales and achieving the outcomes that the exemplars Joseph studied were aiming for.

The customer's choice alone no longer dictated their outcomes, the salespeople felt empowered to say "no" to a customer. They gathered information solely to assess if they could genuinely help the customer and to make their own decision on whether to proceed further in the sales process. Effectively, they took on the role of the *Trusted Advisor* for the customer.

This distinctive approach set these exceptional salespeople apart from the prototype of type-A, high-performing individuals, often measured solely by their aggressiveness, determination, and eagerness to close deals. Most salespeople believe their job is to go to the customer, convince them by presenting features and benefits, and sell what they have, aiming for the deal and the associated financial gain.

The typical sales attitude is often:

"I am here to make the sale!"

We have all encountered overly eager salespeople and we all know how it feels to be subjected to their sales tactics. This attitude alters the dynamics of the customer relationship, triggering resistance since the perspective is:

"I am trying to sell you!"

Every question asked by the salesperson creates a sense of being sold in the customer. It's no wonder customers feel this way; the salesperson has already decided they want the customer to make a purchase without knowing if it genuinely benefits them. Many salespeople (and often the sales managers who guide them, pushing for "numbers" at any cost) are indifferent to this fact; their sole aim is to close the sale, leading to a high degree of negative manipulation.

Although this approach may generate some and even a lot of short-term sales, it does not align with the strategy presented in this book. If your intention is solely to push sales to customers or through your sales team, then this book may not be suitable for you. Instead, this book is a tribute to "anti-selling" tactics in sales.

Satisfaction Selling begins with a willingness to let go of the intention to sell anything when interacting with potential customers. This idea is a profound departure from how many sales managers and salespeople think about selling, and what is also presented in many sales processes as well. In the *Satisfaction Cycle* model, the crucial question is not about selling, but about genuinely assisting the customer to buy what they want and need to achieve their goals and get what they truly want. Within this model the ideal is about creating real value and therefore more satisfaction, not just with the end result of achieving the sale, but also with the customer's experience of the sales process itself.

The crucial question for the professional salesperson using the *Satisfaction Cycle* model of selling is:

"How can I serve and help my customers acquire what they want?"

Sometimes, this may involve walking away from potential customers when you and your offering will not truly benefit them. *Satisfaction Selling* is for those aspiring to be and act as true *Trusted Advisors*.

In consultative selling approaches, the ideal salesperson is often described as a *Trusted Advisor*. On paper, the goals may seem similar to how we describe the *Trusted Advisor* above. However, the true distinction lies beneath the surface. Other methods primarily focus on teaching salespeople how to sell, emphasizing tactics such as questioning, handling objections, presenting offers, and utilizing forceful closing techniques. What the *Satisfaction Cycle* approach offers extends beyond mere sales and solving customers' problems. We illuminate the path to becoming genuine partners in our customers' success. While many people talk about this concept, we, from the *Satisfaction Selling Movement*, go beyond mere words and the facade of empty promises.

Other sales approaches also discuss partnering with customers, but often focus more on closing tactics and turning a "no" into a "yes" during sales training. They believe that obtaining the sale is the ultimate goal for the salesperson. Their advice is to persistently ask the customer three more times when faced with a "no". In contrast, we teach salespeople to discern early on whether they can genuinely improve the customer's situation. If meaningful improvement is not possible, we guide the salesperson on gracefully saying "no" and moving on to the next potential customer, where they have a greater chance of making a positive impact.

Knowing when to say "no" enhances effectiveness and ensures the efficient utilization of everybody's time and energy. If a salesperson realizes that their products and services cannot genuinely assist the customer in creating real value, there is no need to continue discussions, even if a good relationship exists between them. Something much better awaits them elsewhere.

In all fairness, many salespeople already possess the attitude of serving and genuinely caring for their customers. When asked about crucial elements in sales, they often emphasize nurturing relationships or providing education and sharing expertise. Some prioritize building relationships, going to great lengths to create and maintain them - even offering excessive effort, time, and service without leading to a proper sale. However, relying solely on relationship-building as the starting point for a sales process *can* be both risky and dysfunctional, as discussed in Chapter 1.

Contrastingly, technical salespeople often perceive themselves as educators rather than traditional salespeople. They aim to educate customers about their product and share their expertise, hoping that eventually, the customer will possess sufficient knowledge and interest to make a purchase. While this attitude is a good starting point for customer service, it may not be enough to consistently generate sales outcomes and maintain good customer relations.

Both attitudes – focusing on the relationship or on the technical aspects – have something good in them. What will make them better is for the salesperson to have clarity about the customer's desired outcome and their own outcome. Then, going even further and combining relationship building and consulting with an outcome in mind, a powerful mindset appears. When all these aspects are applied simultaneously, you have the foundation for the ideal attitude for *Satisfaction Selling*. By maximizing relationships and outcomes simultaneously, with the help of expertise and consulting, the salesperson becomes what *we* call a *Trusted Advisor*.

The Mindset of a *Trusted Advisor*

Being a *Trusted Advisor* holds significant power. Unlike a typical salesperson a *Trusted Advisor* assumes the role of a true consultant first focused on helping the customer to achieve their desired outcomes, not on selling them but on discovering how to assist them by providing resources that generate the outcome. In this capacity the primary goal is to serve and assist customers in achieving their desired outcomes for themselves and their organizations. This mindset diverges from that of a salesperson fixated on selling a product or service. A *Trusted Advisor* recognizes that customers are not interested in the product or service itself; they care about the positive changes and improvements it enables them to achieve. This is what we the call the *Outcome of the Outcome* which we will discuss more in detail in Chapter 6.

The question at hand is:

"What distinguishes someone as a Trusted Advisor?"

The role encompasses two vital components: being *"Trusted"* and being an *"Advisor."* In the *"Advisor"* role, the focus is on prioritizing customer interests over personal outcomes. It begins with a fundamental inquiry:

"What benefits or advantages can I bring to my customer to improve their situation?"

And advisors continue to ask themselves what would make things better for the customer, their organization, their processes, or whatever they are doing. This mindset becomes an inherent part of the interaction with customers. The *"Trusted"* aspect signifies that the customer views the advisor as reliable, truthful, and capable of delivering according to their guidance. Thus, a *Trusted Advisor*, unlike a conventional salesperson, adopts a customer-centric mindset instead of a self-serving one.

Trust, the second essential aspect of being a *Trusted Advisor*, is intangible and challenging to quantify. However, individuals can recognize the feeling of trust. Often described as "gut feelings," these internal signals provide clear indications of our level of trust or mistrust. *Trust* within a relationship is built upon the ability to understand and anticipate the other person's behavior over time.

When interacting with a salesperson, potential customers instinctively tune into these internal trust signals. They assess whether the advisor is reliable, truthful, and capable of fulfilling their advice. Customers possess an innate ability to discern whether a salesperson genuinely aims to assist them or is merely making empty promises. Nonverbal cues and signals reveal authenticity, congruence, and consistency with the information presented. While much of this evaluation occurs at a preconscious level, customers intuitively sense a salesperson's trustworthiness.

Building trust involves making it easy for others to predict your words and actions. Aligning your actions with your words consistently over time is the shortest path to achieving this, i.e. "walking the talk," instead of just "talking a good game." This alignment fosters an experience that makes it easy for others to trust you as a person and trust what you say and do.

Sales success starts with adopting the attitude and mindset of a *Trusted Advisor*. However, it's essential to clarify that this doesn't negate the salesperson's legitimate desire for a personal sales intent. Salespeople must have a clear purpose for engaging with customers, ensuring a mutual benefit. The critical factor lies in balancing the *Trusted Advisor's* focus on giving and getting.

The interplay between a *Trusted Advisor's* attitude and a salesperson's intent continually influences each other. This dynamic interaction allows the salesperson to authentically communicate their intentions. This involves expressing a genuine desire to serve the customer and assessing whether they can provide a beneficial product and service. Simultaneously, they acknowledge the expectation of compensation for the value they bring.

Salespeople are tasked with generating revenue and profit for their company. This straightforward approach requires working with customers who can pay and are willing to support the sales process. Transparency regarding one's intent is crucial; ideally, professional salespeople live and work at the intersection where the wants of the customer and their own wants overlap.

The key aspect of the *Trusted Advisor's* attitude and mindset is always initiating the interaction from the customer's perspective, considering their wants and needs rather than solely focusing on one's own wants and needs. Ultimately, if you intend to build long-term, sustainable business results you can only get what you truly want by effectively serving the customer. If you are unable to assist a customer and create real value for them, it is best to move on and provide support and service to the next one.

In summary, sales success thrives on maintaining a delicate balance between a *Trusted Advisor's* attitude to be of assistance and a salesperson's clear intent to effectively serve the customer by selling them what they need to achieve their outcomes. Authenticity, transparency, and a customer-centric approach are paramount in building meaningful and mutually beneficial interactions.

The Freedom to Walk Away

The distinction of a true *Trusted Advisor* is essential. It might already be clear what the difference is between a true *Trusted Advisor* who is there to help the customer and the *"Trusted Advisor"* who is really there to sell as their first and foremost priority at any cost. Customers can sense genuine interest from a salesperson and distinguish when it's lacking. Either way, the customer will know.

Customers may not understand why they feel a salesperson is inattentive or distracted. Non-verbal cues transmit a wealth of information, revealing what's happening in the salesperson's mind. This feeling may for example stem from the salesperson not genuinely listening to understand but just waiting for the customer to finish before resuming their sales pitch.

While skilled actors might be able to control these cues, adopting the right mindset is simpler. Then, your non-verbal communication will be congruent and consistent with what you are presenting. When you are confident that you can truly help the customer, it also shows. All of this is communicated, partially with words but mostly non-verbally, and eventually, it gives the customer this sense that you are truly present and care for them.

Much of this process is preconscious to the customer, making it impossible to fake being a *Trusted Advisor*. If a salesperson pushes a customer to buy for personal gain rather than the customer's benefit, *Satisfaction Selling* won't work. *Trust* is fundamental; the customer must emotionally buy into you as a person before they can or will consider your offering.

You cannot implement the *Satisfaction Cycle* effectively and be unethical at the same time. A true, *Trusted Advisor* naturally becomes an ethical sales-person. Because what you are doing is listening to customers' intentions, values, and desires. If their desires do not match what you have to offer, you know you have to move on. You qualify when there is and is not a match, which establishes the ethics in selling. If your solution does not work for the customer, there is no reason to continue.

Then you can say to the customer:

"Now may not be the best time for us to continue, because I don't believe I have a solution that would benefit you the way you want. Perhaps in the future or on a different project I may have just what you need, and I'd be thrilled to assist you then. In the meantime, it's possible that another company might better suit your needs."

Ethics in selling revolves around achieving mutually beneficial outcomes. Compromising your intent and the customer's wants would be unethical. Unless it benefits both the seller and the buyer continuing to sell is unethical, the way we define it. What defines an excellent salesperson is that they are willing to walk away. Even if they think a sale is possible, they understand its possibility doesn't mandate necessity.

Consider a potential customer, a person with whom you feel that maybe you do not want to get the outcome of the sale. Perhaps you realize this person represents something that would make the creation of the outcome unreasonably challenging, that, in some way this person and situation would prevent a mutually rewarding outcome. While you know it *would* be possible for you to help the customer, you also believe it is not necessary.

A great example of when to walk away might be when the situation, or the customer themselves, would cause the sale to become unprofitable if you made it. It's critical in ethical selling that both parties get their outcome and remaining profitable is essential to that end for the salesperson. We will discuss the concept of ethical persuasion in more detail in Chapter 4.

The Value of Uncertainty

One crucial aspect that prepares a salesperson for success is embracing uncertainty about how to serve the customer. While you may believe your product or service can benefit them, the specifics are unknown. Starting from a position of *Not Knowing* allows for discovery with the customer.

In sales you often confront a customer who is questioning you, or you experience something else that you might call resistance. The customer might be unsure whether there is a possible match, and the more you can acknowledge, accept, and contain their insecurity, the faster you can move the process in the right direction. While the customer is uncertain, you maintain your own certainty and give them time. A salesperson's ability to be self-referenced, self-organized, and self-directed is enormously powerful. These abilities set you free. They ensure that you remain open and mentally flexible.

Still, you have a solid external reference: knowing what you want with the customer, why you are there, and being sure how you can serve them. At the same time, you recognize that you cannot control other people. Instead of imposing your agenda on them, you pay attention to them – where they think they are and where they want to go. This open state of mind will give you the edge.

Every decision involves rejecting alternative possibilities. Adopting the *Trusted Advisor* mindset means refraining from self-serving selling tactics. Even if you've found success in such sales, consider the potential benefits of being a true *Trusted Advisor*, helping customers make informed buying decisions rather than just selling them a product.

Imagine the positive transformations and significant improvements your business could experience over the next few years. Our experience suggests that you will likely enjoy high customer satisfaction, loyalty, and recurring business, leading to a more stable, healthy, and solid business. Satisfied customers may even become your *Positive Activists*, enthusiastically promoting your business to their friends and colleagues.

This way, your existing customer base will provide a solid foundation for future success, and you will attract new customers who remain loyal beyond their initial purchase. Think of it as the journey of top athletes who are consistently working towards reaching the podium. By consistently embracing the *Trusted Advisor* mindset, you'll be on your way to achieving your own aspirations. This transformative approach converts a salesperson into a consultative partner, fully committed to contributing to their customers' success by facilitating informed and high-quality decision-making.

In the next chapter, we will explore the physiological and psychological aspects of being in an open and receptive excitatory bias - the *Green State* - that we introduced in Chapter 2, and the opposite - a closed and inhibitory bias associated with problems which we call the *Red State*.

Furthermore, we'll examine the critical shift within the Satisfaction Cycle model, emphasizing the importance of both the salesperson, as a *Trusted Advisor*, and the customer operating from the *Green State*. This approach marks a departure from traditional sales and consulting tactics, which often start by placing the customer in the *Red State*. Such traditional strategies focus on identifying and addressing customer problems by leveraging the negative emotions tied to these issues.

4

BECOMING A BRAIN TECHNICIAN

Building Emotional and Logical Certainty in High-value Complex Sales

Prior to embarking on my transformative journey with Henrik and Joseph, I often found myself trapped in negative emotional state during customer meetings. I could sense my heart racing within the confines of my constricted chest. The rush of blood pulsating through my veins seemed almost audible, making movement feel hard. I was sluggish, weighed down by the burdens of negativity. The tension in my voice mirrored the unease I felt within.

Regardless of the specific label for such a mood, the physiological manifestations were unmistakable and exposed my emotionally negative state to others. Needless to say, this mindset was far from conducive to achieving success, let alone the toll it took on my overall well-being in enduring prolonged periods of stress.

Fast forward a mere two years into my learning journey; vividly, I recall a customer meeting. While the focus was on negotiating commercial terms and prices rather than sales, this scenario showcased the transformative power of mood. The meeting room buzzed with numerous participants, and a number of individuals appeared to be in a bad mood, their voices pitched high, and their facial expressions etched with dissatisfaction. However, armed with my newfound knowledge and skills, I resolved to maintain a state of calmness and positivity, and kept my positive emotional state, regardless of the prevailing dispositions around me.

As the meeting unfolded, complaints and objections filled the room. Neverthe-less, my ultimate mission became preserving my positive mood hoping to ignite a contagious influence that would permeate the atmosphere. Of course, this did not change the fact that there was a significant price increase on the table, but it helped turn the meeting into a more constructive one and ease the path for future collaboration.

The deliberate attention to maintaining a positive mood not only paved the way for potential future collaborations but also enabled the customer to approach the pricing negotiation with a more receptive mindset. Even within the realm of sales, the extraordinary power and impact of the mood should never be underestimated. Its ability to shape the trajectory of interactions and foster fruitful relationships is truly remarkable.

The *Green State* and the *Red State*

Surely, you've experienced emotionally positive moments in your life - those instances that bring forth a sense of calmness, leaving you balanced, satisfied, and brimming with unwavering confidence. This feeling not only impacts your inner self but also influences the world around you. People catch glimpses of this emotional balance and harmony, witnessing its reflection in your very being and presence, because you express this state of being physiologically.

In this state, your voice emanates a captivating resonance. Those who speak in such a way fascinate and entrance everyone who listens. This vocal quality is not mere coincidence; it stems from the depth and regularity of your breaths - a physiological characteristic of an emotionally positive state. As your eyes meet the gaze of those around you, they are met with an irresistible allure. Your pupils naturally dilate, creating a magnetic appeal for those who behold you. Deep within your chest, your heart orchestrates a symphony of tranquility. Its beats resound slowly and steadily, echoing the rhythm of peace.

You are liberated from the chaotic rush of the outside world; your heart embraces a cadence that mirrors the serenity of your body-mind, the conjunction of your body and mind that arises when both are deeply aligned and congruent with one another. In this way, guided by a clear purpose with each step you take, time becomes a companion rather than a master. Life's external hustle and bustle fade into insignificance as you navigate with unsurpassed clarity and unwavering determination. Every interaction becomes an opportunity, every challenge a steppingstone, and every encounter a chance to surpass past achievements.

It is within this kind of state of emotional positivity that the most potent sales mindset takes root. When you harness your inner balance, your sales competence reaches its peak. Your confidence becomes infectious, igniting curiosity and inspiring action. All of this propels you toward success like never before.

Moods and emotions may seem irrelevant when discussing business and sales, but they hold significant power in reality. Moods and feelings are contagious. Let's consider two scenarios. In the first one, your boss arrives in high spirits, radiating positivity. In the second, your boss comes in a lousy mood, venting about a terrible weekend. Now, think about the ripple effect in these contrasting situations. If you were to seek approval or action on an important matter, when would you have a better chance of achieving your desired outcome? It's natural to keep your distance when your boss is in a bad mood.

You may have noticed that when someone at work is in a bad mood, it soon affects your colleagues as well, and vice versa. The person with the most power in the room has the influence to spread their mood more easily to others. If someone is angry and ranting, it's easy for others to mirror that negativity. Conversely, if someone remains calm amidst the chaos, that calmness can also spread. It's like the presence of the Jedis in the Star Wars saga, who were skilled at spreading a sense of tranquility, enabling sound decision-making and action. As a salesperson, you bear significant responsibility for your mood. Whether you've had a good or bad morning, it shouldn't be shown to the customer. Be mindful of your mood when you enter the world, as it will undoubtedly influence those around you, including your customers.

However, the reason we emphasize the importance of mood is not that we think it is all just about spreading happiness. Psychologist Daniel Goleman explains an even more critical point: our mood directly impacts our ability to perceive things. Goleman and his fellow researchers refer to this as emotional intelligence. In the Preface of their book: *Primal leadership*

(Daniel Goleman, Annie McKee, Richard E. Boyatzis, Harvard Business Press, 2002) they put it this way:

"The fundamental task of leaders, we argue, is to prime good feeling in those they lead. That occurs when a leader creates resonance - a reservoir of positivity that frees the best in people."

When people feel good, they tend to have a positive outlook and notice opportunities. Conversely, when people feel bad, they often focus solely on the negatives. Their perceptions and thinking differ significantly in these contrasting states, and since mood influences our thinking, it also drives our behavior and actions. Your mood, as well as your customer's, substantially affects the sales situation and your chances of creating value and achieving success. In other words, the outcome will differ if a salesperson approaches a meeting anxiously rather than with contentment and confidence. Moods play a crucial role in our thinking capabilities, with a good mood leading to better results.

Our underlying neurological state is crucial in shaping our mood. We can oscillate between two distinct positions that define our state of mind - the excitatory bias, characterized by positivity and openness, and the inhibitory bias, characterized by negativity and closure. Depending on which state is active, we are either in the inhibitory or excitatory bias. These states impact our mood and physiology. Henrik simplifies this concept by using the terms *Red State* and *Green State*, respectively.

The *Red State* represents the inhibitory bias, also known as the fight-or-flight response. This stress response, triggered by our sympathetic nervous system, prepares us to face real or perceived threat and dangers. In ancient times, this response was vital for survival. However, in our modern lives, genuine threats are scarce or nonexistent. Nonetheless, we are familiar with the sensations associated with the stress response.

In the *Red State*, our hands become sweaty, our heart beats faster, our vision narrows, and our mouth becomes dry. Blood rushes to our internal organs, away from the external peripheral limbs, our arms, and legs. Movements become more hesitant and inhibited because there is less blood flow. Our responses slow down, and a sense of jitteriness or even shaking may arise. We may become nauseous. All these physiological changes accompany the *Red State*; others can perceive and feel them.

When someone is in the *Red State*, experiencing a stress response, their perception of the world is filtered through a lens of threat and stress. Their thoughts revolve around avoiding potential dangers, what they must avoid, and getting away from the threat or danger they perceive. If we are talking about salespeople, this might involve evading competition, steering clear of the sales manager, sidestepping price discussions, or avoiding conflicts with customers. They must avoid, avoid, avoid, avoid... The threat orientation is strong, leading to hyper-attentiveness to specific elements that are perceived as threatening or dangerous.

Our neurology shapes our perceptions, similar to the "blue car effect." When you buy a new blue car, every car you notice suddenly seems blue. You become oblivious to red, green, or black cars, only focusing on the blue ones. The same principle applies to the *Red State*, where our neurology prioritizes our survival by being hyper-attentive to the most critical factors. The more we enter the *Red State*, the narrower our focus becomes. In a sales situation, we might become fixated on one direction, attempting to force the customer to follow our lead. The *Red State* of mind is not what you would wish for yourself. In selling, it is not helping you either.

The *Green State* is the foundation for successful human engagement and the basis for the *Satisfaction Cycle* as a strategy. When in the *Green State*, you remain neurologically and mentally open, embracing the notion that there are multiple paths to follow and answers to discover. You are receptive to a range of possibilities and ready to explore new avenues. In this state, your parasympathetic nervous system takes charge, and you no longer feel the need to avoid potential harm. Instead, you actively seek out possibilities.

The *Green State* of mind is not only a mental state but also expressed physiologically. It stands in stark contrast to the clammy sensation of sweaty hands. When your parasympathetic nervous system is activated, you exude confidence. Calmness and self-assurance radiate from you. Your heartbeat slows down, settling into a steady rhythm. Your eyes dilate, and you are not sweating. You embrace a leisurely pace, taking your time. As you speak, your voice carries resonance, enhanced by deep and deliberate breaths. There is no stuttering or feeling that you need to take a breath before speaking.

All these physiological expressions become part of your non-verbal com-munication. You may not consciously realize that you are exhibiting these signs, just as the recipient of your non-verbal communication may not be consciously aware of their own response to it. Despite all of this occurring outside our conscious awareness, the neurological state wields a tremendous influence over sales situations. You cannot conceal your state and emotions. As Paul Ekman often gets quoted,

"Your thoughts may remain private, but your emotions are public."

Operating from the *Green State* means that the parasympathetic part of your autonomic nervous system is active. In this state, you possess a range of options and choices. Your mind becomes more open to possibilities, and you become more creative, flexible, and adaptive. Being in the *Green State* allows you to let go of the need to control everything, including the customer and the sales process. Operating in the *Green State* liberates salespeople from fear and doubt, enabling them to function like artists who can adapt and work in a flow, ultimately producing results. So, as discussed in Chapter 2, the starting point counts, and it all begins with the salesperson's ability to get into and remain in the *Green State*.

It's important to note again that the positive *Green State* is not synonymous with being overly energetic or exuberantly happy. Instead, it simply signifies a neurologically open state. Negative feelings may still arise in this state, but they are viewed as information rather than emotionally defining the overall state. It is unwise to suppress negative feelings, as life encompasses both positive and negative emotions and feelings. An open neurological state - the *Green State* - allows you to accept the entirety of the spectrum while maintaining an overall mentally open state.

While the *Green State* is associated with positive energy, it can be experienced at various energy levels, as displayed in Figure 4.1. The *Green State* should not be confused with high energy alone. In a low-energy *Green State*, you experience a sense of calm and contentment, which proves beneficial for sales activities such as planning, preparation, and deep curious listening. On the other hand, a high energy level Green State manifests as confidence, excitement, and passion, serving as a powerful tool for energizing and inspiring others. Starting with a lower energy level is generally preferred in the sales process to avoid overwhelming customers. However, higher energy levels may be appropriately employed to generate enthusiasm and excitement when it is time to present the solution and motivate the customer to act.

The Starting Point Counts !
- High versus Low Energy

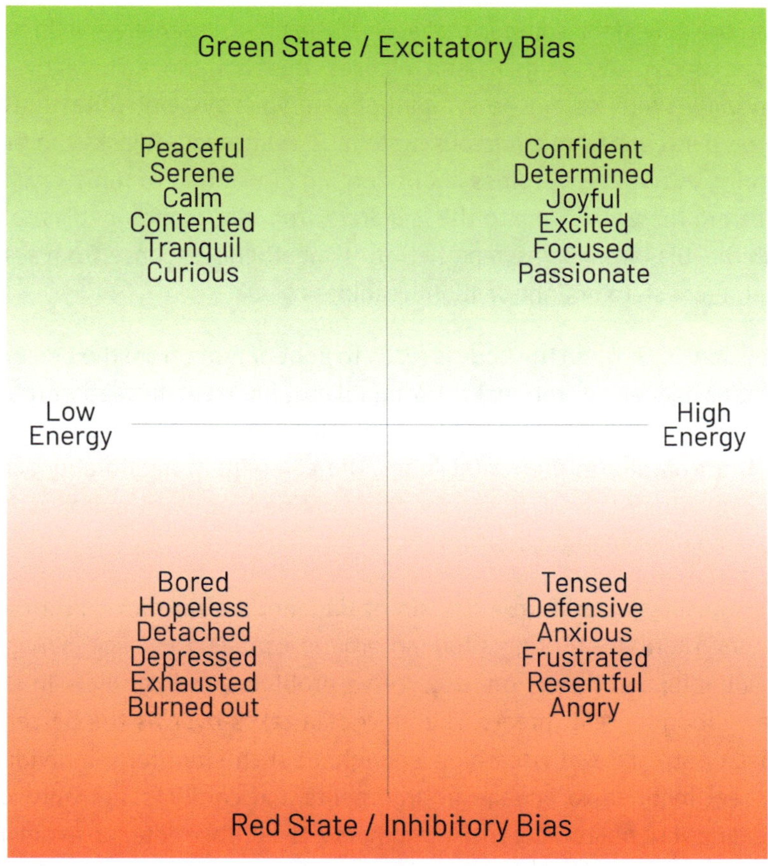

Figure 4.1 Starting Point Counts! High versus Low Energy

Soothing Your Mental and Emotional Hijacker

When faced with emotional disruptions, the brain preferences the limbic system - a primal structure within our brain. An integral part of the limbic system is the amygdala which is the primary sub-organ of the brain responsible for processing threats, anxiety, and aggression. Whenever we feel threatened or stressed, whenever we build up to a sense of aggression or feel like we need to defend ourselves, whether by running away or by attacking, the amygdala takes center stage, triggering a cascade of reactions in the brain.

When the amygdala is firing, it takes over the brain. It perceives a threat or danger, sends distress signals, and releases stress hormones. This activation eventually switches on the sympathetic nervous system while shutting off the parasympathetic nervous system. The amygdala hijacks the brain, meaning everything becomes about fighting or wanting to run away. It's a shift from the *Green State* to the *Red State*, from the excitatory bias to the inhibitory bias, from parasympathetic to sympathetic response, from a state of calm to a state of fight-or-flight readiness.

In the *Red State*, when the body is ready to fight or flight from the perceived threat or danger, our rational thinking takes a backseat. Instead of relying on the cortical brain structures, such as the right and left hemispheres and the frontal and prefrontal lobes, the cerebellum gets highly active. The cerebellum is responsible for coordinating high-level motor actions, preparing us to take physical action.

In the business world, true threats or dangers are rare for white-collar workers. There are no tigers lurking around corners. However, managers, salespeople, and others often perceive problems and conflicts in their organization as real threats. The amygdala takes over as the perceived threat or stress level rises high enough. In such situations, individuals may feel inclined to engage in arguments and conflicts, not only with colleagues but potentially with customers as well. They enter an avoidance mode, simply wanting to escape the situation as swiftly as possible. The cerebellum generates a strong urge to take action and move away from the perceived problem.

In business, what most people do is that they quiet their cerebellum. Even though they may feel the urge to get up and run away or even to physically confront the other person, they remain seated in their chair. They internalize and suppress their impulses due to the constraints imposed by societal norms. This repression can lead to elevated levels of adrenal stress chemicals like cortisol, further impeding brain function. What anyone in this situation would do is just wait for the thing and situation to end right there. The system is frozen.

In such circumstances, when a salesperson enters the scene, promising to solve the problem, the person experiences relief. As the issue is resolved, stress dissipates. One might think this presents an excellent opportunity for sales. As discussed below, many traditional sales models actually leverage this mechanism, assuming that customers must be in a state of distress and perceive themselves as having a problem they want to fix. They start from the premise that the customer must be in the *Red State*.

However, a person consumed by stress and cortisol is not thinking clearly. Being frozen, they are just hoping for a savior. They become passive, surrendering their responsibility of getting the outcome and leaving the decision-making to the salesperson. They *may* achieve a favorable outcome; or they may *not* because they are not truly engaged. They are simply relieved not to have the problem, allowing their exhausted brain to recover from the turmoil of the *Red State*.

The reason for redirecting the brain away from awaking the amygdala that leads to the *Red State* and switching to activating the excitatory bias - the *Green State* - is to promote high-quality thinking, benefiting both the salesperson and the customer in the long run. In the *Green State*, the left cortical hemisphere can process information analytically, making sense of both obvious and subtle details. Simultaneously, the right cortical hemisphere becomes more accessible and adept at recognizing patterns. Patterns emerge from the intersection of what is present and what is absent.

The right cortical hemisphere can notice both positive and negative information about what is there and what is *not* there. For instance, the right cortical hemisphere helps us see a tree by also perceiving the spaces between leaves and branches. In the *Green State*, the brain prioritizes the cortical brain, engaging both the left and right hemispheres, and the forebrain. However, it's important to note that the entire brain remains active in both the *Green State* and in the *Red State*. The preference lies in where the brain directs its energy and attention and what is the most prominent way of processing.

In the *Green State*, this interaction between the cortical brain's two sides enables high-level pattern recognition and accurate assessment. Moving to more integrated cortical processing also moves the cognitive process forward in the brain to the frontal and prefrontal lobes, often referred to as the "executive brain", where consequential thinking is processed. We become capable of considering the possibilities and their implications when we are in the *Green State*. When we access the forebrain and cortically process in the *Green State*, we begin to see both the opportunities and the obstacles.

When we are in the *Red State* cognitive processing moves back to the mid and rear brain which are more reactive, and more specifically the amygdala and limbic system, the center of emotive responses, become active and dominant so all we see are obstacles, unable to recognize the options and possibilities that lie beyond the immediate circumstance or situation.

That is why it is crucial to not activate the amygdala - to "soothe" the hijacker - and transition to higher-level cortical reasoning. To some extent, this also suppresses the immediate cerebellar response for a while, allowing us to slow down, pause, and ask the right questions to gain a clearer understanding of our situation and the potential paths forward.

Traditional Selling, The Fear Cycle, And Poor Decision Making

Essentially, all selling revolves around influencing the decision-making process that customers undergo when making a purchase. The most crucial decision a customer makes is one that leads to a future as good as or better than their present situation. For sales professionals operating in high-value complex sales environments, guiding customers through this decision-making process takes top priority.

Customer decision-making generally falls into two categories, depending on the neurological bias they hold:

1. **Addressing past and present problems:** This approach involves tackling problems customers have encountered or are currently facing, with the aim of mitigating their negative effects. Here the customer's decision is typically made in the *Red State*.

2. **Projecting a problem-free future:** This approach focuses on envisioning a future devoid of past problems, fundamentally better and offering options that may not currently exist, resulting in more favorable outcomes. In this case, the customer's decision is typically made in the *Green State*.

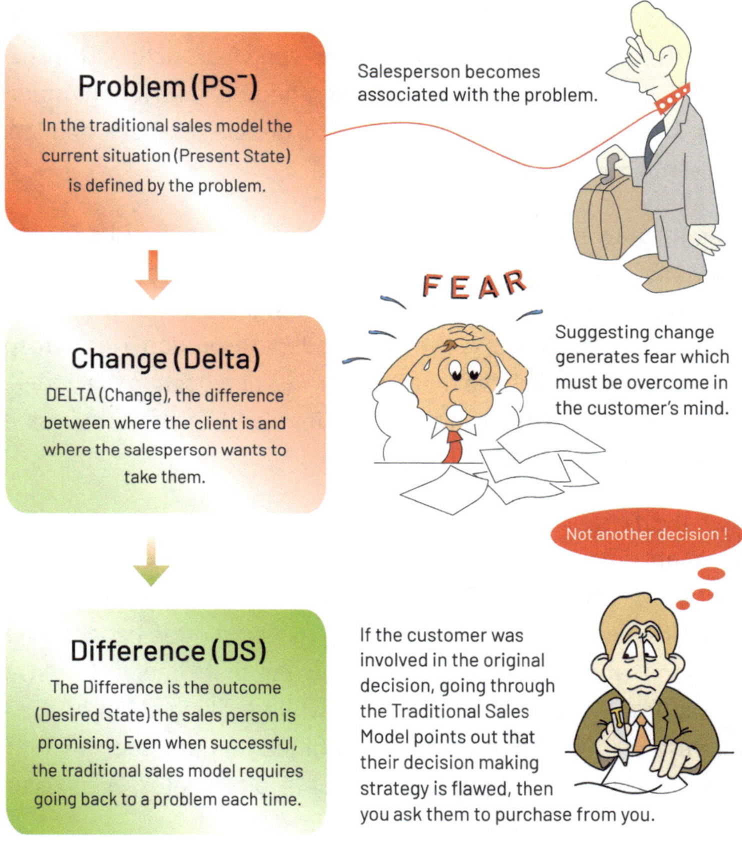

Figure 4.2 A traditional problem-solving sales and consulting model

The first form, addressing past and present problems, aligns with traditional problem-solving models of selling, as depicted in Figure 4.2. Here, the current situation is defined by the problem that the customer is facing. This is the *Present State Negative* - or *PS⁻* for short, where the adjective *"Negative"* indicates that this is a negative state, defined by the problem. The *Change (Delta)* represents the disparity between where the customer is now, and where the salesperson wants to take them which is to their *Desired State* - or *DS* for short - where the problem ceases to exist. Thus, the *Desired State*

(DS) embodies the outcome promised by the salesperson: the resolution of the problem.

In this traditional problem-solving model, a classic persuasion pattern is applied, focusing on persuading the customer to purchase the solution offered by the salesperson by eliciting threats and fears of loss. This strategy deliberately prompts customers to access a neurocognitive inhibitory bias - the *Red State* - triggering the amygdala, as discussed above, and leading to a decision based on fear.

However, by drawing attention to the problem, examining its intricacies, including costs and implications if left unresolved, customers recognize that the problem stems from a previous decision, and they may associate their decision-making process with the need for resolution. This perception can lead customers to believe that decision-making itself is the underlying issue, particularly if they were directly involved in the previous decision-making process.

Additionally, if the same salesperson provided a solution previously, customers might implicitly link that salesperson to their current problem, potentially undermining confidence in their offerings, as indicated in Figure 4.2. In fact, becoming the link to the problem would often happen even for a salesperson who meets the customer for the first time. Just by making the customer talk about their problems while looking them in the eyes is enough to establish that anchor. This highlights a paradox: while the traditional problem-solving approach may result in sales, even recurring ones, it ultimately carries an inherent "expiry date."

During Joseph's original research while developing the *Satisfaction Cycle* model, he indeed observed that clients he interviewed began contemplating changing products, services, and suppliers after four sales cycles rooted in this traditional problem-solving approach, guiding customers through an elicitation process of their problems in an attempt to create new sales opportunities.

The implication was clear: even when the solution the clients were sold had been implemented and was deemed successful, it resulted in new problems, pointed out by the salesperson. This cycle turned recurring sales into a *Fear Cycle* rather than a *Satisfaction Cycle*. Thus, when the problem-based sales process repeatedly forced them to recognize the problems they had also purchased along with the solution, they began looking for new and different solutions without the problems.

On the other hand, when a positive solution-based sales process is implemented, leading from success to greater success in relation to the framing of the decision-making process and the results produced - corresponding to the second form of decision-making discussed earlier, projecting a problem-free future - there was not a limit to the number of times the sales process could be used, and each cycle led to greater trust and satisfaction with the solutions provided.

Establishing a positive framework within the sales process, which naturally results in the projection of a favorable future outcome, is fundamental to *Satisfaction Selling* and the *Satisfaction Cycle* model. This positive outlook typically arises when customers operate from a state of receptivity and openness, i.e. the *Green State*, thereby enhancing satisfaction with the sales process itself.

Creating a positive frame in the sales process that leads to the projection of a positive future outcome that naturally happens when a customer is operating from the *Green State* that also generates a sense of satisfaction in the sales process itself is the basis of the *Satisfaction Cycle* model and *Satisfaction Selling*.

A Counter-Intuitive Approach to High-Value Complex Selling

Starting from the premise that all selling is the selling of certainty about a future outcome that is at least as good or better than the present situation, and that all decision-making is an emotionally driven process, as described above, the most important aspect of the sales process is helping the customer access and sustain a positive outlook about the future from a positively oriented emotional state - the *Green State*.

While it may appear counterintuitive, initiating the sales process by establishing satisfaction with the customers' current situation yields numerous benefits that support achieving a positive outcome. Firstly, when customers recognize the strengths of their current situation, including their choice of product, service, or provider, they begin to view their decision-making process favorably. And when customers perceive their decision-making process positively, they are more inclined to make decisions to progress with your solutions. Furthermore, customers can more easily envision positive future outcomes from the *Green State* than from the *Red State*.

The ability to access and maintain a *Green State* with customers is paramount for sales professionals in managing their customers' emotional state, facilitating decision-making free from mental friction and resistance, and achieving positive outcomes in the sales process. Avoiding inadvertently triggering the negative inhibitory bias or the *Red State* is crucial. Emphasizing problems can elicit the inhibitory bias, leading to emotional hijacking. Several critical issues arise when this occurs. Firstly, customers dwell on the negative past and its implications for the future rather than focusing on potential solutions and their benefits.

Once individuals adopt a particular outlook on the future, they develop cognitive inertia around that projection, which must be overcome. It is therefore preferable to prevent the creation of negative cognitive inertia altogether. We'll delve into the concept of cognitive inertia in more detail in Chapter 5.

Setting Brains up for Promoting the Right Action

As we shift our focus towards envisioning a positive future and the desired outcomes we wish to achieve, our brain preferences the frontal and prefrontal cortex, the brain region responsible for processing projections of future possibilities and engaging in high-level consequential thinking. When we are in the *Green State*, we also access the parasympathetic response of the autonomic nervous system. Once we've shifted to forebrain processing, we begin projecting different scenarios and the brain conducts genuine risk assessment free from the influence of fear, threat, or stress. The brain can now rapidly sort through a wide range of possible scenarios, and with more training it can do so even faster.

Our minds and bodies are intricately interconnected and work in singularity. When our brain begins to explore preferred future possibilities, our physical state also undergoes a transformation. It is impossible for us to think without simultaneously experiencing sensations within our bodies. Through our senses, such as seeing, hearing, and feeling, as well as our sense of balance and spatial orientation processed in the vestibular and proprioceptive systems that create dynamic experience, we construct a mental representation that incorporates a comprehensive sensory experience. This way, we are experiencing the future before it even happens. We are essentially conducting a virtual simulation, so to speak.

When a person envisions what it is like to have achieved a desired outcome, the cerebellum, playing a vital role in motor control, coordination and fine-tuning of muscles becomes engaged and activated. As a result, the cerebellum initiates a micro-muscular process and responds as if the envisioned outcome is happening and afterwards has already been realized. This mental rehearsal gives us a somatic, visceral experience of what it is like to have achieved the desired outcome and the associated value and benefits.

This pre-experience of a future where our aspirations are fulfilled leads us to the decision point, where we commit to pursuing that outcome. While these concepts may seem peculiar initially, they align with the inherent neurocognitive functioning of the brain. Irrespective of the subject of our thoughts, the cerebellum readies us to experience it so that we can take action accordingly.

Once the brain has settled on a solution, the cerebellum is reinvigorated, generating physical, neuromuscular feelings that urge us to take action. It may involve something as straightforward as sitting in front of a computer to write a memo or an email. There is a motor action - physical activity - involved in doing that. This physical activity aligns with the cerebellum's crucial role in motor control, propelling us toward realizing our intentions.

At this stage, communication is taking place throughout the entire brain. The frontal lobes articulate the desired outcome:

"This is the outcome I want."

At the same time, the cortical brain engages in analysis, reasoning, and rational thinking to determine the path toward that outcome:

"This is the way I think we will get there."

And then the cerebellum triggers the necessary actions.

"This is how I will act to create the outcome."

The whole brain is now working synchronously to link intention and action to high-level outcomes.

The situation itself remains unchanged for the person involved, and the available information remains the same. The crucial difference lies in shifting the brain's preference away from an emotional response to the forebrain's frontal and prefrontal lobes, and consequential thinking. Instead of relying on the limbic system, the brain now employs logical and analytical reasoning processes. This shift results in distinct and more advantageous outcomes compared to relying solely on the amygdala, which is limited to fight-or-flight responses, or in extreme cases, freeze responses.

Taking Advantage of Full Brain Power

The *Satisfaction Cycle* is an exceptionally effective sales strategy due to its power to soothe the amygdala and the limbic system response. It emotionally guides the customers into the *Green State* - the relaxed and balanced state of high-level thinking, where they can genuinely think through what they want and consider the outcomes they desire. Quieting the limbic system, particularly the amygdala, instills a sense of well-being. The customers experience positive feelings. They feel good - about themselves, their company, their situation, you, and the solution you are presenting. This positive foundation fosters a deeper level of commitment and, ultimately, compliance. The customer becomes not only committed but also eager to take action. By employing this approach, a salesperson significantly reduces the occurrence of buyer's remorse or the sense of second thoughts.

Altogether there is far less mental friction in the system. This means there is less anxiety and fewer anxious interactions between the buyer and the seller regarding ensuring things go right or avoiding potential issues. There is much more cooperation and a sense of partnership and collaboration. The system operates with an integrated sense of satisfaction, where all parties involved are content with the unfolding process. Minds and brains are free to engage in open communication, leveraging the power of whole-brain interaction rather than being trapped in the trigger response of the amygdala, steeped in threat, and constantly anticipating problems.

When decisions are made solely based on the amygdala response, individuals frequently seek reassurance, repeatedly affirming:

"I'm going to be okay... I'm going to be okay..."

This creates mental friction within the system, resulting in increased costs for you as a supplier, more significant time investment for salespeople, reduced collaboration and less compliance, and a resistance to share information that would be useful. However, when the *Satisfaction Cycle* is embraced both parties actively participate in finding a solution, fostering a collaborative thinking process of exceptional quality. Any obstacles or issues that may arise are simply seen as valuable information rather than threats.

The *Satisfaction Cycle* is a powerful strategy designed using the latest neuroscience and linguistic research on persuasion and influence. It leverages how the human brain works, and you don't need to be a brain scientist to utilize it because its design makes it readily applicable even without scientific knowledge. This technology is an application of scientific knowledge for practical purposes, and it can help individuals transform high-quality dreams into reality.

Fundamentally, the *Satisfaction Cycle* empowers salespeople to become adept "brain technicians" without requiring extensive study in neurocognitive sciences. It provides the code and a practical framework that allows salespeople to utilize their time efficiently and pursue significant successes with the customers.

Ethical Persuasion

While the term "brain technician" may initially sound negative, when applied correctly, the *Satisfaction Cycle* ensures that it operates as a highly ethical approach. It aims to genuinely provide customers with what they truly desire. By strategically influencing them to enter the *Green State* and tap into their full brain potential, we help the customer to achieve their desired outcomes quicker and precisely the way they want.

When this occurs, both the salesperson and the customer reap the highest rewards. Selling this way will be experienced as a value exchange based on a mutual understanding of the desired outcome, and both parties' values are aligned with the outcome and the behaviors along the way. As the salesperson, you act as the customer's *Trusted Advisor*, ensuring the selling and buying process is mutually rewarding and collaborative.

However, some people may associate this with negative manipulation, which could imply an unfair influence for personal gain. It's important to note that all communication and engagement involve some level of manipulation and thinking about it in that way manipulation can either be ethical or unethical depending on one's approach. Ethical manipulation helps your customer adopt a possibility mindset and achieve significant results by incorporating your product or service. Helping customers to buy only when they can achieve a significant outcome makes this way of selling ethical.

Regrettably, numerous individuals in sales don't care about the customer and only focus on making a sale for their own benefit. Many salespeople often seem unconcerned about the outcome that the customer receives. Once they have sold their product or service, they believe they have fulfilled their responsibility and received payment for their job. Their focus is not on assisting the customer getting real value. If they only replace one thing with another for the customer, it will not alter their outcomes, and according to *Satisfaction Selling*, this would be considered unethical manipulation.

Utilizing the *Satisfaction Cycle* offers unique benefits for salespeople compared to other sales models. Approaching sales with an ethical mindset is fulfilling and rewarding. The *Satisfaction Cycle* is designed to work when the salesperson is authentic, congruent, and genuinely interested in helping the customer achieve their desired outcome. It transforms salespeople into consultative partners and *Trusted Advisors* for their customers by focusing on creating value and building relationships filled with real and deep trust.

This approach also allows salespeople to find deeper meaning and satisfaction in their work while achieving successful outcomes for their customers. *Satisfaction Selling* enables you to work in alignment with your core values, which is an exceptional experience. You know what is right for you and what is not. Even if your company's offer is the best choice for the customer, knowing when to opt-out allows you to hand the customer over to someone else confidently. When you are ethical with both yourself and your customers, working in sales becomes even more fulfilling than it already may be for you.

Another ethical consideration that comes with the *Satisfaction Cycle* is determining if your product or service can have a significant positive impact on the customer. Once you thoroughly understand the customer's desired outcome, you must ask yourself whether you truly believe you have the potential to create meaningful change. Will your engagement result in a significant shift or only a minor improvement? This evaluation helps determine whether what you have to offer aligns with their goals. Sometimes, you may even decide to decline to present your solution altogether because there is not a good match between what you have to offer and what the customer wants and needs.

If there is no match, it is crucial for the salesperson to be transparent for the transaction to be and remain ethical. As discussed in Chapter 3, you can then say:

"Now may not be the best time for us to continue, because I don't believe I have a solution that would benefit you the way you want. Perhaps in the future or on a different project I may have just what you need, and I'd be thrilled to assist you then. In the meantime, it's possible that another company might better suit your needs."

In sales, ethics are defined by establishing mutually beneficial outcomes. The sale becomes unethical when either the seller or the buyer must make significant compromises. Unless there is a solution available that is advantageous for the salesperson, their company, and the customer, it would be unethical as we define it to continue with the sales process.

Time is a precious commodity, and by adopting an ethical approach to selling, you can prioritize efforts that offer the greatest return on investment. The *Satisfaction Cycle* and its ethical selling approach make it easy for both parties to determine when to say "yes" and when to say "no." Ultimately, this distinction and choice leads to more meaningful and rewarding outcomes for everyone involved.

Selling is ultimately about influencing and persuading the customer. Ethical persuasion aims to get other people to agree and say yes to something you are proposing while you have ensured that this proposal is getting them what they want. This structure is embedded into the *Satisfaction Cycle*. It has been built as a powerful tool for influencing and persuading, while always working from the ethical premise.

With the *Satisfaction Cycle*, we aim for a long-term relationship; therefore, the ethical approach is the only sustainable option. We must only persuade when we certainly know that we can help the customer achieve their desired outcome while enabling a good business case for ourselves without any compromises.

Win – Win or Walk Away!

In the next chapter, we will delve into how the *Trusted Advisor* mindset, as discussed in Chapter 3, enables a shift from the traditional problem-solving approach found in conventional sales models discussed in this chapter, towards co-creating genuine value with your customers using the *Satisfaction Cycle*. We will demonstrate in practical terms how initiating from the *Green State* influences customers' thinking towards positive outcomes and ignites a *Burning Desire* for success.

In any case, as we have learned in the present chapter, the starting point counts, so:

"Where do you want to start now - from the Green State or the Red State?"

5

BUSTING THE MYTH

Going Beyond Problem Solving to Creating High-Value, Positive Sales Solutions

*F*or years, I believed I knew the right way to sell effectively. I was convinced that a potential customer must have a problem before buying consulting services from our company or, in more severe cases, they should have a Burning Platform. I vividly recall the 2011 memo from Stephen Elop, then CEO of Nokia, who brutally addressed their Burning Platform:

"We poured gasoline on our own Burning Platform. I believe we have lacked accountability and leadership to align and direct the company through these disruptive times. We had a series of misses. We haven't been delivering innovation fast enough. We're not collaborating internally. Nokia, our platform is burning."

I am sure Stephen Elop had sincere intentions with his Burning Platform memo. And so did I when I got inspired by his approach to instill concern about maintaining the status quo.

The same year I had one customer who had severe troubles, and they needed to adopt radical changes to survive in their business. I wanted to help them and do what our company could deliver well at that time. I believed that our company's services would be a good match for them. I wanted to help these people in their daily struggles to see their opportunities. I remember speaking with them in a meeting room, where I used the Burning Platform metaphor with the same brutal honesty as Stephen Elop. I remember first the silence and perhaps even a shock. In the end, my customer was "pleased" they got what they expected in terms of defining their biggest problems, and we had a consulting project together. No pain, no gain, we were all thinking.

This problem-oriented approach was what I believed to be the best approach in customer-centric selling, and what was needed to understand the customer's real needs. Looking back, I cannot pinpoint what led me to learn this way of selling. It probably became my truth through my studies in process engineering and industrial management. What I know is that I could not see it any other way, and I was working to become better at defining customers' problems. I did not like selling at all. The more I did it, the less it felt right. I felt so uncomfortable asking around the issues, so I thought it was just that I did not have skills or competencies in selling.

Because I almost hated selling, most often, I did not actively pursue sales situations. Eventually, I still got business. In those cases, something just fell into place between the customer and me. We had a good rapport. The conversation was flowing naturally, and somehow the outcome and solution emerged naturally. I remember a case like this. I visited a potential customer later the same year after I had used the Burning Platform for selling.

Again, I was in a meeting room. This time it was different. The potential customer was primarily talking, and I was listening. It was easy not to talk about problems because there were no problems yet. They were kicking off a new business, so we were just talking about what they wanted to achieve and what they already had in place. I was not there to sell. We had a pleasant conversation, and I trust the customer had the same experience. After gathering this information, we agreed that I would propose what we could do for them the following day.

So, I went back to my hotel room, made the proposal, and presented it to them shortly the next day. And then, at that moment, I knew I had a new customer. There were still some other stakeholders to convince, but those in the room wanted to take action and get the others to accept our proposal. This was the starting point for a long-term collaboration. However, at that time, I could not clearly see the difference between my different sales experiences. I knew that I didn't like the concept of digging into problems, and I knew this other approach felt much better – both for the customer and me.

Despite occasional discomfort, my curiosity for selling grew. I was aware that there are people who are extremely good at selling. If they can do it, I should also be able to learn it. A few years later, I met a person through one consulting assignment who seemed to do something magical. This magic was present not only when he was selling but in his every encounter with other people. Something was happening there that I had not seen before. I had no idea what it was all about and could not even recognize what made the difference. I could just see, hear, and feel the difference from all the other skilled salespeople I had met before. After every engagement with him, everything was at ease. I had clarity and felt highly energized.

I grew increasingly convinced that there was still something I had yet to learn about selling. More precisely, I had a feeling that there was something that most people in sales do not know. I desperately wanted to know. What was, after all, the most effective way of selling? I went on reading books and tried new things. But something still was not right. The discomfort remained.

To my luck, this exquisite sales professional stayed in touch with me. He could see my search. Bit by bit, the truth began to unfold, and I became even more curious. On his recommendation, I went to see and test what Henrik would have to offer. The first courses with him felt like I was like Neo in the movie The Matrix, who was given a call from Morpheus to take either a red or a blue pill.

Neo took the red pill and got into the real world. I also took the red pill and stayed in the "Wonderland of the real world" to see how deep the rabbit hole goes. Henrik introduced me to the ideas behind the Satisfaction Cycle and busted the myth of problem-solving in sales and leadership. The truth was shockingly simple, yet not so easy to implement. Instead of solving problems, the Satisfaction Cycle takes its starting point in focusing on what is already working making it easier to access the positive possibilities to create success – with and for a customer.

The shift in focus was and is essential for me. When we focus on building solutions in sales where the inevitable outcome is a success, success becomes inevitable. Then, there is no problem to fix because problems do not exist on the path to success. Instead, there are simply tasks to be done. Satisfaction Selling enables the transformation of customers' dreams into reality in a more effective and enjoyable manner.

After the myth of problem-solving was busted for me, I continued studying with Henrik and he introduced me to Joseph to learn more about the Satisfaction Cycle. Surprisingly, this newfound approach made selling feel right and re-spectful, ultimately leading to a career change. Transitioning to global account management was a significant leap for someone who had disliked selling. I was no longer there to sell. My focus shifted from selling to helping customer to buy and succeed. Starting in the Green State with a focus on what was already working transformed my approach, making customer interactions significantly more effortless.

A Customer is Not Meeting You to Have Problems

In high-value, complex selling, meetings are inevitable. There are typically several people involved on both sides that have their say. The solution is often customized and has intangible elements. To tailor a solution that is uniquely suited to the customer requires information from the various stakeholders in the customer' *Buying Center*. There will be meetings when the solution requires substantial budget allocation or efforts in integrating the solution, such as IT systems.

The common presumption for a successful sales meeting is that the customer must address their problem and pain point. Identifying these issues is central to most widely recognized sales models. We have been conditioned to believe that the way to resolve, fix, eliminate, and overcome problems is to find them and solve them. Therefore, in the initial stages, especially during the first meetings with the customer, the primary goal for the salesperson is to gather information about the customers' problems and pain points. This process aims to enable the salesperson to identify the most pressing pain - essentially, what keeps the customer awake at night. A problem they can solve.

Subsequently, the salesperson's strategic approach involves heightening awareness of potential negative consequences of this problem. This is done with the intent of magnifying the pain and instilling a level of angst and fear significant enough to prompt the customer to affirmatively seek a resolution – to say "yes" in order to alleviate the identified pain. All this is still very normal in selling in the 2020's business world. The sales models employ various tactics; some emphasize consultative approaches, while others rely on direct questioning. However, at their core, they all seek to define the problem and then close the sales by providing a solution to this problem, as discussed in Chapter 4.

The meetings at the beginning of a complex selling process are important for listening and gathering information. The more quality information there is, the easier it is to design and propose a solution the customer wants. However, the challenge arises when a salesperson attempts to gather information about problems and therefore often builds resistance and consequently obtains limited relevant information. People typically hesitate to reveal their weaknesses, and customers may not want to discuss their problems openly. Admitting to problems can be emotionally challenging, leading customers to avoid discussing them willingly, unless they are desperate.

And digging into problems is how the customer might end up seeing problems they didn't even know they had. Imagine this feeling after a meeting, knowing how big and severe your issues are. How eagerly would you move on to not have those problems? Or would you feel hopeless knowing how long it will take to solve them and give up? The reality is that a customer is not meeting a salesperson to have a problem, even when they have an existing problem, that they know about themselves.

The One Question

Satisfaction Selling shows us a different approach. When meeting with a new customer, a salesperson is there to listen, learn, understand, and gather information. There are no product pitches. There are no questions about pain points. The salesperson just starts the meeting by asking the customer this one question:

"What is working well for you today?"

and then refraining from further commentary. The meeting is for the customer to talk, and it all begins with this powerful question. How exactly you do this in the right way, is something we will discuss more in detail in Part 2 of the book - The *Satisfaction Selling* playbook.

Starting from what is already working holds immense value as it establishes a relationship based on a positive foundation. It acknowledges that the customer has already achieved success, fostering a positive expectation that, together, you will generate further positive outcomes and success for the customer. Encouraging customers to discuss what's working well for them fosters an environment conducive to open communication.

Initially, it might not be second nature for individuals to share their successes, as this typically isn't the normal starting point in a conversation. However, once they begin, there's a natural inclination to delve into their achievements. Discussing successes is mentally easier and gratifying. As individuals elaborate on what's working, they tend to ease into the conversation, becoming more relaxed. This relaxation facilitates further openness, leading to a richer exchange of information.

The quality of the information a salesperson gets also improves when somebody speaks from a positive point of view because resistance dissolves. By asking this one question, the customer is given the opportunity to set the pace and lead the way. It is common for salespeople to have a natural inclination to rush and get straight to "the point." However, exercising patience and allowing the customer to express themselves will increase the likelihood of expediting the process later on and ultimately achieving success by getting the business.

Allow me to share a captivating anecdote from Henrik's training program involving a private banking customer amid the challenging backdrop of the aftermath of the financial crisis in August 2009. At that time, the private banking sector was grappling with a crisis, and customers were markedly dissatisfied due to the poor returns on their investments or even losses that had significantly affected them.

To exacerbate matters, the private bankers of the bank found themselves under immense pressure, contending with new demands for certifications mandated by evolving legislation. Burdened with heavy workloads and navigating through the challenges of the new legislative landscape, they were not particularly motivated for the training sessions provided by Henrik and his team.

In the midst of this trying period, Henrik persisted in maintaining a positive emotional state despite the palpable weariness and negative atmosphere among the private bankers. At the beginning of the third module, Henrik asked a participant about the practical application of what she had learned from the previous two modules. After a brief pause, she responded,

"I've been so busy that I've only had time to implement one thing,"

and then she paused again. After a while, Henrik broke the silence and asked:

"What is the one thing, you have implemented?"

"Since our last training module, I've started all my customer meetings with a simple question:"

"What is working well for you today?"

she replied, and then she fell silent again. Intrigued, Henrik asked her about the impact this had on her and her meetings. After a few moments of contemplation, she straightened her back and smiled, saying,

"It has created a completely different atmosphere in my meetings - much more positive and productive! My meetings have never been better!"

Cultivating Cognitive Inertia for Positive Thinking About Outcomes

If there's one key takeaway from this book and the *Satisfaction Cycle*, it's the concept of beginning with what is already working - by posing the straightforward question:

"What is working well for you today?"

Asking this question directs your customers' attention to their current successes. It is the most direct and effective way to establish a positive emotional state and atmosphere. Affirming their ability to make sound decisions, this positive approach fosters a robust association between the salesperson and feelings of satisfaction and success.

One of the most astonishing revelations for individuals trained in the use of the *Satisfaction Cycle* is the significant increase in the amount of information customers are capable of and willing to be sharing. This exceeds their prior experiences in terms of customer openness and willingness to disclose. Based on this approach, it is possible to gather much more information about customers' current solutions, how they purchased them, who was involved in decision-making, how the decision was made, and the most important features of the current solution.

Enriched with this information, salespeople gain a clear understanding of what they must deliver at a minimum to keep the customer satisfied. From the positive point of view, customers can easily also reveal things that they are challenged by, things that are missing for them to get things working even better. They share these details because they hope the salesperson can assist in filling those gaps.

Engaging in a positive dialogue about what is missing, once the customer has shared what is already working, differs greatly from focusing on problems. The salesperson acquires high-quality information that can be utilized in later stages of the sales process when designing and presenting their solution to the customer.

Beginning with what is working is crucial for establishing long-term collaboration and strong positive relationships with customers. Commencing interactions with a positive foundation and moving towards an even more positive outcome ensures that each subsequent result becomes progressively positive. This approach enables you to leverage your past achievements.

Constantly searching for problems with your existing customers - the approach in the traditional problem-focused sales models - can lead to customer frustrations, as discussed in Chapter 4. The customers have spent a lot of money on your solutions and still have problems. The question might come to them that maybe they should try someone else. However, by adopting a positive approach, this scenario can be avoided. Why would customers consider switching when they consistently experience improvement and satisfaction?

In high-value, complex B2B selling, a group of people is involved from the customer side –the *Buying Center*, as discussed in Chapter 1. To facilitate swift and smooth sales, it's essential that everyone is aligned. Again, the question to start with is:

"What is working well for you today?"

This gets the whole group to talk about what they do well today. Even those initially resistant will join because everyone wants to be part of success.

The same scenario holds true in high-value, complex B2C selling, i.e.: you may have two or more people making a buying decision that function in the same way as the *Buying Center* does in B2B sales. This could be a couple making decisions about a family purchase, or even a small group of friends deciding to purchase something together like a vacation of maybe a vacation home. Essentially, regardless of the specifics of the selling situation when you have multiple decision makers aligning them right at the start is crucial, and starting from the positive position that asking them,

"What's working well for you today?"

and in some cases,

"What has worked well for you?"

can set the stage for moving forward with little or no resistance throughout the entire sales process.

On the other hand, nobody wants to be a part of a failure which is exactly the situation we are creating when the starting point is identifying problems. Here, it is pretty easy to end up having a conflict. People might even start pointing out who has made the mistakes, or at least start thinking about this which would be a sure way to destroy the meeting. For a salesperson, such an approach does not help to get customers to a position where they actually can and will make a decision together easily.

On the flip side, adopting a positive perspective that emphasizes existing or past successes fosters unity and creates a common ground. This alignment simplifies the process of reaching consensus within the group or team regarding the desired direction and the subsequent steps to be taken.

Allowing the customer to talk about what is working for them helps you understand how they have created their successes and the minimum requirements you must meet. You are uncovering the resources they already have in place, which you can later refer back to in order to bolster your argument. All information you gather becomes part of the sales presentation and arguments later on. By doing this, you are effectively building what we could call a self-referencing case, which means that you are using customers' experiences and specific examples to make your case, when you are presenting your solution.

Your curiosity as a salesperson provides a competitive edge. Don't hesitate to discuss the customer's experiences, including their successes with their present suppliers - your competitors, or the products and services they provide. Remember, when a customer shares a positive experience, they've had with one of your competitors while looking at you, they will subconsciously start to associate you with something positive. The emotional state people are in when they are in your presence will be anchored to you.

You might feel you are not making progress, but be patient, move slow, take your time, and while listening, one little phrase with some additional questions that could become powerful in revealing even more information would be:

"Wow, that is interesting - how did you do that?"

"Please tell me more about that - how did you accomplish that?"

"What worked for you?"

"How did you employ it?"

This tactic works throughout the sales process. Customers may consider their existing solution acceptable and be wary of the salesperson's intentions to sell theirs. They might not be too comfortable with that idea. However, when you acknowledge and appreciate their current situation, showing genuine curiosity about what is working for them, the customer relaxes. You gain information about what you can do to move on the dialog and the process to keep the customer open, relaxed, and satisfied all the time.

Uncovering what works well for the customer establishes a positive mindset towards possibilities. This is a neurocognitive phenomenon common to everyone termed cognitive inertia. In short, it's the tendency for someone to continue thinking in a direction they are already thinking in, and they remain inclined to continue thinking that way unless something interrupts them. They intrinsically resist changing this orientation. That's why it is so important to set up the right direction from the beginning of the meeting you are having with the customer so that you don't need to work on changing the direction later in the conversation. Cognitive inertia is a powerful force that makes shifting from one direction to another difficult.

In sales, a customer may also be stuck because of cognitive inertia with another solution, so they first need to give up the idea that their current solution is the best before considering any other options. It's not possible to make a direct jump from one solution to another without first deciding to leave the direction that their current thinking leads them to.

When cognitive inertia revolves around negative considerations, individuals persist in thinking and talking about problems. Very often this negative problem consideration spiral leads nowhere. On the other hand, when cognitive inertia is built around what is already working - the positive point of view - a person begins to see their current and past successes which can help them think about the positive future successes they most desire. This way, a virtuous cycle organized in relation to creating more success starts to build, which continues to work both in the customer's and the salesperson's favor.

Salespeople certainly meet plenty of customers who only want to talk about their problems. Customers have been conditioned and trained well in this approach too. They can also start by talking about what is working well, and then something might take them off track to the deep dark waters of problems in the *Red Sea*. An exceptional salesperson is a skilled listener and communicator who can establish and sustain cognitive inertia in a positive direction. Even when customers express negativity, the salesperson can use that to build rapport without connecting themselves to the negative.

For example, they can begin by acknowledging the customer's viewpoint:

"It must be challenging to face such a tough year and witness people seemingly not doing their jobs."

"I understand that it is often easy to focus on the people, who are not performing and thereby running the risk of not noticing those who are silently performing."

"Who in your team are examples of someone you believe is making an effort to do the right thing?"

"What, specifically, have they been doing the past year?"

Therefore, inquiring about what is working demands skills. In this example, the salesperson cannot ask the customer to tell everything that is working well, right away. They would face a huge resistance. Still, the point is not to talk about the problem but to use whatever the customer presents to lead the discussion to the positive. The salesperson's expertise lies in structuring questions to elicit positive responses, regardless of what the customer says. The salesperson's job is to ask:

"What is working well for you today?"

By asking this question, or some variation of it, you engage in genuine conversations with customers and ensure they feel positive from the very beginning. This is what makes the *Satisfaction Selling* uniquely powerful. It is a genuinely unique way of selling because it operates from the beginning to the end with a positive perspective.

The Starting Point Counts

Cognitive inertia is a powerful force influencing how we perceive and respond to information. It describes the tendency for individuals to hold onto their existing beliefs, thought patterns, and mental frameworks even when faced with contradictory evidence. Our brains naturally seek cognitive consistency and efficiency, leading us to maintain our established beliefs rather than undergo the challenging process of reevaluating and changing our points of view.

In sales, the implication of cognitive inertia is that framing the attention in one direction at the beginning of the customer's buying process makes the process generally smoother and faster. Framing plays a critical role in shaping our perspective. It refers to the conscious or unconscious frame that guides our thinking, directing our attention and focus.

In the context of traditional sales, where the parties often adopt a problem-focused frame in which they identify a problem and work together to find solutions. However, this limiting frame results in inside-the-box thinking. While it may solve immediate problems, it may not address the underlying questions that truly matter.

An optimal frame, on the other hand, aligns all participants around the purpose of the conversation. Starting from a positive standpoint that focuses on what is already working creates a mindset of possibilities and directs attention toward opportunities. Creating this positive frame generates cognitive inertia towards success rather than getting trapped in a cycle of problem-solving. This approach opens the space for out-of-the-box thinking and sets the stage for a process that leads to even more successful outcomes. Achieving more extraordinary results becomes easier when we have a process that encounters minimal resistance.

From Positive Present to Positive Future

Another aspect that distinguishes the *Satisfaction Cycle* as a unique model for persuasion and selling is its approach to the future. By looking at the future from a positive present viewpoint, which we shall refer to as the *Present State Positive* (*PS⁺* for short), individuals automatically position themselves for success. When customers start from their *PS⁺*, they naturally engage in discussions about how things can work even better for them and how they can achieve their desired outcomes.

While in their *PS⁺*, the customers become receptive to multiple possibilities and cultivate a positive expectation of success. They envision what that success will look like, creating a vibrant dream from where anything is possible. Starting from a positive perspective and envisioning an even more positive future builds a compelling desire, often referred to as a *Burning Desire*. In this state of success which we shall refer to as the *Desired State Positive* (*DS⁺⁺* for short) any potential problems are non-existent in people's minds.

Most traditional selling is based on the concept of a nightmare - a *Burning Platform*. It is about identifying things that don't work and what happened in the past to create that situation. After identifying the problem, the salesperson first brings the customer into the past to identify the root cause of the problem and then makes them look into the future from the past. The positive intention of the salesperson is to make sure that the customer's nightmare doesn't continue - that the fire can be put out - and the salesperson then encourages the customer to envision a future without that problem.

However, in establishing the nightmare from a *Burning Platform* they have unintentionally also established negative cognitive inertia leading the customer further aware from becoming open to considering solutions. This is the fundamental principle of traditional selling: the belief that by solving problems and fixing issues, the future will inevitably improve. However, problem-solving approaches inherently and inevitably place individuals in a negative mindset.

When people are consumed by present issues, they cannot envision and create the future they truly want and desire. As discussed in Chapter 4, we shall refer to this state as the *Present State Negative* (*PS⁻* for short).

When in this problem-focused state, the customers' minds are not wired for positive, solution-oriented thinking. The best-case scenario is that they find themselves with a future - in a *Desired State (DS)* - that has just one less problem.

It is an undeniable fact that problems do exist in the world. Customers may face genuine concerns and issues which they need to deal with. Given this reality, one might wonder why we don't believe in problem-solving in sales. One reason is that problem-solving approaches are often inefficient in making problems disappear. Problem-solving in itself is ineffective. Typically, it tends to address the effects or symptoms of a problem rather than resolving its root cause. As a result, individuals find themselves stuck in a repetitive cycle dictated by the underlying cause of the issue.

In fact, attempting to solve a problem can unintentionally reinforce one's commitment to the very cause that initially led to the problem. However, the most significant reason for our skepticism towards problem-solving in sales is that focusing on problems hinders people from achieving what they genuinely desire.

The *Satisfaction Cycle* offers a powerful strategy for building *Burning Desires* rather than *Burning Platforms*. It takes a positive approach by emphasizing what is already working, starting in the PS^+. Interestingly, this shift in perspective often leads to eliminating root causes for problems. This can happen in two ways: either the present circumstances have changed so significantly that the previous problem is no longer relevant, or the fulfillment of desires (achieving the DS^{++}) directly addresses the root cause, causing it to disappear.

Let's be clear: we don't advocate for ignoring or suppressing problems. Instead, we believe that the *Satisfaction Cycle*, with its positive orientation, is far more effective in creating success and even solving potential problems - without fixating on them. Or as Albert Einstein put it:

"A clever person solves a problem. A wise person avoids it."

The bias that selling can only happen when the pain is big enough sits firmly in many people's minds. The trick in many traditional, problem-solving based, sales models starts with:

"What problems do you have?"

Asking this question, fundamentally creates the same effect as if asking:

"What's wrong with you?"

The premise of *Satisfaction Selling* is centered on making customers feel good for their own sake, not for the salesperson's gain. Rather than focusing on customers' pains and problems, it operates from a positive perspective, the PS^+, naturally directing attention toward possibilities. By helping customers break free from problem-centric thinking and shift their mindset towards possibilities, they begin to perceive a wealth of opportunities available to them. This approach unveils their authentic dreams, desires, the DS^{++}, and the motivation that drives them.

Consequently, not only do customers gain greater clarity, but you also create an environment that maximizes their chances of real success. They have the opportunity to transform their dreams into reality and gain a deeper understanding of their true aspirations rather than merely resolving a specific problem.

The quantitative difference in the value of the solution, created for the customer, when following the trajectory from a *Present State Positive* - the PS^+ - to the *Desired State Positive* - the DS^{++} - that the *Satisfaction Cycle* promotes, as opposed to following the traditional problem-based trajectory from the *Present State Negative - PS⁻* - to the *Desired State - DS* - with one less problem is indicated in Figure 5.1.

The Starting Point Counts !
- Where do you start?

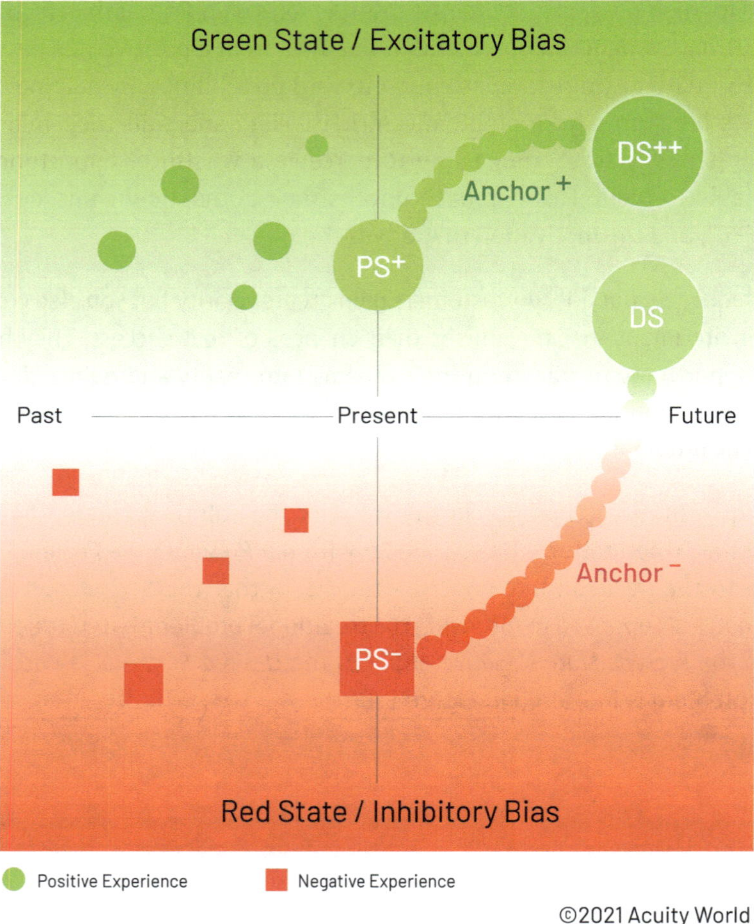

Figure 5.1 The PS+ to DS++ trajectory versus the PS- to DS trajectory

Future Memory

With the *Satisfaction Cycle*, you go beyond helping potential customers envision the future; you actually take them to a future where they have already achieved their desired outcome, the DS^{++}, and gotten what they wanted to have. As a salesperson, you can guide potential customers to experience what they have gained and achieved when your solution has been implemented. This is how we create a *Future Memory*.

Using a process we call *Time Sliding*; you can mentally position the customer to consider an outcome from the point in time where they have already achieved it. From the future position the customer can consider that now, i.e.: when they have achieved their outcome, they can understand why it was so valuable for them to go through what it took to get here. Holding the future as a memory alters their emotional response and reinforces the agreement you've made together.

Ultimately, two things make the *Satisfaction Cycle* uniquely powerful and work better than any other sales strategy: working from the excitatory bias, following the trajectory from the PS^+ to the DS^{++}, and building a *Future Memory* from there. No other sales model we know of contains these two elements that make the *Satisfaction Cycle* so effective. With these factors, you can help a person restructure how they process reality. In essence, the *Satisfaction Cycle* allows you to become a brain technician utilizing the fundamental way that neurocognitive processing, i.e.: thinking, works, enabling you to help your customers realize their dreams, and from there to help them buy the right solution faster.

Guiding customers from a positive present - the PS^+ - to a positive future, the DS^{++}, ensures customer satisfaction at every step of the process. Literally, the name of the *Satisfaction Cycle* implies what it is all about. This strategy represents the most direct and efficient method for establishing an emotionally positive feeling and atmosphere. It also associates the salesperson and the company it represents with a positive feeling of satisfaction. The *Satisfaction Cycle* is a unique approach to building long-term relationships and ultra-satisfied loyal customers – those customers we refer to as *Positive Activists* - as discussed in Chapter 1.

While this concept of *Future Memory* may not be fully clear at this point, we will delve much deeper into it and explain why it is so powerful in the next chapter.

6

TRAJECTORY OF INTENT

How to Build a Future Memory

*A*s I reflect on my journey in learning Satisfaction Selling, one particular concept stands out – Future Memory. At some point, I realized that it is not only a tool for engaging customers, but also a profound concept in personal leadership - the art of leading yourself and others.

One particular experience demonstrated the power of Future Memory in every aspect for me. I was entrusted with a new, challenging task in global account management - a situation common to many account managers. Due to its complexity - spanning the marketplace, customers, a high number of stakeholders, cultures, and diverse perspectives - many colleagues perceived it as insurmountable. However, I was able to envision the desired outcome with absolute clarity. The task was so significant, though, that I anticipated it would take at least a year, if not longer, to achieve.

It was clear to me what would have changed once we reached the outcome. Even before I properly began working toward it, I felt certain that we would achieve it one day, as if it had already happened. This certainty signaled that I had created a Future Memory for myself. It felt as definite as knowing that the sun will rise again in the morning, or as unwavering as knowing that I will love my children forever.

With this unwavering certainty about achieving the outcome, the only thing I needed to figure out was how to get there. The overall idea of what needed *to happen was clear to me, and with a strong pull from the Future Memory, I could easily propel myself into action, making decisions and utilizing every opportunity that arose to steer closer to the envisioned outcome. With this mindset, something that could have been perceived as a challenge by someone else became just another opportunity for me to act. It was about finding the optimal path to the outcome in a way that I saw could maximize the positive consequences and minimize the negative ones.*

Finding the optimal path towards the outcome felt smooth and effortless. I found myself experiencing a flow and enjoying every moment regardless of what actually happened. There were moments and events that temporarily threw me off, but I easily rediscovered the next steps by tapping into my Future Memory. I felt clarity at all times and accepted that I did not need to be anywhere else in the process. Somehow, I gained patience in a way I had never experienced before. I just knew in each moment that I was on the right track and exactly where I needed to be. Utilizing the Satisfaction Cycle approach for my personal leadership created a deeply satisfying experience.

As the journey progressed, I realized that Future Memory wasn't just a personal tool or sales tool; it was also the essence of transformational leadership of others. It became clear that to achieve the outcome, there needed to be a shift in the attitudes and behaviors of the key stakeholders. By instilling this approach within my colleagues, I helped them adopt and experience a shared vision of success which helped them cultivate their own Future Memories of achieving it.

Over time, I witnessed a profound shift among most of my key colleagues in the sales team - they too began to embody a belief in our shared outcome, resulting in a singular focus. This shared view of the outcome fostered a sense of unity and clear purpose within the team, propelling us towards our goals with great synergy.

I realized that my colleagues had fully embraced a vivid Future Memory of our desired outcome when they began to take ownership of their respective responsibilities and subsequently proactively and creatively fulfilled their roles. It was as if they intuitively understood what to do and how to execute their tasks. For me, this experience also provided a highly satisfying and cohesive teamwork experience. Describing this kind of experience in words is not easy, but it instilled in me a profound feeling of contributing to something greater than myself, fostering a deep sense of fulfillment.

Naturally, throughout this journey, our focus remained on the customer. Following the Satisfaction Cycle guidelines, I sought to understand what was already working for the customer and what they wanted to become even better. Once the customer's desired outcome became clear, I ensured that key customer stakeholders envisioned a compelling Future Memory of the positive changes they aimed to achieve. When our desired outcome aligned with the customer's, we collaboratively began to develop mutual activities that would ultimately fulfill both parties' desired outcomes. Ultimately, the customer's goals became the driving factor for me and my colleagues.

One day, it dawned on me that everything had fallen into place. The customer had reached a decision, and we seamlessly transitioned into the delivery phase. The subsequent impact on growth and profitability proved to be substantial. However, upon reflection, what stood out the most was the remarkable smoothness of the entire process. Mental friction within the system had diminished significantly.

It's challenging to articulate just how satisfying the journey was and the profound sense of vitality it instilled in me. I felt an immense gratitude for the opportunity to just be alive and to contribute meaningfully. In the end, this was "just" a fairly regular task within the global account management team. That being said, it wasn't all smooth sailing. We encountered our fair share of challenges and a range of emotions along the way. However, having a solid foundation in the Green State and a strong Future Memory allowed me to navigate the path effectively.

For me, this experience demonstrated for the first time the immense power of Future Memory in navigating complex scenarios, serving as another pivotal moment for my personal growth and reflection. It not only sparked a further interest in mastering the Satisfaction Cycle but also provided clarity regarding my purpose and professional aspirations.

All Decisions are Made in the Future

One of the fundamental principles of the *Satisfaction Cycle* model is the premise that all decisions are made in the future. Specifically, this means that decision-makers base their choices on their anticipation of the outcomes resulting from those decisions.

While it may seem obvious when stated, that decisions are made with consideration for the results they will produce, this understanding isn't necessarily apparent to either the individual making the decision in the present moment or to someone attempting to influence or persuade them in a particular direction.

This lack of clarity is especially pronounced when a problem-solving paradigm is in place and the decision is being made to fix or rectify a problem that the decision-maker is experiencing in the present. In fact, the decision-maker may perceive the effects of their decision as being solely confined to the present, without fully grasping the consequences that may unfold in the future, through time.

Self-Resolving Problems or "No Problems At All"

What sometimes makes this confusing is the assumption from a person operating from the *Red State* that the present conditions and context will remain stable over time – i.e.: that the problem will be there forever.

A simple example illustrating this idea is being bitten by a mosquito. When someone is bitten and the bite itches, it may seem that if they take no immediate action, the itching will persist. However, in reality, if they do nothing, their body will naturally relieve the itching by breaking down and flushing away the proteins causing it, without any additional intervention. This is a good example of how, if you try to do something about the problem, like scratching, then the problem just gets bigger. Instead of just having a small mosquito bite, you end up with a bleeding wound.

The consideration that if a person experiencing a problem does nothing, the problem will continue or worsen, is one of the two conditions required for a problem to exist. The other condition is that the current conditions or context are not as the person desires them to be in the present or in the future.

If either of these two conditions is absent - meaning

1. the person believes that the situation will improve without their intervention, or

2. the current conditions or context are satisfactory.

then the person will not perceive the situation as a problem. In other words, as soon as someone believes the current conditions or context will positively change, even without their action, the notion that it's a problem for them is immediately relieved.

Going to Where the Problem is Not

Within the *Satisfaction Cycle* model, we operate on the premise of envisioning a positively structured future, which we have termed the *Desired State Positive* or DS^{++} as introduced in Chapter 5. This premise of envisioning a positively structured future entails the belief that the current conditions and context experienced by the customer will improve by selecting future conditions conducive to success. When conditions conducive to success lead to the realization of the DS^{++}, this state becomes the *Present State Positive*, the PS^{+}. When the DS^{++} has been realized, it immediately creates the possibility for achievements that were not feasible before it was in place, leading to outcomes that are beyond the DS^{++} in time, i.e.: further in the future. We refer to the future beyond the realization of the DS^{++} as the *Outcome of the Outcome* - the results achieved by attaining the DS^{++}. Making customers aware of the *Outcome of the Outcome* is critical for establishing a compelling future motivation to move towards.

To simplify, customers typically do not buy products and services to possess them "as is"; rather, they are investing in future possibilities enabled by these products or services. Even when someone is buying something as non-functional as a certificate of investment, say a municipal bond or certificate of deposit that earns them interest or appreciates in value, they are not buying the investment or the certificate that comes with the investment.

When someone makes an investment represented by some kind of certificate of investment they are buying future value, maybe in the form of an increase in their wealth, or a hedge against a loss of buying capacity due to inflation, or security for their future needs, not a certificate. This same thinking can be applied to any purchase in terms of customers buying desired futures and not products or services, even when the desire is purely abstract or intangible.

This is what makes the *Satisfaction Cycle* model so compelling to customers: it positions them in their desired future. We do this in three different ways.

First, we disengage them from the problem-state in the present and bring them into PS^+.

Next, we move them through time to the *Future Memory* of the realization of their DS^{++}. Third, we help them see the path they can take to achieve the realization of the DS^{++} in a way that makes sense to them and fits with their *Evidence Strategy*. This is detailed via the narrative of the *Solution Experience,* which we will delve more into in Chapter 8, where we go through the *Satisfaction Cycle* step by step.

By disconnecting from the negative aspects of problem-based thinking, individuals who establish a DS^{++} - made up of the future-based outcome they desire and the *Outcome of the Outcome* - liberate themselves to envision and project a future free from the continuation or implications of present problems. Instead of projecting a future based on problems or the endless loop of resolving problems, the DS^{++} always presents an expression of an improved future. Considering the positive aspects of the PS^+, we can build further on that state to create an even better future outcome, as discussed in Chapter 5.

Achieving the *Outcome of the Outcome* triggers the creation of what we refer to as *Future Memory*, as briefly introduced in Chapter 5. The *Future Memory* induces a neurocognitive shift in the perception of the future, which is then reflected backward through time to the present. It establishes a trajectory through time from the present to a future "where the problem is not" - i.e., where the problem does not exist or is not relevant. Simultaneously, it creates a trajectory back through time to the present, describing the steps needed to reach that future point, regardless of current conditions or context. The pathway that extends from the *Future Memory* to the present is called the *Trajectory of INTENT* within the *Satisfaction Cycle* model.

Specifically in the *Satisfaction Cycle* model, the pathway of steps that had to have been taken, starting from the PS^+ to arrive at the DS^{++} is referred to as the *Trajectory of INTENT*. Viewing the trajectory that led to the DS^{++} from the position of the *Future Memory* - when the DS^{++} has been realized, or beyond that point from the *Outcome of the Outcome* - identifies the steps that had to have been taken to arrive at that point in the future back to the present with clarity.

Trajectory of INTENT
Teleological Design

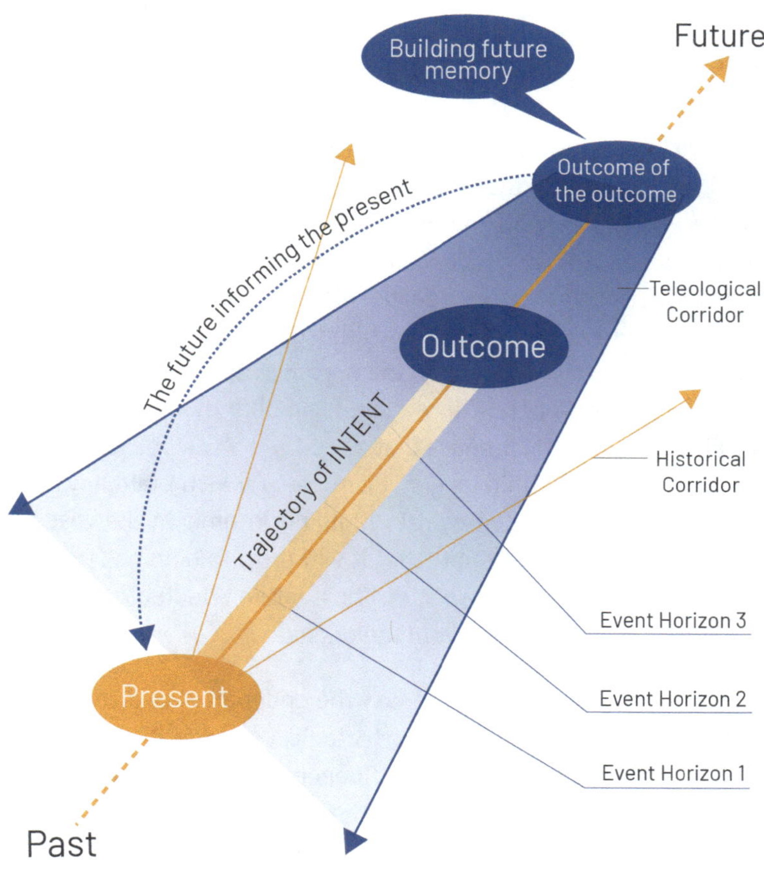

Figure 6.1 The Trajectory of INTENT model

Structuring and Using Time in the Satisfaction Cycle Model

The concept of *Future Memory* is rooted in teleological principles and forms an integral part of the *Trajectory of INTENT* model, developed by Joseph, as we apply it within the *Satisfaction Cycle* model. This teleological model, illustrated in Figure 6.1, commences by envisioning oneself in a future state where the desired objectives have been realized. Operating within the *Trajectory of INTENT* facilitates decision-making that is aligned with future outcomes, thereby guiding individuals toward their intended goals and the ultimate realization of the *Outcome of the Outcome* in an optimal manner.

The *Trajectory of INTENT* is structured around the concept of the "arrow of time." The *Trajectory of INTENT* model values the teleological corridor as having more information available that can be used in making high-quality decisions, beginning with the endpoint and tracing the sequence of events back to the present through an uninterrupted series of steps. Viewed from the future, these steps inevitably culminate in the realization of the outcome. This is distinctly different from the historical corridor (also illustrated in Figure 6.1), where *Event Horizons* blind the viewer to anything that might occur, or be occurring, beyond them, as discussed below. Teleological processes, which are inherent in nature, exemplify this principle. For instance, it is a fundamental premise that a seed will always develop into the specific plant encoded within its genetic material, which is already present at the beginning of the teleological unfolding in time. In the case of an acorn, it is a teleological certainty that it will grow into an oak tree, never into a maple tree or any other species. Thus, within teleological processes, the endpoint is predetermined from the outset.

What's not always consistent is the way the endpoint is realized in teleological systems. An example of how teleological systems can play out can be found in the way bonsai growers influence the end shaping of the tree that grows from the acorn, mimicking the kind of events that happen in nature. While an acorn will always produce an oak tree, the form that the growing path takes cannot always be known ahead of time. The growing path has a direct influence on the way the tree grows and, to a great extent, even on what the outcome of that growth becomes.

So, when the acorn germinates into a small sapling in an environment where the roots cannot dig too deeply into the earth, the growth of the tree is stunted, and it remains small in stature. If an oak sapling is exposed to sunlight growing from only one direction or strong prevailing winds blowing from a single direction forcing the tree to conform its growth to compensate, the oak tree may become lopsided with branches pointing to just one side instead of being evenly dispersed as per the usual pattern of growth.

Bonsai growers utilize this knowledge of how the growth path of a sapling will compel the tree to conform and shape its eventual form as it matures into a tree. In nature, the constraints that affect the growth of an oak tree are a function of the context in which the acorn that will become the tree lands and takes root. In the artificial environment of a bonsai gardener, the gardener applies constraints to force the growth of the oak sapling to conform to the outcome they desire. Yet despite the constraints imposed by nature or the bonsai gardener, the acorn becomes an oak tree.

We can argue that many of the constraints that occur in nature, or that the bonsai gardener applies, are knowable. But even in those conditions where much of what happens is knowable there are unknowables - those things that can, did, and will happen that could not and were not known until after the fact. In systems theory, the boundary condition of those things that cannot be known before they happen, which will happen in the future, are known as *Event Horizons*. Since we cannot see beyond the *Event Horizon*, we can only know with any degree of certainty what will happen up to the next *Event Horizon* (as indicated in Figure 6.1).

The actual path to achieving any outcome when viewed from the present moving towards the future unfolds gradually and is limited by those *Event Horizons* – the points in space and time beyond which it is impossible to perceive, when standing in the present. Within the *Trajectory of INTENT* model, moving forward to reveal the teleological pathway requires taking one step at a time, allowing each step to reveal the next, and making suitable adaptive adjustments, to ensure consistent directionality of action that links the present with desired outcomes.

One of the paradoxes in the model of the *Trajectory of INTENT* is contained in the concept of the *Event Horizons*, described above. The paradox with the Trajectory of INTENT model is that every action you take at every step in the process of moving toward and creating the outcome, and the *Outcome of the Outcome*, changes the pathway by introducing new information into the system, which requires a response that also adds new information to the system.

As the paradox of *Event Horizons* unfolds within the *Trajectory of INTENT*, each action taken at every step in the process keeps the outcome position stable and determines the next action, which then becomes the subsequent step in the process. In terms of the sales process used within the *Satisfaction Cycle* model, this requires an ability to remain present to what actually happens, not what is presumed to happen, or the desire for the perfect sales scenario to unfold as planned.

To ensure the desired outcome is realized with a customer, each interaction where there is an exchange of information must include the result of that exchange, i.e., the information that has now become present and revealed, in whatever happens next to maintain the alignment with the intended outcome. This may mean adjusting the relationship to what has already happened to re-establish alignment with the outcome. The constant adjustment to keep the alignment in place with regard to the outcome, regardless of what happens along the way to attaining it, is what we mean by directionality.

Adapting to what actually happens and adjusting what happens next to conform with what happens at each step in the process is a key skill in the successful application of the *Satisfaction Cycle* model in sales. One example of this is the use of backtracking, where what someone has said is repeated to create a logical chain with what is said next. Using logical chaining establishes an embedded *Yes Set* in the dialogue, i.e., eliciting a series of "yes" responses from the customer to the things you say - a powerful technique which we will discuss more in detail in Chapter 9.

An example of such a dialogue could be:

Salesperson: *"You mentioned that you need the outcome within three months, and you have a small team currently working to integrate the existing process with the new one, which you expect to complete by the end of this month. At that point, it's critical for us to be up to speed with programming the new system to take over operations control, including the new dashboard you requested, correct?"*

Customer: *"Yes. Everything must be in place for us to make the transition within the next three months; otherwise, we'll face significant impacts, and the costs will dramatically increase for us."*

Salesperson: *"Okay, so we're clear: this needs to happen by the end of the month from our end. We can definitely do that, guaranteed. We'll add two additional people to the development team to ensure we finish ahead of* *schedule, allowing time for any last-minute fixes that might be needed. It will be slightly more costly to accelerate the process, but this cost is far less than the expense of missing that deadline. Does that approach make sense in terms of maintaining your schedule?"*

Customer: *"Well, yes, we need this to happen without fail, but we are concerned about incurring additional costs."*

Salesperson: *"I understand your concerns about unnecessary expenses. If I understand correctly, we have two potential paths we can explore together..."*

Salesperson: *"The first option is to stay on schedule "as is". If we do that, you're facing a delay that will require you to pause your operations here, put your internal team on hold, and cause the rest of the organization to continue working in the existing sub-optimal environment. This will not only increase your current operational costs but also add significant additional costs to the transition into the new system when it is eventually implemented. We can proceed without any additional cost from our side, delivering the project exactly as promised. That's, of course, your choice - just let me know, and we'll leave things as they are."*

Salesperson: *"The other path is to update the project, adding a couple of developers on our side to ensure that the project is delivered by the end of the month. This would allow your team to continue working without delay or interruption, completing the entire project, including the transition to the new system, within three months. Once operational, the increased throughput and output will significantly boost productivity and the operational cost savings will more than cover any additional costs incurred to keep the project on the timeline you initially wanted."*

Salesperson: *"It really comes down to where you feel most confident about incurring additional costs and whether the value of being where you need to be in three months justifies any additional investment. From our experience with numerous projects, customers who keep their timelines tight often tell us six months or a year later - after enjoying the operational cost savings and increased productivity - that the upfront investment was worth it, and they are glad they didn't hesitate."*

Customer: *"Sure, but we really need to keep costs tight on this project and do everything we can not to exceed the original budget we set."*

Salesperson: *"Well, we can stick to the original schedule "as is" if that's the right decision for you. However, to ensure we meet the updated deadline, we would need to add a couple of people to the project. Unless I misunderstood, and the original delivery dates still work for you, adding two developers is the only way we can meet the new delivery dates for our part of the project by the end of this month."*

Customer: *"No, we definitely need those in place by the end of the month, or it will be very costly to shift the project timelines."*

Salesperson: *"So, it's really up to you. We can initiate a new work order to change the scope of work and move things forward with a minor adjustment in cost now or keep the original timeline if you'd prefer to absorb the higher costs later in the project."*

At this point, it is challenging for the customer to dispute the options after agreeing with the entire rationale that began the process of updating the sales conditions. While the decision remains in the customer's hands, they are now well-informed and a strategic design to create the desired outcome has been established.

In this example, the salesperson has used time to establish a logical chain and build cognitive inertia, pulling the process forward toward a future desired outcome. First, by backtracking, the history of the exchange is included and brought up to date. From there, the customer can be moved to a future position in time where the outcome has been realized by them as a conceptual experience.

Seen from the present looking forward, each step beyond the first remains unknowable. However, when viewed from the position of having attained the outcome, these steps appear inevitable and fixed in terms of the actions taken.

The organizing principle guiding the steps in the *Trajectory of INTENT* is the attainment of the outcome, viewed as an inevitable future reality that is preserved as the *Future Memory*. From the perspective of the *Outcome of the Outcome,* as a point in time beyond having achieved the outcome, and looking back to the present, all necessary steps are contained within the *Trajectory of INTENT* in a teleological manner.

At the starting point, while any potential outcome, including possibilities of both failure and success, remains within the realm of possibility, at the endpoint where the outcome has been achieved, only the possibility of successful attainment remains. Consequently, all steps leading up to that outcome become fixed in time. In addition, when progressing through the path that the *Trajectory of INTENT* describes, all the *Event Horizons* that were present at the start of the process of attaining the outcome are resolved as a result of the action taken at each step as the steps in the process were revealed.

All of the information that is contained on the *Trajectory of INTENT* toward the attainment and realization of the outcome is present in the *Future Memory*. When looking back through time, from the position of the *Outcome of the Outcome*, in the future, all of the information contained on the *Trajectory of INTENT* can be accessed. This view is called the *Teleological Corridor*, as indicated by the triangular shape in Figure 6.1. The *Teleological Corridor* contains and shows all of the potential possibilities that were eliminated in the progress toward attaining the outcome and realizing the outcome of the outcome.

Viewing the future from the present within the *Trajectory of INTENT* model describes the *Historical Corridor*. Within this corridor, the present possibilities seem narrower compared to those observed when looking back from the future through the *Teleological Corridor*. Therefore, the point of view on the historical opens up many more potential possibilities moving forward as you look to the future from the present, and the singularity of attaining the desired outcome therefore becomes more and more uncertain.

By accessing the *Future Memory* from the position beyond the realization of the desired outcome in the future of the *Outcome of the Outcome*, the entirety of the *Teleological Corridor* on the *Trajectory of INTENT* becomes available, including all of the changes that occur as each *Event Horizon* is revealed and resolved by the actions taken. By maintaining the *Future Memory* as the organizing principle that aligns your responses, you ensure that your actions are consistently moving toward the realization of your desired outcome. When your actions are aligned and consistently moving toward the realization of the *Future Memory* you hold, every outcome along the way creates more information that you can use and narrows the possibilities at each step, pointing the entire system to the eventual attainment of the outcome.

Inside the Brain's Black Box

Consciously contemplating the *Outcome of the Outcome* within the *Trajectory of INTENT* entails projecting oneself forward in time to the moment when the *Future Memory* is fully actualized. This mental projection constitutes a neurocognitive process originating in the frontal lobes of the cerebral cortex, which then integrates with the functions of the limbic and rear brain in the cerebellum. This mental process of projecting a *Future Memory* translates into decisions that drive and manifest the necessary actions to achieve desired results.

When the neurocognitive process driving the *Trajectory of INTENT* is called *Future Memory*, it is because it functions similarly to memory creation of what has happened in the past. This process involves the hypothalamus, a core component of memory creation in the brain. By mentally projecting oneself into the future and associating into that state, the hypothalamus generates the *Future Memory*. This occurs because, from the future point where the *Future Memory* is projected, the present is perceived as a memory of events leading up to that moment.

As this future projection becomes fully realized, to the extent that one feels present in that moment, the future also becomes a neurocognitive memory. This process can be enhanced by considering the *Outcome of the Outcome*, projecting further into the future where the desired *Outcome of the Outcome* also becomes a memory. This process profoundly influences individuals, motivating them to take action to realize their intended outcome.

Once the hypothalamus engages in creating a *Future Memory*, that memory begins to replay itself in the mind, inducing an effect psychologists refer to as nostalgia. This phenomenon makes individuals nostalgic about experiences they've already had, strengthening their expectation of attaining the future outcome and instilling unwavering confidence in the certainty of realizing additional outcomes. This process of establishing a complete, deep neurocognitive representation of attaining the desired future outcome creates a frame, or as Joseph puts it ...

"It creates a memory of it having already happened, just not yet."

Consequently, this memory of the future alters people's perception of reality and how they structure and process their experiences in relation to time, while letting go of what one has already "had," having mentally and emotionally experienced the complete benefits and value of a solution, becomes psychologically and emotionally demanding. When the memory pertains to the future, individuals must take action to realize those benefits or let go of them entirely, a process that holds significant emotional weight.

Transforming the Emotions Involved in Selling

Understanding the dynamics between your emotional state (*Red* or *Green State*), your past, and the formation of memories is crucial. As discussed in Chapter 4, the amygdala, positioned in the limbic system, is the emotional center of the brain. The amygdala serves as the gateway to the hippocampus, acting like a conduit to the memory center of the brain. Memories originating in the hippocampus extend to the prefrontal cortex, where we envision our future.

Thus, your past shapes the way you envision your future, and your emotional state dictates which memories you can access. In a negative state - the *Red State* - your emotional state triggers accessing negative memories of the past, which in turn become future-paced projections influencing your perception of a negative future - an approach common to virtually all traditional problem-based sales models, as discussed in Chapter 4 and 5.

The *Satisfaction Cycle* introduces a transformative shift in selling. Instead of dwelling on negative experiences, i.e.: problems, we focus on creating a positive present state experience – the PS^+, as also discussed in Chapter 4 and 5. By doing so, we unlock access to positive memories, paving the way for the realization of the positive future you genuinely desire, and the positive *Future Memory* that it represents. This distinction sets the *Satisfaction Cycle* apart, offering a uniquely powerful approach that extends beyond mere techniques like questioning. It delves into the core of authentic human engagement, particularly when collaborative creation is the objective.

Commitment to instantiating their *Future Memory* diminishes any inhibitions or fears of consequences that may have initially held back the individual holding it, significantly reducing the likelihood of objections arising later. The *Satisfaction Cycle* is designed to ensure that the positive emotional tone that allows access to the *Future Memory* in the first place continues throughout the entire process. It also aims to build up the experience of satisfaction from the beginning, paving the way for a mutually beneficial setting where both the salesperson and the customer are aligned in their commitment to bringing about the desired outcome.

Commitment to creating the desired outcome engages another processing center of the brain, the cerebellum. The cerebellum acts as the center for controlling the bodily function of movement. When the cerebellum is engaged there is a literal sense of movement as the body acts out micro-muscular responses that replicate the gross motor movements required to create the behaviors required to produce the outcomes intended.

Imagine standing on a basketball court, ready to take a shot. As you prepare to shoot the ball, your body automatically engages in a complex series of movements, including flexing your muscles and focusing your eyes. Even before the ball leaves your hands, your body already has the experience of shooting it. In your experience, before you release the ball for real, you feel the satisfaction of a successful shot or the disappointment of a missed opportunity.

Athletes train their minds and bodies to visualize success because the body follows the path the brain has prepared. In the context of sales, customers undergo a similar process. They focus on their desired outcome and imagine what it will be like to have already achieved it. As they envision a future where their desired outcome has been achieved, their body automatically responds by taking action to move toward their outcome.

For example, consider a customer seeking to enhance their CRM workflow, desiring faster access to information. They begin by focusing on their desired outcome, visualizing a future where they effortlessly access all the necessary information for their work without any delays or frustrations. As the customers construct this *Future Memory*, their body instinctively responds by taking action to bring it closer to reality. They invest in new software that allows them to streamline their workflow and provide instant access to the information they want and need.

Being able to provide answers promptly and with confidence is an em-powering experience for the customer. They no longer worry about lacking the necessary information and can concentrate on their work with ease. By building a *Future Memory*, the body-mind prepares to take action and bring the desired outcome into reality, as described above. By taking action the neurocognitive chain that begins with imagining and projecting a positive outcome in the future is satisfied. This aspect of managing the customers' emotional process in this way is unique to the *Satisfaction Cycle* model of high-value, complex selling.

Creating a *Future Memory* with the customers and enabling them to experience it is a powerful technique in sales. This is the essence of what makes the *Satisfaction Cycle* so effective. When a customer has a body-based experience of satisfaction, the *Future Memory* becomes a vivid and tangible recollection, allowing them to immerse themselves in the feeling of already having achieved their desired outcome. The customers experience a genuine sense of satisfaction, and the thought of letting go of this *Future Memory* and returning to their current reality and old solution can pose a challenging choice.

It is undeniably difficult to let go of the satisfaction associated with already having realized what their *Future Memory* allows them to embody. Once *Future Memory* takes root in the customers' minds, they become fully committed to taking action and have already tasted the satisfaction that comes with it. By harnessing the power of *Future Memory* sales professionals can deeply connect with their customers instilling a sense of possibility and achievement. As customers experience the satisfaction of their *Future memory*, their motivation to instantiate it and turn it into a concrete reality intensifies.

Moving Time

In order to create a powerful experience of *Future Memory*, one of the most important aspects integral to the *Satisfaction Cycle* model is the idea of moving your customers through time. This involves shifting their perceptual experience from the present to the past, the past to the present, the present to the future, the future to the past, the past to the future, and the future to the present. In other words, an important skill to develop is the ability to connect all permutations of movement through time, including past, present, and future.

The way we move the perceptual position in time within the Satisfaction Cycle model is through the structuring of verb tenses in language. For example, to refer to the present, we use the form of the verb "to be" by saying,

"I am/he-she is/we are/they are."

To describe a position in the past with the verb "to be" we say,

"I was/he-she was/we were/they were."

When referencing the future use of the verb "to be" we say,

"I will be/he-she will be/we will be/they will be."

By using the available verb tenses, we can place the message we are communicating in a specific position in time. Being able to position a customer in a specific time when they are making sense of what we are referring to as we communicate with them is especially helpful. This is combined with the *Trajectory of INTENT* model, having them consider the idea of attaining the outcome they want and then building a *Future Memory* of having achieved that outcome. When a customer gains the perspective of having achieved the desired outcome, it creates the distinct feeling of having also completed the required actions, positioning these activities in the past as already done.

There is deep value in helping a customer move smoothly through time to consider the current situation as the future, the present, and the past. It's also valuable to have them consider the outcome they want to attain as either the future or the present. Then, moving in time beyond the attainment of that outcome, they should consider the outcome they have achieved as if it were in the past. When a customer thinks about the outcome they want to attain as if it were in the past, they have moved to a position in time where they are experiencing the *Outcome of the Outcome*, as indicated in Figure 6.1.

We can build powerful representations of *Future Memory* that are experienced physically as full-body sensations. These create the emotional connection to having the outcome we want our customers to experience, from the position in time of the *Outcome of the Outcome*, where the outcome is experienced as having already happened in the past.

Here's an example of what the dialogue might look like when we consider using language, and specifically using verb tenses, to help us move our customers through time:

Starting in the present:*"So you stated that you are currently able to sustain great relationships with your current customer ...,"*

then moving from present to past *"... and this is actually a continuation of the decision your made to make customer services levels a priority, which you've been very successful in accomplishing for at least the past five years."*

then back from past to the present

"Realizing how valuable it's been to have made and kept that commitment to customer service levels, and how it's helped build the business to the current level of success you're enjoying today, you want to leverage that to scale beyond the current growth to double your revenues in the next two years."

and finally moving from present to future and further on to future-past.*"As you consider what it will be like to have achieved the result of doubling your business, what will be true as a result of having done that already?"*

You have now moved your customer conversationally through time from the present to their past, back to the present, and into the future, and then you've asked them to consider a question from the perspective of having accomplished the outcome they desire, looking back through time to consider the implications of achieving that success.

The process of moving a customer through time from the present to the future, where the outcome has occurred, allows you to use these conversational skills to take them beyond the outcome to the *Outcome of the Outcome* position. The deep value in taking your customers to the *Outcome of the Outcome* position is that from there, they can experience the return on investment you're asking them to make a decision about investing in here in the present, where the investment for the return they haven't yet realized.

Conversational *Time Sliding*

The dialogue presented above serves as an example of conversational *Time Sliding*, an advanced communication skill. *Time Sliding* refers to the ability to intentionally navigate through time semantically using verbs and their tenses. This technique allows you to position a person in a specific time frame conversationally. However, it extends beyond merely using the past, present, and future tenses of a language. The real mastery lies in seamlessly guiding people's minds from one temporal position to another.

For instance, one might transition from discussing the present to envisioning the future, then speak as if that future is already the present, effectively linking the desired future outcome with the current moment. The essence of *Time Sliding* is to fluidly move from one time frame to another and then discuss that time as if it is occurring now.

Intentionally employing *Time Sliding* in sales allows for a connection between the present, future, and past, facilitating a smooth transition that helps individuals visualize a desired outcome as illustrated above. Delving deeper into *Time Sliding* in Part 2 of this book, we explore how this language usage guides our brains to consider events that have not yet occurred as if they are happening right now. This cognitive ability is linked to the neocortex, organized semantically around abstract ideas. The frontal and prefrontal lobes, in particular, are instrumental in this forward-looking capability, enabling us to 'experience' future events in the present. Thus, the brain organizes actions today that will lead to desired outcomes tomorrow.

Yet, the brain's preparation for future events isn't limited to semantic organization. The limbic system, brainstem, and the posterior part of the brain collaborate to craft imaginative sensory representations based on sensory data. These representations condition our body to be ready to perform in a certain way when we encounter future stimuli.

The ability to slide time verbally and conceptually to navigate semantically through time underscores the potent interplay between language and the human brain. By leveraging our brain's propensity to predict and prepare for future events, we can better position ourselves to achieve our objectives. Employing narrative structures that immerse individuals in an experience enables decision-making that transcends logical reasoning alone.

By intentionally using language and verb tenses, you guide customers through various temporal positions. Ultimately, *Time Sliding* is a technique that allows customers to genuinely feel the achievement of their future goals. When they can embody that sensation, they are much more inclined to take the necessary actions to realize those goals.

In Chapter 7, we will discuss how the *Satisfaction Cycle* serves as a practical framework for navigating complex and dynamic environments, emphasizing adaptability and the alignment of sales processes with factors such as people, relationships, politics, and market dynamics. The *Satisfaction Cycle* becomes a strategic tool for traversing uncertainty and chaos by fostering an understanding of stakeholder dynamics, optimizing the system as a whole, and focusing on strengths over weaknesses.

7

ALL SELLING IS CONTEXTUAL

Optimizing Your Sales Approach for Success in Complex, Dynamic Systems

One effective method of learning is to teach someone else. During my journey to learn the Satisfaction Cycle, I encountered various courses and training sessions. When it was time to take the next level in my training, I had a mind-blowing experience when Joseph first asked me to assist in a training session about the Satisfaction Cycle.

For those unfamiliar with Joseph's or Henrik's training sessions, they are un-conventional. They eschew PowerPoints and traditional presentations in favor of a more dynamic story-telling approach that ensures participants leave with life-changing insights and the ability to change their behaviors. Even though the purpose was for me to learn, the bar was set high for my performance as an assistant trainer.

Suddenly, I found myself in front of seventy people, discussing the Satisfaction Cycle without any prior preparation. Although my expertise may lag twenty to thirty years behind Joseph's and Henrik's, the audience was content with what I shared. Of course, at this point, I already knew the basics, so it was more about the way I was delivering the content than the content itself. This was a pivotal moment for me; I realized that for me to be able to do this must mean that as part of my learning, I had learned to let go of the need to control every aspect of the session. I was fully present, without expecting anything in particular from the audience, allowing the session to unfold naturally while maintaining engagement. Embracing the unknown, I felt completely at ease.

Whenever I faltered, Joseph was there to offer guidance and make additional remarks, ensuring the training stayed on course. His interventions ensured a high standard of excellence in the overall training program, even as he entrusted parts of the session to a novice like me. None of these things were planned, they just happened on the course towards the desired outcome of that session.

When reflecting this experience, it reminded me of a story Joseph often recounted about jazz legends Miles Davis and Herbie Hancock. Herbie Hancock, an esteemed American jazz pianist, had the privilege of being part of the Miles Davis Quintet early in his illustrious career. Miles Davis, an iconic and influential figure in the history of jazz, and Hancock found themselves in a live performance in 1963, interpreting Davis's classic composition, "So What."

In the midst of Miles Davis's enthralling solo, the unexpected occurred - Herbie Hancock struck a chord that resonated as discordant and seemingly amiss, a notable deviation from the musical script. In response, Hancock froze, halting his playing altogether. A palpable moment of tension hung in the air as the audience and fellow musicians absorbed the unexpected twist.

However, Miles Davis, as the formidable force and strongest player in this dynamic musical equation, approached the situation with a unique perspective. Rather than perceiving Hancock's "wrong" chord as a mistake, Davis recognized it as an opportunity for innovation and creativity. In a brief pause, Davis skillfully incorporated complementary notes, transforming the dissonant chord into a harmonious expression that seamlessly blended with the overall performance.

The music, once interrupted by an apparent misstep, now resonated with an unexpected beauty. The collaboration between Davis and Hancock continued, reaffirming the power of adaptability and the transformative potential within the strongest component of a dynamic system.

For Miles Davis, the incident wasn't a disruption but a chance to redefine the trajectory of the performance. His ability to embrace unforeseen challenges and turn them into opportunities showcased the strength inherent in the most influential part of any dynamic system. Davis, with his exceptional skills, exemplified the capacity of the strongest player to shape and redefine the system's capabilities. Davis' playing turned the" wrong" chord right.

Complex and dynamic systems cannot be controlled. There was a time when I believed only in rigid plans and a single path to success. But the most valuable lesson I've learned with the Satisfaction Cycle is the art of embracing the unknown and being content in every moment, without the longing to be elsewhere. After all, both business and life are replete with constant changes and surprises. It's only now that I truly grasp what Joseph means when he says:

"You cannot know what you don't know until you know it."

"You cannot do what you can't yet do until you can do it."

No one knows exactly what will happen until it unfolds. Possessing the ability to remain present, coupled with the flexibility and adaptability to respond to situations as they arise, is invaluable.

In the realm of business, this has meant shedding linear thinking in favor of a broader perception of complexity. Guided by the principles of the Satisfaction Cycle, I maintain clear intentions and outcomes, even if they seem uncertain at first. My focus is on the present reality, taking actions based on what is actually occurring, rather than what I anticipated might happen.

I don't know my exact future in relation to the Satisfaction Cycle and how my journey with Henrik and Joseph will continue. Henrik and Joseph will certainly continue educating more people like me. What I know, based on my ultimate professional desire, is that I am going to continue learning and gradually learn to train and teach this approach so that more people can learn this way. I want to show those people who have an interest... a world without limitations and boundaries—a world where everything is possible.

Where you, dear reader, go from here is a choice we leave to you.

When Sales Become Transformational

Sales should generally be kept simple and not unnecessarily complicated. For instance, if a customer runs out of paper for their printer and wants to buy two boxes of printing paper, the focus should be on selling the paper without unnecessary effort. If you happen to have an offer of three boxes for the price of two, you can communicate this to the customer and ask if they would like to have three boxes instead. Upon agreement, proceed to dispatch three boxes and continue with the transaction!

In such sales contexts, there is no need to overanalyze the customer's brain states or over-optimize decision-making. If the sales can be conducted easily, it is best to take the shortest route. Transactional sales are generally straightforward, although there are cases where they might become complicated; however, they are never truly complex.

Grasping the difference between something which is complex and something which is complicated proves valuable in identifying the most effective approach in sales. Consider for example the repair of modern car engines as an illustration. Engine repair is no longer a simple task; it has become complicated due to advancements in design. However, while fixing the engine may pose challenges, a thorough understanding of engines, encompassing their components, rules, and algorithms, enables successful repairs.

Consider now the complexity that arises when evaluating the engine's performance in diverse conditions. It extends beyond the mere mechanics of the engine and its components. It involves factors such as the driver's influence, the prevailing atmospheric conditions - encompassing temperature, humidity, and oxygen levels in the air. These variables collectively contribute to a multitude of factors affecting the engine.

To illustrate, let's envision an engineer tasked with designing a Formula 1 engine to optimize a race car for victory. Formula 1 introduces a certain level of complexity due to the driver and specific conditions on race day, although it is not overwhelmingly intricate. In the process of engine design, a reasonable understanding of racetrack conditions can be achieved - encompassing factors like location, track profile, surface material, and more.

So, Formula 1 cars are complicated. It is hard to drive the races, but certain rules, recipes, and algorithms can be applied. By design the variables in Formula 1 racing are limited. Logical processes can resolve the conditions and requirements of Formula 1 car engineering.

The scenario for an engine for a rally car is different. For a rally driver, driving is a much more complex thing, and designing an engine for a rally car therefore presents a much more complex challenge. Rallies are located in different altitudes changing the oxygen available to the engine. The quality of the road varies a lot. Sometimes it is hard, sometimes gravel, and occasionally muddy. Also, the road conditions can vary dramatically from day to day, depending on the weather.

Thus, the engineering solution for Formula 1 optimization does not work well with rally cars. Rally driving involves too many unknowns, changing variables, and interrelated factors that cannot be reduced to a limited set of rules. The variables involved represent the distinction of complexity – in an almost race-by-race fashion – in Rally car racing.

The *Satisfaction Selling* approach we are discussing here is more akin to rally-driving sales, where uncertainty and constant changes are the norms. You can never be sure what is around the next corner, as the situation changes constantly as it unfolds. Complexity is inherent in systems that possess the ability to change rapidly. Dynamic systems, by definition, are always inherently complex.

Joseph and Henrik use an illustrative example to highlight the contrast between mechanical and dynamic systems. They draw upon Gregory Bateson's *Rock and Dog* metaphor, originating from his 1972 work *Steps to an Ecology of Mind*. Bateson, an English anthropologist, social scientist, and cyberneticist, focused on system theories.

If you kick a rock that is lying on the ground at a specific angle and with a predefined amount of energy and disregard any wind resistance or friction, you can easily calculate precisely where the rock will land. If you repeat the experiment - put back the rock and kick it again at exactly the same angle and with exactly the same amount of energy - it will land in precisely the same place. In other words, there is a well-defined linear connection between cause and effect for this simple mechanical system.

If you then replace the rock with a dynamic, living system, such as a small dog that weighs the same as the rock and kick it at the same specific angle and with the same predefined amount of energy, ignoring the variables of form such as size and shape, it could be that it will comply with Newton's laws and land in the same place as the rock. However, there are many other possibilities. It might fly through the air for a bit and then run away with a whimper or it might turn around and bite you on the leg before you can get around to kicking it. Even if you would go and kick the same dog on a different day, you might get a different response.

In other words, the same predetermined and repeatable, well-defined linear connection between cause and effect does not exist in non-linear, dynamic systems in the same way you can apply and count on them in linear, mechanical systems.

Dynamic Systems Are Always as Strong as Their Strongest Part

Bateson's *Rock and Dog* metaphor underscores that people are more akin to dogs than rocks. It highlights the systems theorists' departure from applying the classic cause-and-effect model to living, dynamic systems. Bateson extends the analogy by demonstrating that a mechanical system like a machine or chain, consistently reacts the same way and is never stronger than its weakest part. In contrast, a dynamic system, exemplified by a dog, has infinitely diverse ways of responding to external actions, such as a person attempting to kick it.

These principles also apply to high-value complex sales that occur within dynamic systems. Linear processes and fixed rules are inadequate in this context. To succeed in non-transactional sales, an alternative approach that accounts for the complexity of the situation and can handle unforeseen contextual changes is required.

In high-value complex sales, the context is defined by multiple interrelated elements. There might be a lot going on in complicated systems, though the system itself does not change. In a dynamic system, however, changes are emerging at a high pace. In a high-value complex sales context, sales typically get complex when the offer has some intangible elements, service components, or level of customization. It also becomes complex when more people are involved from both sides.

In complex, non-linear, dynamic systems the strongest part - usually the one with the greatest adaptability and tolerance to variability - will determine the trajectory of the system, and the final outcome achieved. When a salesperson represents the individual in the system with the greatest range of tolerance and adaptability by moving flexibly and creatively to changes as they arise in the interactions, they maintain the ability to set the course of the exchange as it unfolds.

In mechanical systems, the performance of the whole system is defined by its weakest part. For instance, if your car has a flat tire, it impacts how fast you can drive; the weakest part, the flat tire, limits the performance of the entire system - the car. However, the situation is actually the opposite in dynamic systems. In dynamic systems, it's the strongest part that defines the strength and performance of the entire system. To optimize the system to perform at its highest level, everything should be organized around the strongest part rather than focusing on fixing the weak parts. This is because, in dynamic systems, the strongest part limits the outcomes the system can produce.

The idea that the strongest part determines the strength of the system is akin to how a professional athlete, through their talent and abilities, can change the course of a single play or the entire game, even elevating the level of play for the whole team with their creativity, capability, and action. Joseph articulates this concept succinctly:

"The strength of a dynamic system is always defined by its strongest part."

This realization is fundamental and crucial. To make a dynamic system stronger or better, you need to focus on finding the strongest part, not the weakest. That's why, in *Satisfaction Selling*, we begin by uncovering what works - the strong part of the system - rather than starting by identifying the problem and what doesn't work - the weak part of the system.

Again, this idea is evident in sports teams. When you have a team with a star player who can score many goals, that single player can raise the quality of what everybody else is doing. The team gets better with a high-scoring player. The performance of a team is not diminished by the player who scores the fewest points. In team sports, the team begins to play around the strengths of the best player and feed him the ball and create positions for him to score. This way, the whole team wins. Everyone plays their part, and even the weakest player has a role because you cannot only play team sports with one person. It does not work. Instead, the teams always organize themselves around the strongest part to leverage the entire team's performance.

Instead of singling out the weakest player and asking everyone else to slow down to accommodate their limitations, which would only result in subpar team performance, in team sports, the coach allows great players to stand out and puts them where they can do their best. The coach of a winning team takes advantage of the strengths of the most outstanding player and then considers how the rest of the team can operate in relation to and around the strongest player. Then the reality might very well be that the star player can even compensate for the fact that the weakest player does not run that fast, throw far, or bring explosive strength to the team. Adjusting how the team plays also turns the weakest player's capabilities and limitations into assets rather than detriments.

To further illustrate the point, consider first these five examples of systems that are best described as mechanical, where the weakest part sets the limit for performance:

- **A chain**: The strength of the chain is determined by its weakest part, as a single weak part can cause the entire chain to fail.

- **A car engine**: The performance of the engine is limited by its least powerful component, such as the smallest cylinder or weakest piston.

- **A water pipe system**: The flow of water is restricted by the narrowest or weakest point in the pipe, affecting the overall water flow.

- **A computer network**: The speed and efficiency of data transmission are limited by the slowest or weakest device or connection in the network.

- **An assembly line**: The productivity of the entire line can be hindered by the slowest or least efficient workstation, causing bottlenecks and delays.

Now look at these five examples of systems that are best described as dynamic systems, where the strongest part sets the limit for system performance:

- **A racing team**: The overall performance of the team relies heavily on the skills and capabilities of the fastest or most skilled team member.

- **A sports team**: The success of the team can be determined by the abilities and performance of the star player who sets the standard for the team's performance.

- **An orchestra**: The quality of the performance is often set by the most talented musicians or the skill of the conductor, influencing the overall musical experience.

- **A research team**: The breakthroughs and advancements made by the most innovative and knowledgeable researchers push the boundaries of the team's capabilities.

- **A technology company**: The ability to develop cutting-edge products and solutions is driven by the expertise and creativity of the top engineers and designers in the company.

People, Relationships and Politics

Context determines the best approach and the most efficient utilization of resources to facilitate sales, and the *Satisfaction Cycle* provides a useful frame for complex and dynamic sales contexts. In the context where the *Satisfaction Cycle* is intended to be used, implementing the product or service requires the customers to change their business practices to some extent. So, one way to look at a sales context and the most efficient way of selling is to consider what the product or service means for the customer.

"What will be different for the customers, when they have bought and implemented your product?"

When the customer will get a significant change or improvement in their situation, and when it requires effort and commitment from their side to make this change and improvement happen, we are in the field of selling that can be called transformational sales.

Transformational selling always has an impact on the customers' businesses. For example, in the case of software sales, buying a new customer relationship management system is almost by definition transformational, especially when it is happening for the first time. The buying company must adapt its operational practices to accommodate the new system. Once the system is implemented and functioning, the seller-buyer relationship may become more transactional. For instance, if the company acquires additional user licenses or opts to provide training for a specific number of individuals, the interaction becomes more transactional.

At this stage, the focus shifts to negotiations regarding terms and conditions, such as quantity and pricing. It is no longer a transformational process; instead, it becomes transactional. By its very nature, transformational sales are complex and typically occur within dynamic systems. This distinction arises from the understanding that customers will need to modify some aspects of their business operations, self-perception, or perception of the seller. In these instances, implementing the sales process using the *Satisfaction Cycle* can make a tremendous difference.

Complex transformational sales most often involve multiple individuals. Several people from both the customer's and the seller's sides may be participating in meetings. Salespeople often create stakeholder maps to identify the individuals involved in the buying process. These stakeholders form a *Buying Center*, sometimes called a decision-making unit, as introduced in Chapter 1. The *Buying Center* comprises members of an organization engaged in the buying process and making purchasing decisions.

Here, people have different roles that are not necessarily tied to their formal position in the organization. Typically, a *Buying Center* includes roles such as

- *Users*

- *Influencers*

- *Buyers*

- *Decision-makers*

- *Gatekeepers*

While significant attention is usually given to the *Buying Center* in sales literature, it is important to note that the seller's side also often form a team in high-value complex sales, known as the sales or selling team. This team consists of individuals with different roles and responsibilities related to sales strategy, sales process, product/service, customer service/follow up, and management.

While stakeholder maps of the *Buying Center* are straightforward at a conceptual level, the real-life maps are often hard to draw due to the complexity introduced by various factors. Each stakeholder brings their unique personality to the situation. People have their individual agendas. There are politics involved. These people have relationships with each other, and their nature creates additional complexity in the system. All of this influences the buying process and customers' decision-making, whether the people are physically present in the room or not.

Imagine that in a sales meeting there is one person who is primarily focusing on what has already happened, they are oriented to the past. The person who is past-oriented discusses potential issues and is fear-driven, constantly seeking signs of possible problems. There might be another forward-looking person in the same system as the person who is oriented toward the past. The future-oriented person also recognizes the challenges and acknowledge that there are solutions to them. You need to deal with both characters. Individuals who are problem or past-oriented, and those that are solution or future-oriented, preference and use different parts of their brains.

The difference between individuals who are problem-seeking and those that are solution-seeking brings and adds to complexity. The fear-driven individual who references the past and is problem oriented relies on the rear brain and activated limbic system; while the forward-looking, solution-oriented individual is front-brain driven, actively engaging the frontal and prefrontal lobes.

A critical consideration about how individuals preference different and unique ways of using their brains is that each part of the brain communicates differently, almost as though they speak in different languages. "Brain language" begins with sensory processing and moves through emotional response before it becomes the language we speak with one another, knowing this distinction and how to specifically apply it is extremely powerful. As the number of participants in the room increases, the complexity arising from the unique characteristics of each person also grows, and so does the complexity arising from the unique characteristics of each person.

Another consideration in high-value complex sales involving multiple stakeholders and interactions between buyers and sellers may be that not all significant stakeholders are or will be physically present. When selling in complex contexts you need to be aware of who is present in the moment, and who is not present but may be influencing the decision-making process. In a complex sales context, it is important to remain mindful of what needs to happen to satisfy those who are not present. The salesperson needs to handle this complexity in real-time.

Each person who will influence the decision-making process, whether in the room or not, brings their own unique intentionality and outcomes that they have set themselves. The ability to navigate these dynamics and make the necessary adjustments is essential for success in complex sales. The salesperson who can remain present to the interactions as they are happening and also continues to remain adaptable and creative becomes the strongest link in the engagement who can and will set the trajectory for the outcome that is achieved.

All of these interactions among unique individuals with their own biases, intentions, and outcome creates politics, and politics is always complex. So, politics always play a role in complex transformational sales. When a decision-maker within the *Buying Center* accepts an offer, it often means saying "no" to someone else. It is important for the salesperson to ask him- or herself:

"Who will be affected by the decision-makers positive decision?"

"How is that going to affect the relationship with both the decision-maker and the organization that is buying?"

For example, if a line manager says "yes" to purchasing new software and at the same time, the company's IT manager maintains a friendly relationship with the competitor, potential challenges may arise. Could we anticipate resistance from the IT manager, potentially jeopardizing the project? In the sales process, it is crucial to anticipate and mitigate such risks. If there is a possibility of the project being undermined, it is essential to incorporate that into the sales process and structure it in a way that prevents such occurrences.

The approach taken in any sales process will vary depending on the specific situation and context, as all sales are contextual. One essential question to consider in the example of selling a new software solution may be how to get the IT manager on board, encouraging him or her to work with the software despite his or her friendship with the competitor. The political question in the example of potential conflicts in the sale of new software is that the decision-maker's "yes" means "no" to the IT manager: he or she is not getting the opportunity to have his or her friend supply the software.

When there is a conflict between a third-party decision-maker and the IT manager because of a previous relationship they have, the IT manager will most likely want to defend the current software because they are loyal to their friend. Conflicts of interest become a political and relationship issue that needs to be managed in the sales process. The salesperson has to manage the relationship between themselves and the decision-maker, other influencers, and even external parties like a previous supplier that may have existing relationships within the organization. Managing all these relationships that may influence a sale becomes critical for a smooth and successful sales process.

In complex transformational sales, the *Satisfaction Cycle* provides a contextual and adaptive framework. It prompts questions such as:

"Where are we?"

"What's going on?"

"Who are the key players?"

"What opportunities exist?"

"Where do we want to go?"

"How do we avoid getting caught by the situation?"

"How do we navigate the situation effectively?"

Asking these questions as an individual, internally, or in the sales team during a meeting, will assist in helping to clarify the movement of the sales process, i.e.

1. Where you are in relation to that movement.

2. What needs to be done to complete a step in the process.

3. How to move the sales process forward.

4. What roles need to be filled and by whom.

Each case and each situation in complex selling is unique. Based on the situation and the context, the *Satisfaction Cycle* allows you to adapt and change the rules of the play and deal with complexity and contextual changes, securing that everyone is aligned with the goal and going in the same direction.

Market Environment

The marketplace and the external environment significantly impact the sales context. Competitors might engage in unpredictable actions, and environmental or political events can have a sudden and profound impact. Over the last decades, we have witnessed several examples of such game-changing events; consider the 9/11 terror attacks in 2001, the financial crisis in 2008, and right now we are standing at the brink of an AI revolution that most likely will constitute a bigger change than going from the typewriter to the PC and from sending physical letters to sending e-mails.

The Covid-19 pandemic in 2020 serves as an example of an unforeseen event that led to rapid shifts in travel behaviors due to government regulations enacted in response to the emergence of new variants. Additionally, the Covid-19 pandemic disrupted the balance of supply and demand, resulting in numerous supply shortages and increased prices. During this period, companies were forced to adapt their strategies, adjust their supply chains, and seek alternative sources to meet their resource needs.

External factors, like the Covid-19 pandemic, directly influence sales. In addition to considering people, relationships, and politics, the marketplace context adds another layer of complexity. The *Satisfaction Cycle* provides a valuable tool for managing this complexity. It allows companies to create effective sales strategies and determine where to focus and optimize their efforts. In other words, the *Satisfaction Cycle* can also be used to optimize the decisions within your own organization which is also in itself a complex system.

For instance, let's examine the strategy for targeting specific markets and segments. Instead of fixing the areas where the company might be weakest, the *Satisfaction Cycle* guides to start from what is already working well (in some cases this can also be a way to identify and align with the strongest part of the system). We want to understand what it is about the current markets and segments that are already working well. In other words,

"What are the company and their salespeople already doing that works?"

Let's say that a company wants to increase its sales next year by 20%, and they are already successful in markets A and B but struggling in market

C. Unless the individual markets a company is operating in are entirely saturated, it is most effective to start maximizing what the company can get out of markets where they are already successful. Building on existing strengths provides easier wins. For example, if the company is already successful in markets A and B, they can allocate resources and develop capabilities to strengthen a less successful market, such as market C.

Unfortunately, it is common for companies to redirect resources from the successful markets to support a market where they face challenges. This decision can be counterproductive as it yields lower returns and greater uncertainty. Yet this often happens. This may involve reducing the investment budget for successful markets to allocate more resources to a less successful market, such as marketing resources. Basically, the company is asking people to produce the same outcome for their existing successful markets with fewer resources so that someone else can try to solve a struggle in a less successful market.

In contrast, the *Satisfaction Cycle* can be applied to maximize the entire system and its overall performance by focusing on strengths and areas of success. What eventually might be the best for the company is to eliminate their least successful market from its target market mix entirely, or at least for the time being until they can support it fully without cutting support in their existing successful markets.

Even though the company could serve all three markets, it might achieve the same outcomes as focusing only on the two biggest markets. By concentrating efforts on the two largest markets and reallocating resources from the underperforming market, the company can channel all its energy, brainpower, ideas, and creativity toward serving markets that are already highly productive. This strategic approach can lead to significant increases in profitability rather than persisting in developing an unprofitable market.

When navigating through the ever-changing external business environment, the most effective approach to dealing with unknown and unpredictable events is precisely what we have previously discussed. It involves beginning with what is already functioning effectively and leveraging existing strengths. By shifting the focus away from constantly addressing crises, firefighting issues, and isolated challenges, this approach promotes a more holistic and systemic perspective, ensuring a comprehensive approach to real value creation.

Leading the Sales System

High-value sales inherently involve complexity, each case being unique. The market environment, people, relationships, and politics create a unique context to be dealt with. To achieve effective results in such complex contexts, salespeople and their managers must be adaptable and align the sales process and its content with the context.

When considering organizations, the essential question is how to optimize the entire system, not just one part. Understanding the importance of optimizing the entire system, not just one part, is crucial in the sales context, where all components must work together. Companies consist of various departments, such as Management, Research & Development, Production, Marketing, and Sales, each with its own ideas and objectives.

Research & Development may want to bring a particular idea strongly to the market. Production seeks to increase the production of what they already know. Marketing likely has its unique perspective on the marketplace. Sales has their distinct idea possible different from the other arms of the organization of what successful interactions with the customers could be like. Management brings something else they want to happen in terms of goals and profitability when interacting with customers.

These ideas of how to approach the customer often clash in the real-life corporate environment and lead to internal conflicts. Sometimes pushing and doing one thing from one department's perspective minimizes the outcome the entire company can get. Recognizing the presence of silos, management needs to address them and their issues individually. This approach is widespread even though it entirely contradicts the principles of dynamic systems thinking. To optimize outcomes for the company, the idea that the strongest part sets the limit of the dynamic systems is an essential insight, but not at a cost to the system-at-large.

Another principle in systems dynamics, in addition to the idea that the strongest part determines the strength of the system as a whole, is that optimizing any one part of the system will compromise the system as a whole. To optimize the system, all of the parts of the system must be aligned and working together to allow the strongest part to perform at peak efficiency and effectiveness within the system-at-large.

Sales plays a critical role in generating revenue from customers. To really benefit from this, the whole system must function optimally. The sales team can interact with a certain number of people in a month, and by doing the maximum, they can get the most significant number of sales. If you just go and optimize the sales team's performance, what might happen is that they sell so much that the production team will be so overworked that the quality will decrease. While there might be a lot of sales in the first few months, the quality issue might pop up a few months later. That would put much pressure on the aftersales and service.

If all the parts of the system do not have the capacity to accommodate the input, throughput, or output of the strongest part in the system the system-at-large can fail. The system can fail if the strongest part of the system overtaxes the system-at-large. For example, a company's reputation may be damaged or destroyed because their customers' expectation of customer service and their actual experience aren't met and fall below acceptable levels of performance, and the seller cannot adjust quickly enough to compensate and deal with it.

In order to unlock the full potential of a highly productive sales team, management should concentrate on optimizing the entire company's system across all departments. It is crucial to acknowledge that the sales team acts as the powerhouse in achieving sales goals, determined by reaching a specific customer count. While hiring more salespeople can boost sales resource capacity, it's essential to recognize the limitations on the sustainable level of sales activity that the rest of the company can handle. This includes delivering products or services to customers and meeting their expectations for post-sale support, ensuring a comprehensive and efficient customer experience.

Like a high-performing sports team, a well-managed organization strategically centers its operations around the strongest part of the system. For instance, if the sales team demonstrates exceptional strength, effective management involves orchestrating other departments to provide optimal support, ensuring the sales team consistently performs at its highest potential. Realizing the full potential of the sales team might necessitate an increase in production capacity, while marketing may need to realign its focus and activities to penetrate new markets.

This holistic approach to maximizing the entire system involves aligning and coordinating capacities with the strongest part of the system, ultimately enhancing the overall quality of outcomes the company can achieve. This optimization of the system at large exemplifies the application of the *Satisfaction Cycle* to strategic leadership, providing a framework to navigate complexities within the organization.

When the entire organization is fine-tuned to support the sales department and its team, the challenge is to identify and harness the capabilities of the top performers within the sales team. To achieve this, it's crucial to understand who in the organization is already achieving exceptional results and what strategies contribute to their success. Rather than aiming for average performance across the board, the focus should shift towards recognizing the unique approaches that performers employ.

Consider that the highest achievers in your organization likely employ specific strategies that consistently yield positive results. This approach involves the practice of *Generative Exemplar Modeling*, where exceptional performance is observed and emulated to be transferred and replicated by others. Joseph utilized this method in developing the *Satisfaction Cycle* model, the unique sales approach presented here, as discussed in Chapter 2. Although others may not reach the same level of excellence as the very top performers, they can learn from them how they create their extraordinary level of performance and leverage their individual assets to improve their own performance.

Another key aspect of optimizing the sales team is organizing the team around its strongest players. By strategically positioning and supporting these top performers, the entire team can collaboratively achieve outstanding results. This involves directing opportunities and resources toward the most effective contributors, ensuring a collective effort that leads to excellence across the entire sales team.

A common error among sales managers is establishing uniform goals for the entire team. In pursuit of the sales target, a manager might determine a specific number of customer appointments required monthly. For example, instructing the team to each secure 30 customer appointments. The key issue lies in imposing the same target on everyone, regardless of individual capacities or circumstances.

A 30-customer appointment target in a month may be effortless for one salesperson, even achieving 40 appointments. However, another team member might find reaching 20 appointments challenging. Setting the struggling salesperson's goal at 30 becomes demoralizing. While they may hit the target on occasion, it's not their current capability. Imposing uniform goals is counterproductive; individualized targets are more potent and productive for the team.

The focus should be on optimizing the sales team's performance to reach the overall goal for customer appointments. Maybe the best salesperson who could easily make 40 appointments should be getting 20 of the most challenging cases because they have the best skillset in turning those appointments into sales. It would be beneficial for the team to give the more straightforward cases to those who would struggle to get 20 regular appointments. Maybe they can do at least 30 easy ones or even more. As a result, the team achieves the same overall number of meetings but in a much more productive manner overall.

Shifting to task optimization based on individual capabilities is crucial in transforming average sales teams into high performers. The *Satisfaction Cycle*, when applied, changes the perspective on leading and incentivizing the sales team. Team members start viewing themselves collectively, working towards the organization's overall success rather than individual achievements.

Unfortunately, prominent companies often make the mistake of doing the opposite - excessively rewarding top performers, punishing the weak, or even ignoring the best and investing heavily in the weakest. This misguided approach creates a moral dilemma, destroying both employees and the organization. Organizations failing to recognize the unintended consequences of their reward and punishment strategies subject the rewarded to constant stress, risking elimination for underperformance. Management unaware of the costs of unintended consequences can lead to severe financial repercussions, impacting revenue, profitability, and short- and long-term equity.

In times of severe financial repercussions, individuals or organizations may recognize the downward spiral and feel compelled to take drastic measures. Fortunately, some companies have successfully navigated this challenging situation. Their initial move involved a shift in leadership strategy, fostering a more sustainable morale within the organization. This transformative approach mirrors the method employed by sports coaches with their teams. Just as coaches identify the team's strongest aspects and assess the unique strengths and weaknesses of individual players, they then determine how each player can best contribute to the team's success. Great coaches assign clear roles to each player based on their strengths, aligning with the team's overall needs and desires to maximize collective contributions to the company's success.

The benefits of the *Satisfaction Cycle* extend beyond individuals. Through Joseph's and Henrik's work with various companies, tangible improvements have been observed for sales managers upon implementing this approach. Sales managers play a crucial role in guiding their teams by providing direction, setting goals, and offering training, coaching, and mentoring. Having a shared strategy, represented by a map, creates a common platform, process, and language.

With the *Satisfaction Cycle*, everyone can easily determine their position in the sales process, whether it's gathering information about the customer's current state, collecting data on their desired future state, defining necessary components for solution delivery, building evidence to secure a positive response, designing, and proposing the solution, presenting it to the customer, or negotiating terms and conditions after obtaining the first and soft "yes."

By adopting the *Satisfaction Cycle* as a sales strategy, similar to using a map, sales managers gain the ability to manage the sales process and the behavior of their salespeople effectively, rather than solely focusing on outcomes. Many sales managers attempt to drive sales outcomes by setting goals, such as increasing sales by 20%, and constantly monitoring progress toward those targets. If sales fall behind the target on a particular day or month, the questions arise:

"Why are we behind?"

"What more must be done to achieve the goal?"

"How many additional meetings are required to meet the numbers?"

In this approach, activities are determined based on the gap between the target and current sales figures. However, adopting the *Satisfaction Selling* strategy shifts the focus to managing the entire sales process, including behaviors and even micro-behaviors, rather than solely fixating on outcomes and activities.

When driving the process, sales managers can ask their salespeople more specific questions, such as who they are engaging with and at which stage of the sales process, they find themselves. This enables managers to define the necessary actions for each case. The emphasis becomes less about making arbitrary phone calls and more about strategically selecting whom to contact and how to conduct those conversations. In doing so, sales managers can assist their salespeople in focusing not only on what to do but also on how to do it effectively.

Furthermore, sales managers can better support and motivate their salespeople to take the next appropriate actions, instead of merely making calls to earn their salary. The next action may not always involve making phone calls; it could include other activities that advance the customer through their buying process and the sales cycle. For example, if a customer requires evidence of the solution's effectiveness, the salesperson might need to contact the R&D department for a sample or a design blueprint. By updating the selling strategy in this manner, sales effectiveness can be enhanced, leading to improved returns on sales efforts.

Another crucial consideration is optimizing and prioritizing the salesperson's and the company's time to maximize potential rewards. When the time investment outweighs the potential sales reward, it is wise to redirect time toward other endeavors. Salespeople need timely information to assess the feasibility of a sale. In turn, sales managers can guide their sales teams more effectively, as selling is not always about securing "yes" responses. A wise sales manager encourages salespeople to be willing to accept "no" when it becomes evident that obtaining a "yes" is exceedingly challenging or impossible.

Identifying early whether there's a mismatch between customer wants and needs and the offered solution enables organizations to make swift decisions. This allows them to pinpoint customers and projects worth pursuing, where a positive outcome is feasible. Acquiring what we refer to as a qualified "no" early in the sales process is a compelling aspect of the *Satisfaction Cycle*. By employing this approach, it becomes possible to identify the necessary steps for achieving a sale at each stage of the process. Sales managers and salespeople together can assess whether the cost and effort required to deliver the solution outweigh the potential rewards. Such an approach empowers them to allocate their time and energy in a manner that maximizes return on investment.

The *Satisfaction Selling* Mindset

In these first seven chapters of the book, we have introduced, step-by-step and layer-by-layer, the underlying mindset in *Satisfaction Selling* that redefines sales and sales leadership. It encourages ethical practices, transparency, and a focus on long-term customer satisfaction for success in dynamic business environments. Key elements include:

- Embracing an infinite mindset for sustained success in dynamic markets.

- Playing a positive-sum game, shifting the focus from short-term profit to customer loyalty and lifetime value, creating more *Positive Activists*.

- Leveraging neuroscience to guide customers from a positive present to a future-oriented mindset.

- Guiding customers through significant purchases by applying professional competence and authenticity, listening to, and understanding what the customer really wants.

- Adapting sales approaches based on contextual complexity and distinguishing between transactional and complex sales.

- Shifting from traditional selling to a *Trusted Advisor* mindset, genuinely assisting customers in achieving desired outcomes.

- Understanding the impact of emotional states on sales success, emphasizing the importance of the *Green State* for effective sales.

- Optimizing the entire system, considering external factors, and fostering a holistic perspective for effective sales strategies.

- Encouraging ethical practices, transparency, and a focus on long-term customer satisfaction for success in complex business environments.

Thus, the *Satisfaction Cycle* not only aids customers in fostering a positive mindset but also offers a transformative experience for sales professionals. Imagine the possibilities when you navigate the sales journey with calm, contentment, or even joy and passion.

- Embrace the opportunity to enjoy the process alongside your customers, maintaining an emotionally positive state throughout!

- Witness the customer's profound sense of satisfaction at every stage of the sales process!

- Strive not to be labeled as merely a "salesperson" but to embody the qualities of a consultant and a *Trusted Advisor*!

- Find fulfillment in serving and assisting customers in attaining their desired outcomes!

Fundamentally, selling is about assisting individuals - the customers - in acquiring what they genuinely desire. Instead of adopting the narrow focus of a "salesperson" pursuing personal and organizational gains, envision yourself as a consultant and Trusted Advisor. Your role is to facilitate customers in obtaining what they truly want and need for themselves and their organization.

In Part Two of this book - the *Satisfaction Selling* playbook - the *Satisfaction Cycle* model and the entire *Satisfaction Selling* process will be introduced step by step - first as an overview, and the subsequently more in detail, where a whole chapter is devoted to each stage of the *Satisfaction Selling* process.

PART 2

MASTERING SATISFACTION SELLING

THE HOW-TO PLAYBOOK

8

SATISFACTION SELLING

Implementing a Positive Approach in High-Value, Complex Selling

*S*everal years ago, I crafted my own sales model by synthesizing insights from various sources. This model, resembling a well-scripted play, delineated precise steps and actions for each stage. However, when reality diverged from this scripted approach, I erroneously concluded that my sales talent was lacking.

It soon dawned on me that relying on an imaginary script is an impractical gauge of real-life success, unless the other side is reading off the same script and using the carefully crafted dialogue it contains. In intricate contexts involving complex human dynamics, scripted or fixed processes are bound to falter due to inherent unpredictability. What's crucial, I realized, is an adaptable approach and strategy to navigate complexity efficiently.

The revelation occurred when I first came across the Satisfaction Cycle - a seemingly simple framework of five straightforward steps easily depicted in a diagram. However, as you delve into the following chapters and explore the Satisfaction Cycle in more depth, you may come to the same conclusion I did: simple should not necessarily be confused with easy.

While collaborating with Joseph and Henrik on this book, I was still in the early stages of learning about the Satisfaction Cycle while working in global account management. The context I faced was already complex and difficult due to the extensive networks of internal and external stakeholders. Additional factors affecting the sales process beyond just addressing the expectations of internal and external stakeholders made effectively managing global accounts even more complex and difficult. However, as time passed, I discovered that everything became increasingly easier. What intrigued me even more was the growing satisfaction I derived from my work.

During that period, I also participated in other sales training programs within the company. Fortunately, these programs shared some principles with the Satisfaction Cycle, such as adopting the mindset of a Trusted Advisor, being consultative, and reserving solution presentations for later stages in the sales process. I recognized the value these programs brought to the organization by emphasizing essential skills applicable to every sales professional. Notably, there was a strong emphasis on questioning and information gathering, which is vital for exceptional sales performance.

The Satisfaction Cycle training not only enhanced my skills but also brought about profound changes in other aspects: who I knew myself to be as a sales professional, my behavior and performance in real-life. These transformations cannot solely be attributed to improved skills. I began to see tangible evidence that both skills and strategy contribute to successful outcomes in complex contexts.

First and foremost, abandoning my previous scripted sales processes and embracing a new model proved advantageous. The Satisfaction Cycle acted as a new map, providing simplicity amidst complexity, and offering clarity regarding our current position and desired destination. Rather than strict scripts, it served as a flexible framework that fostered creativity and adaptability. It heightened my situational awareness, enabling me to define the context for each conversation and guide the discussions effectively.

I could precisely identify our progress with potential customers in the sales process, which helped me realize necessary resources I needed to bring to move forward. Whether it involved engaging the product team, the contract team, or seeking legal counsel, I became more adept at making informed decisions and determining the next steps. This significantly improved my ability to personally lead the sales process.

Another notable improvement was my enhanced capability to optimize and prioritize time, both for myself and others. Over time, I became better at recognizing situations where the customer's needs did not align with what our solution could deliver. In such cases, I became more proficient at saying "no" as a means to redirect our efforts towards opportunities where we had a higher likelihood of securing a "yes" from the customer because we could create real value.

I can confidently attest to my own personal experience of the profound transformation I went through. As I progressed in writing this book with Joseph and Henrik another shift occurred for me, I reached a point where I eagerly looked forward to each morning, excited to engage in the work I was doing. My work flowed effortlessly, and I experienced a profound sense of fulfillment.

While there may be alternative paths to achieving such deep satisfaction, for me, it was realized through deep learning and a commitment to implementing the Satisfaction Cycle as the basis of my approach to working with clients and customers, as well as coaching and leading my team through the sales process.

The Satisfaction Cycle - Step by Step

It's now time to introduce the five steps in the *Satisfaction Cycle* model and strategy as depicted in Figure 8.1. While we touch upon all the major aspects of the *Satisfaction Cycle* model in this introduction, it is important to remember that the following chapters - the *Satisfaction Selling* playbook - are devoted to a much more comprehensive description of how to successfully carry out the steps and stages involved in *Satisfaction Selling*.

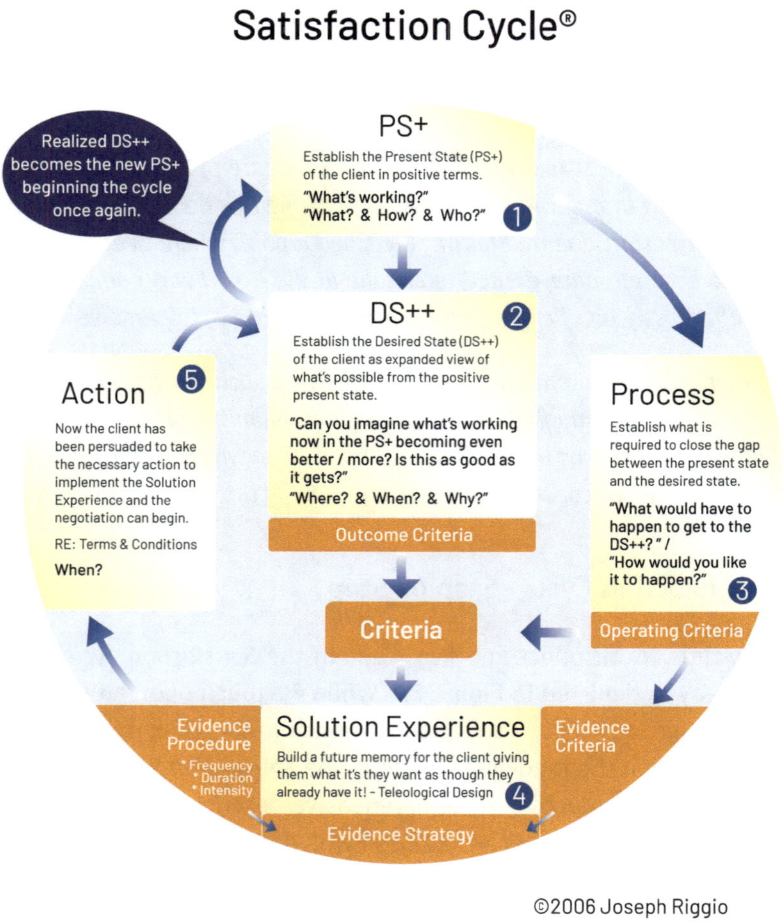

Satisfaction Cycle®

Figure 8.1 The Satisfaction Cycle

Step 1: Present State Positive (PS⁺)

The *Satisfaction Cycle* begins by establishing the *Present State Positive (PS⁺)*, as we defined it in Chapter 5. In other words, we start with the simple question,

"What's working?"

or, more specifically,

"What's already working well for you today?"

With this question, we lead the customer into accessing the neurocognitive excitatory bias, or what we refer to as the *Green State*. From the positively organized *Green State* we lead the conversation to a position from which we are discussing the successes the customer has already experienced by beginning from eliciting what's already working for them and framing their existing situation in a positive frame.

This approach allows us to highlight the customer's successes and re-inforces their ability to make sound decisions. It also establishes a connection between the customer, you, and your company, fostering positive associations. Gathering information on the PS^+ becomes easy because the customer has nothing to hide or fear. They are only discussing their successes and have received permission to demonstrate how clever they have been and can continue to be.

One of the most powerful outcomes of beginning the sales process in this way is the amount of information the customer will become capable of recalling and willing to share with you. You can easily gather information from the PS^+ about the current solutions they are employing today, including specific suppliers and often specific budgets associated with maintaining their current solution.

You can also find out how they arrived at their existing solutions, such as who was involved in making the decision to implement the current solution, how the decision to implement this solution was made, and what the outstanding characteristics of the current solution are.

Step 2: Desired State Positive (DS^{++})

The next logical step that naturally emerges from starting with the PS^+ is the *Desired State Positive (DS^{++})*. The means to move into DS^{++} is by asking the simple and straightforward question:

"What do you want, that would be even better/make that even better?"

... than what they've shared about the positive aspects of their current solution in the PS^+ elicitation you've just completed. And you can become even more effective and specific in your questioning,

"Given that you know that what you have done ...

specifically backtracking to what they've shared they have done

... and that you are currently doing

specifically backtracking to what they've shared that they are currently doing

... that is working for you as we've discussed, what would make your current situation even better than it has been or is now?"

What's so powerful about this longer and more specific question is that it contains an implied future-paced positive frame, i.e.: the current state is already working and there's a reasonable presumption that working from that success of what's already working, even greater success is possible.

You want to put the customer in a position to consider the outcome they would most want if there were no limitations to achieving it. The DS^{++} in simpler terms is an amplified version of the existing PS^{+}. It represents more of what is already working well for the customer that their current solution has not yet delivered. This point is critical.

When you follow the path from PS^{+} to DS^{++}, the customer maintains the *Green State* - a positive emotional state - along the whole path (see Figure 5.1). The customer will therefore continue discussing what is working for them and what will work even better when they achieve DS^{++}. This allows them to consistently experience a sense of satisfaction. In fact, you are now starting to amplify and intensify that experience. The customer will continue associating the satisfaction experience with the sales process itself and you - the salesperson - facilitating it.

At this point in the process, it is critical to remind the customer that this is the experience they will be having after engaging with you, establishing a *Future Memory* with them. The *Future Memory* uses the technology of *Time Sliding* to move the customer's perception from the present moment to a future time where what they desire has already happened for them, as discussed in Chapter 6.

"So, when you've taken the action, you'll need to, you'll have created ...

their description of the ideal future that would make the current situation even better,

... and because of that what will now be possible for you as well?"

You can do this by using a structure like the example above and allowing them to envision the position they will experience after achieving the outcome they desire. This is the *Outcome of the Outcome*, as also discussed in Chapter 6 which represents the benefits associated with creating the initial outcome the customer desires. What's critical about this step is that the customer can only answer the question about what else will be possible for them by considering having achieved their initial outcome. When the customer has considered achieving the outcome with enough clarity and detail to determine what else will be possible for them (the *Outcome of the Outcome*) they will have established a neurological state that is literally a memory of the future, the *Future Memory*.

Establishing the *Future Memory* via this *Time Sliding* technique creates a sense of both clarity about the outcome and begins to build a compulsion for making the commitment and taking the necessary action to achieve it. This is a critical and distinctive step in the *Satisfaction Cycle* selling process.

The *"What"* information is gathered in the second step of the *Satisfaction Cycle*, the DS^{++} as described above, and is referred to as the *Outcome Criteria*. This represents what your customer wants in terms of the outcome they want to achieve comprised of the intended outcome, and the *Outcome of the Outcome*. The second part of what you need to know is the *"How"*. Not only does your customer desire a specific outcome, but they also want it in a particular manner. Ideally, they want to create and achieve it their own way.

Step 3: Process

In the *Process* step, you elicit the *Operating Criteria* which pertains to the *"How,"* described above, or in other words, what the customer needs in order to achieve their *Desired State Positive (DS^{++})*. By asking a few targeted questions, you gather all the specifics regarding the *"How,"* such as available resources, including time frames, finances, human resources, skills, and knowledge. The resource question is critical for understanding what they currently have available and their commitment to allocate the necessary resources to achieve DS^{++}.

Step 4: Solution Experience

Once you have a clear understanding of the customer's *Criteria* (the *Outcome Criteria* plus the *Operating Criteria*), you are equipped to craft a solution that will deliver a satisfying experience. Aligning your efforts with the specific desires and needs of the customer, you can create a tailored solution that meets and exceeds their expectations. This customer-centric approach ensures that every interaction and touchpoint is designed to provide maximum value and contribute to overall satisfaction of the customer.

By focusing on their *Criteria* and designing a solution accordingly, including aligning the *Criteria* in terms of hierarchical importance - the *Rank Scale Order* of the *Criteria* - you lay the foundation for a successful and mutually beneficial relationship with the customer. Within the *Satisfaction Cycle*, we refer to this step as the *Solution Experience* - a narratively organized presentation that incorporates all of the criteria you've elicited from the customer as opposed to simply stating the solution in a purely descriptive manner, like a series of bullet points, e.g.:

"We'll do this and this and this and that ..."

that addresses the points in their *Criteria*. To effectively present the story-based style of the *Solution Experience*, it's crucial to lead the customer to the *Green State*. This involves completing the elicitation of their decision-making process, *Outcome Criteria*, and *Operating Criteria*, as well as their *Evidence Strategy*. This story-based style of presenting is done in a dialogical way that sounds very conversational, e.g.:

"Well, you've shared with me that what you really appreciate in your current situation are ..."

Here, you enumerate the information obtained in Step 1 - the PS^{+}.

1. The solution they've implemented.

2. The quality of the products or services they are using.

3. The relationship with their current vendors

before continuing:

"... and yet what you'd love to see as well are ..."

Here, you list the *Outcome Criteria* you've elicited in Step 1-2 - the PS^+ and the DS^{++}- and continue:

"We can definitely design a solution that will work with you that will deliver ...

Here, you mention the specific aspects of the *Outcome Criteria* you can meet, and continue:

"And we'll deliver it ..."

Here, you include a description of the way you'll work with the customer that's aligned with their *Operating Criteria* that you've elicited in Step 3 - *Process*.

This way of communicating becomes story-like especially when you weave in examples from previous work you've done or references to your specific way of working. We will cover how to do this in the following chapters - the *Satisfaction Selling* playbook.

The intention of using the story-based *Solution Experience* presentation style is to highlight that in addition to meeting the customer's logical expectations the aim is to create an emotionally gratifying experience. In fact, the customer's primary decision on whether to proceed or not is heavily influenced by their emotions. Subsequently, this decision is rationalized and justified with logical arguments, which is why it is crucial to provide the customer with a compelling emotional pull and reasons to move forward.

There is no better-known way of creating both a compelling emotional state supported by the necessary logical information and arguments than via story-based communication. First, the story-based presentation style of the *Solution Experience* shows customers how effectively you have gathered relevant information and genuinely listened to what matters to them.

Second, it provides an opportunity to address any potential areas that may have been overlooked. During your presentation, make sure to address all new information in order to maintain alignment with the customer.

The final step in presenting the *Solution Experience* involves guiding the customer through the *Process* and the step-by-step journey they will undertake to achieve their DS^{++}. One effective approach is to start from the DS^{++}, building a *Future Memory*, as described briefly above, and in more detail in in Chapter 6, and present the main events in reverse order until reaching the pivotal initial step. It is not necessary to explain the intricacies of the process; rather, focus on emphasizing what you will do for the customer and the positive outcomes it will yield.

Before you rush to present your solution, you need to verify how the customer will decide that your solution satisfy all their *Criteria*. Therefore, throughout the process, you also need to gather information about their *Evidence Strategy*. There are two significant parts to an *Evidence Strategy*: The *Evidence Criteria* and the *Evidence Procedure*. Although most people have a well-defined and consistent way to judge whether they agree or disagree with something they are presented with most of the time, their *Evidence Criteria,* and their *Evidence Procedure,* that comprise their *Evidence Strategy,* remain out of conscious awareness for most people.

The *Evidence Strategy* shows the way someone forms beliefs and decide whether or not to believe something is true or false. Specifically, the *Evidence Strategy* defines the threshold conditions of belief that must be fulfilled and complete for someone to accept something as being believable, true, or valid.

The *Evidence Criteria* refers to a specific kind of evidence that's most meaningful to the person making the decision. The two kinds of criteria that form the basis of the *Evidence Criteria,* are either *Internal Criteria* or *External Criteria.* A simple way to describe the distinction of *Internal* versus *External Criteria* is whether the evidence that determines if something is believable, true, or valid is based on knowledge that is within the individual or if the evidence is outside of the individual.

An example of *Internal Criteria* might be if someone decides they like something because it pleases them subjectively and uniquely, such as the taste of chocolate or vanilla ice cream, or the way they think they look in a particular piece of clothing, or maybe if they prefer massage using a softer or stronger touch. More specifically in a buying situation the person may possess personal information or expertise that determines their buying decision-making process, e.g.: whether a particular pair of skis are engineered correctly for the kind of skiing they intend to do or whether the pair of skis they are using feels right to them when they are skiing.

These are all examples of internal criteria that are dependent upon internal references.

On the other hand, an example of one type of *External Criteria* is social proof, which is agreement and testimony of others that will verify some piece of information or some kind of offer that is presented. Social proof can come from a respected individual such as an icon or expert, or from the weight of crowds, e.g.: fans or satisfied buyers. A respected individual or a crowd can become the reference source for information that the buyer doesn't believe they possess themselves, so they depend on these external references. The external reference does not have to be based on or given as in-person communication, for example written references and testimonials are classic examples of social proof. Another kind of *External Criteria* would be information-rich data, which is either historically or scientifically verifiable. A common example of this kind of data used in a buying situation is a case study.

The other aspect of the *Evidence Strategy* apart from the *Evidence Criteria* is the *Evidence Procedure*. The *Evidence Procedure* is comprised of three specific qualities: *Frequency, Duration,* and *Intensity*. These qualities are sequence independent, meaning that you can gather the information about the customer's *Evident Procedure* in any order in which the qualities appear in conversation, or you can choose to enquire about them specifically.

Frequency is about how many times the evidence needs to be presented. *Duration* refers to the amount of time or over what time period the evidence must remain present. The third quality of the *Evidence Procedure, Intensity,* refers to the amount of emphasis or force with which the evidence is presented.

The best way to elicit this kind of information from the customers is to ask about how they made other similar decisions in the past. It can be useful to literally enquire about the unique qualities of someone's *Evidence Procedure* directly, e.g.:

"When you made the decision to replace your last software system how long did the process investigating and deciding to move forward with that purchase take?"

which will tell you something about the customer's *Duration* preferences, or

"In deciding to purchase your previous home what put the decision over the top for you?"

uncovering their *Intensity* preferences, or

"How many times did you need to review the decision to change the previous law firm you worked with to your current legal representation?"

eliciting their *Frequency* preferences.

The information you gather about your customer's *Evidence Strategy* needs to be woven into the narrative of the *Solution Experience* you offer in your story-based presentation. An example of this is to speak to the customer's desire for working with a trusted partner they can count on to deliver what's promised on time to someone who has a rather high *Frequency* demand, e.g.:

"We understand your need to be confident that we will do what we've promised when we say we do it, so the project is completed on time by completing each step on time or before the deadlines we agree to before we've begun the work. We've completed over three hundred projects in the last five years with similar requirements and have delivered each one on time or earlier than promised."

If that same customer is also using *Internal Criteria* as their *Evidence Criteria*, you might add,

"I'm sure you know how important it is to work with someone who has ample experience making and keeping promises with a track record that matches your expectations."

If on the other hand this particular customer is more dependent upon *External Criteria* you might say,

"Our clients are all aligned that it's critical to deliver what and when as promised and I'm sure you know how demanding customers like (name of a well-known customer) can be, and we didn't just satisfy them, we thrilled them by meeting every deadline!"

The key to success in using the *Evidence Strategy* in delivering the *Solution Experience* is keeping conversational and dialogic within the structure of the story-based presentation you make regarding what you are offering.

Step 5: Action

At this stage, your aim is to guide the customers to a position where they are left with only one decision to make: a commitment to take *Action* and implement the *Solution Experience* you have presented. If you have executed the previous steps correctly, this decision should be relatively straightforward. Essentially, you have achieved a sale, in principle. While there may still be a need to negotiate the terms and conditions, the customer has already made the definitive purchase decision.

The *Action* step propels the customer towards the realization of their DS^{++}. In any persuasion scenario, the initial step involves reaching a point of agreement with others. This agreement represents a commitment to take *Action* and move forward. However, it is crucial to recognize that an agreement is not the same as taking *Action*. In the realm of sales, a customer's *Commitment* alone remains an empty promise - you lack a valid reason to send your invoice just yet.

Through the *Satisfaction Cycle*, you not only obtain the customers' *Commitment* but, more importantly, you gain their willingness to take *Action* - what we refer to as *Compliance*. By *Compliance*, we mean that the customer, after agreeing with you, follows through on their agreement by taking the necessary steps to implement what they've agreed to do. It goes beyond a mere "yes" and reflects genuine intention and the implementation required to take the agreed upon *Action*.

The *Satisfaction Cycle*, by its very design, naturally motivates *Action*. Successfully employing this strategy guides the customer to a *Future Memory* position, where you lead the customer into a mental state in which they have already envisioned the outcome of working with you. This creates an innate pull - a *Compulsion* - towards their *Future Memory*, compelling them to act. Not taking *Action* would require the customer to relinquish the envisioned outcome they hold in their mind. The *Future Memory* serves as the driving force behind their *Compliance* and subsequent action, pulling them into the future, as discussed in Chapter 6.

Within the *Satisfaction Cycle* model, the negotiation of terms and conditions, including pricing and delivery, occurs toward the end of the process, after the customer has made their buying decision. There are several reasons for this approach. First, discussing terms and conditions, such as pricing and payment schedules, is often impractical until there is a comprehensive understanding of what the customer intends to buy. Second, proposing terms and conditions prematurely, without the customer fully understanding the overall solution design and its value proposition, may make the discussion irrelevant or, worse, undermine your ability to secure a commitment to buy.

Therefore, we recommend initiating negotiations only after you have a clear understanding of the customer's wants and needs and have ensured they understand how your solution will specifically benefit them. Only after the full *Solution Experience* presentation can the customer truly appreciate the potential value your solution offers. If the customer does not understand the value your solution provides, it will always seem too expensive, and you will struggle to achieve agreement and get *Compliance*. Or as one of our customers phrased it:

"Price is only an issue in the absence of perceived value!"

Case: Sales Training Consulting Services for an IT Solutions Company

In the following case study, we meet Mike, a seasoned sales consultant, and Karen, the Director of Sales at IT Solutions Inc. The case demonstrates the main features of the five steps of the *Satisfaction Cycle* discussed above.

Step 1: Present State Positive (PS⁺)

Mike: *"Hi Karen, thank you for taking the time to meet today. To get started, can you tell me what's currently working well with your sales team?"*

Karen: *"Hi Mike. Overall, our team has been hitting their targets consistently, and we've received positive feedback from our clients about the consultative approach we take."*

Mike: *"That's fantastic to hear. It sounds like your team is doing a great job building relationships and meeting their goals. What else has been contributing to this success?"*

Karen: *"I think the regular training sessions and the supportive team environment have really helped. We have a strong culture of collaboration."*

Step 2: Desired State Positive (DS⁺⁺)

Mike: *"Given that your team is already performing well with their consultative approach and collaboration, what would make your sales process even better?"*

Karen: *"Well, I think we could benefit from more advanced training techniques. Some of our competitors seem to be closing deals faster, and I suspect they have some sales strategies we're not using yet."*

Mike: *"So, you're looking to build on the current strengths of your team with new strategies that could help them close deals more efficiently. Anything else that would help?"*

Karen: *"Yes, I'd also like to see more consistency in our results across different sales reps. Some are excelling, while others are just meeting their targets."*

Step 3: Process

Mike: *"That makes sense. What do you think has to happen to bridge the gap between where you are today and where you want to be? How do you envision expanding on what's working to reach your desired outcomes?"*

Karen: *"I believe we need a more structured training program that incorporates the latest sales techniques. Additionally, personalized coaching for each rep might help bring everyone up to the same high standard."*

Mike: *"A structured program with the latest techniques and personalized coaching sounds like a solid plan. How do you see this being implemented?"*

Karen: *"We could start with a comprehensive training session for the whole team and then follow up with individual coaching sessions. Regular reviews and updates to the training content would be necessary to keep it relevant."*

Step 4: Solution Experience

Mike: *"That sounds like a great approach. Let me share a story of how we've helped another client in a similar situation. They had a strong team but wanted to boost their closing rates and ensure consistency. We started with an intensive training workshop where we introduced new sales strategies and tools tailored to their industry. The reps were excited to apply these new techniques, and we provided ongoing coaching to support their development. Over the next few months, they saw a significant increase in their closing rates and more uniform performance across the team. Their clients noticed the difference and appreciated the enhanced consultative approach."*

Karen: *"That's exactly the kind of outcome we're aiming for. It's encouraging to hear that your approach has worked for others in a similar situation."*

Step 5: Action

Mike: *"I'm glad to hear that, Karen. Let's talk about the next steps. Based on what we've discussed, it sounds like starting with a comprehensive training session followed by individual coaching is the way to go. How soon would you like to get started with the initial training workshop?"*
Karen: *"I think we should get started as soon as possible. How quickly can we schedule the first session?"*
Mike: *"We can arrange the first workshop within the next two weeks. I'll prepare a proposal outlining the training schedule, the topics we'll cover, and the follow-up coaching sessions. Does that sound good to you?"*
Karen: *"That sounds perfect. Let's move forward with it. I'm excited to see the positive impact this will have on our team."*
Mike: *"Excellent, Karen. I'll get the proposal ready and send it over to you by the end of the day. We'll make sure your team has the tools and support they need to reach their full potential."*
Karen: *"Thank you, Mike. I'm looking forward to working with you and seeing the results."*

In this dialogue, Mike effectively transitions Karen through the Satisfaction Cycle, culminating in the *Action* step. He begins by eliciting the PS^+, understanding what's currently working well for Karen's team. He then explores the DS^{++}, identifying what would make the current situation even better. In the *Process* step, Mike gathers Karen's vision for bridging the gap between the present state and the desired future.

Mike then presents a *Solution Experience*, sharing a success story that aligns with Karen's goals. This builds confidence and a positive expectation. Finally, in the *Action* step, Mike connects the positive expectations to the specific actions needed, leading Karen to initiate the process of scheduling the training workshop. The dialogue concludes on a high note, reinforcing the decision and setting the stage for continued positive interactions.

The Seven Cs of *Satisfaction Selling*

When you guide customers through their buying process within the *Satisfaction Cycle*, you navigate them through a series of decisions, starting from their choice to engage with you, the salesperson. Customers have their own decision-making processes, and your role is to facilitate these decisions. Thus, *Satisfaction Selling* represents a distinct shift from merely selling to actively helping customers buy.

As you guide the customer through the five steps of the buying process, described above, both you and the customer move through seven stages of engagement - although, in reality, the first step involves only you. These stages are known as the Seven Cs of *Satisfaction Selling*:

1. **Centering:** This initial stage prepares you for the first meeting with the customer. You prepare yourself to enter the *Green State*, gaining access to understanding your own PS^+ and DS^{++} so that you can create a clear intention for the upcoming meeting. This preparation allows you to enter the meeting in the *Green State*, fully present and with a clear INTENT.

2. **Connection:** At this stage, establishing rapport and building a trustworthy relationship with the customer is crucial. Effective *Connection* occurs when both you and the customer are in the *Green State*. Psychologically, this *Connection* fosters familiarity and certainty, reducing resistance and feelings of threat by addressing cognitive dissonance. A strong *Connection* facilitates the smooth elicitation of the customer's desires without resistance, setting the stage for positive future expectations.

3. **Curiosity:** The next stage aligns with the first step in the *Satisfaction Cycle* and involves the PS^+. It starts with recognizing what already works for the customer, including *Curiosity* about competitor products they may be using, creating a sense of contentment that leads to the positive neurological state of accessing the excitatory bias - the *Green State*. We are immediately aiming to establish a sense of satisfaction with the sales process right from the beginning. This approach aims to bring the customer into the *Green State*, where they are open and receptive. By achieving this, customers can access their true desires, leading into the next stage.

4. **Clarity:** Following the steps in the *Satisfaction Cycle*, this stage delves into the DS^{++}. Here, the customer begins to feel a sense of positive expectation and enthusiasm for enhancing something beyond its current state. By guiding the conversation, you allow the customer to view their thinking as entirely their own. In the *Clarity* stage, you elicit not just the customer's desired outcome, but also what the customer ultimately desires - the *Outcome of the Outcome* which is the DS^{++} that the *Future Memory* should be based on.

5. **Compulsion:** Matching the *Process* step in the *Satisfaction Cycle*, this stage involves asking what it would take to bridge the gap between the DS^{++} and PS^+. *Compulsion* involves fostering an intense desire for a specific outcome, which becomes apparent as the customer discusses their desired outcome and what achieving that outcome would get them. Furthermore, when they articulate what they believe is necessary to achieve their desired outcome, this sense of the pull to commit and comply is only strengthened. The metaphorical stretching of the elastic represents the creation of *Compulsion* towards achieving the *Outcome of the Outcome*. Notable enthusiasm from the customer about their DS^{++} during the interaction signals this *Compulsion*.

6. **Commitment:** This stage involves the design of the *Solution Experience* and its presentation. In the *Commitment* stage, the customer decides first to turn their desired outcome into reality. The second decision in the *Commitment* involves the customer agreeing to the *Solution Experience* offered by the salesperson. It simply means the customer says, *"Yes, let's do this."*

7. **Compliance:** This stage involves the final step in the *Satisfaction Cycle*, the *Action* step. *Compliance* entails ensuring that the customers not only express their intention but also follows through with concrete *Actions* to achieve their desired outcome. A strong *Commitment* to the desired outcome facilitates the customer's readiness to take *Action*, especially when they see that there is a process that can take them all the way. And when the first step is perceived as easy and simple with a low perceived risk for the customer, it becomes easy for them to act, resulting in *Compliance*.

A sale is completed when both the salesperson and the customer have navigated all seven stages of *Satisfaction Selling*. Utilizing the *Satisfaction Cycle*, you secure not only the customer's *Commitment* but also their *Compliance* and willingness to take *Action*. Achieving this *Compliance* and willingness to take *Action* is the ultimate goal of *Satisfaction Selling*. Customers don't just say "yes"; they demonstrate their "yes" by taking concrete *Actions*. In this way, the structure of the *Satisfaction Cycle* naturally cultivates motivation to act.

Personal Skills in High Value Complex Selling

In the realm of high value complex selling, a successful strategy and model, like the *Satisfaction Cycle* is of course not a standalone entity. The intricacies of complex sales require a certain level of expertise and skill. It's crucial to acknowledge that a strategy, no matter how effective, cannot be executed without individuals driving its implementation. A strategy offers a general approach, guiding resource utilization and determining actions for successful outcomes. However, the efficacy of a strategy ultimately relies on your personal capabilities.

Think of a strategy as musical notes of a beautiful song; its true beauty is realized when played on a properly tuned instrument. In the context of selling, you - the salesperson - serves as the instrument bringing the strategy to life. Yet, even the most skilled salesperson cannot guarantee success if the strategy itself is flawed. Both the strategy and your skills are indispensable.

Primarily, every salesperson should possess a fundamental understanding of the product or service they are selling. This knowledge enables you to identify its value and effectively communicate it to individual customers. However, it is important to note, that while some salespeople may have deep expertise, achieving mastery is not always possible for you in complex selling scenarios. The true skill of high-performing salespeople lies in recognizing the limits of your expertise. You do not need to be a product or service expert, but you must know when to seek assistance from a product manager, a finance professional for specific terms and conditions, or a legal team for contract arrangements. Competence, therefore, lies in understanding your own knowledge and limitations.

Secondly, successful salespeople possess business acumen. You must be able to understand the financial drivers both within your own company and for the customer. This will enable you to see the bigger picture and identify opportunities to create a mutually beneficial business case.

Thirdly, high value complex selling demands robust personal, and social skills. Having the right mindset is not enough. A crucial skill is the art of asking high-quality questions. As a skilled salesperson, you must be able to grasp the entire process of questioning, from framing the questions to knowing the desired outcome. Furthermore, experienced salespeople excel in communication, building rapport, interpreting gathered information, and utilizing persuasive language techniques such as storytelling and metaphors.

Above all, exceptional salespeople exhibit personal leadership skills. You need to be able to remain composed, open, and adaptable, and you need to maintain focus and direction, even in challenging situations that may derail someone else. You must possess the ability to maintain a *Green State* and effectively manage your mood and mindset.

In the next chapter, we will share with you the necessary personal and social skills that will enable you to become a master in *Satisfaction Selling* - with the right mindset, the right strategy, and the right personal skill set.

9

PERSONAL AND SOCIAL SKILLS

For the *Satisfaction Cycle* to function effectively, a solid relationship is essential since the quality of this relationship dramatically influences the results of any persuasive effort. Two parts in a relationship impact the outcome of persuasion: the person or people you're having the relationship with and you. Only when you know both yourself and others can you succeed in influencing. All leverage in persuasion and selling comes from knowing who the other person is, understanding the relationship between you, and, most importantly, knowing who you are yourself. Specifically, knowing yourself in this context means recognizing the distinction between how you respond to what you experience and what you experience as distinct from your response to it.

You Are the Instrument in Sales

As a top sales professional, your own self-awareness and ability to access and maintain the *Green State* are fundamental. To truly understand yourself, you must first pay attention to your internal experience. This requires an awareness of your own signals. Knowing yourself also means being able to intentionally shift to the *Green State*. Only then can you fully utilize your experience and skills to optimally operate your brain. If you and your sales team adopt the principles presented in this chapter, your business will already improve dramatically.

Successful salespeople are like artists or musicians. Just as musician's instruments require attention and tuning for a piece of music to come to life, salespeople can tune themselves and organize their internal experience in relation to possibility. Every master of persuasion and influence knows precisely how to use their body to access this state. When you are in the *Green State*, your neurological system is open and receptive to new data. You can absorb and process information right away. In this state, your mind is open, and you can pay attention to and gather new information. But it doesn't stop there. When you are in the *Green State* and meeting customers from this perspective, you will influence them so that they also can enter the *Green State*.

As discussed in Chapter 4, every human operates from one of two neuro-logical biases: the excitatory bias - the *Green State* - or the inhibitory bias - the *Red State*. These states operate at both neurological and physiological levels. You can notice "signals" within yourself to recognize which state you are in. Physiological changes, such as a slower heart rate and deeper breathing, indicate that you are in the *Green State*. Being in this state is often described as feeling balanced and totally attentive. How you specifically recognize the state is unique to you; only you can know your internal signals for this state.

Free Yourself

In the *Green State*, you feel fundamentally OK and truly yourself. From this position it is possible to act with true integrity. You are yourself at your best, and your mind is neurologically open. When your parasympathetic nervous system is active, your frontal and prefrontal lobes become engaged in con-sidering possibilities, as discussed in Chapter 4. The frontal and prefrontal lobes then utilize this information and feed it back to the cerebellum, the part of the brain responsible for motor control. Your brain works highly optimally, and you can imagine very quickly, almost instantaneously,

"If I go after this outcome, it would be like this..."

"If I go after that outcome, it would be like that..."

In this state, it becomes easy and natural to adopt the mindset of a *Trusted Advisor*. *Trusted Advisors* focus on what they can control and let go of what they cannot control. In every influencing situation, you can totally control one thing: yourself. What you cannot control is the other person or persons. Accepting this makes you free to notice who the other person is and the possibilities to influence how they respond.

Your ability to be self-referenced, self-organized, and self-directed is incredibly powerful and enables you to remain open and flexible. Instead of imposing your agenda on the customer, pay attention to where they think they are and where they want to go. When you are free of the urge to control, you can at the same time still know what you want with the customer, why you are there, and how you can serve them. By maintaining an open state of mind, you gain an edge and the ability to succeed in all these things.

So, the first step in training to master *Satisfaction Selling* is to have the ability to access and stay in the *Green State*, regardless of what happens.

Accessing the *Green State*

All humans possess the ability to transition between neurologically open and closed states, but fewer are aware of how to consciously put themselves in an open state - the *Green State*. As noted in Chapter 4, the amygdala plays a crucial role in triggering the switch from a *Green State* to a *Red State*, from the parasympathetic to the sympathetic nervous system. However, the amygdala only works in one direction. Therefore, we need to use other methods to reverse the switch and return from a *Red State* to a *Green State*.

The vagus nerve plays a central role in the parasympathetic nervous system as it calms down the amygdala. It is part of the "gut-brain axis," which involves bidirectional communication between the brain and the gastrointestinal tract. The vagus nerve can regulate stress responses; up to 80% of its transmission is from the body upwards toward the brainstem. This means that the state of the body can significantly stimulate the vagus nerve, and this is the mechanism to utilize in accessing the *Green State*.

Intentionally practicing how to access the *Green State* can make it easier to achieve it, even in challenging situations. With regular practice, you can build resilience and enhance your performance. Practicing also helps you recognize the *Green State* in others as well. You can help the customer get there when you can do it yourself.

In *Soma-Semantic Modeling*™ developed by Joseph, the neurologically open state, which we refer to as the *Green State*, is called the *Generalized Desired State* or *GDS* for short. Some books that discuss these models in more detail include *The State of Perfection* by Joseph Riggio, *Mental Fitness for Warriors – Be Authentic* by Henrik Wenøe and Erik Schwensen, and *Do What You Do Best* Vol 2 by Henrik Wenøe and Joseph Riggio.

Re-experience Past Successes

One way to tap into the *Green State* is by recalling a time when you succeeded, whether it occurred recently or in the past. In the sales context, you can also more specifically recall your past successes in sales. You have surely experienced moments in your life where you turned out to be doing something successful. Something that when you now look back on them, you think,

"If I could consistently recreate, replicate, sustain, and hold this experience and level of excellence... my life would be perfect."

These moments of success serve as examples of what you know of who you are at your best. Take a moment to contemplate the specifics of one of these experiences. The first step in creating a consistent shift toward a life resembling those moments is to notice how it was for you when you were like that:

"Where you were?"

"Who was with you?"

"What happened when you were at your best?"

Engaging in this mental exercise inevitably propels you into an excitatory bias, the *Green State*. When we reflect on our past successes, our bodies instinctively adopt the same postures and way of being that we had when we were at our best. The more vividly we recall a particular memory, the more our bodies reenact the same physical state as they were in that situation. At that time, there was a certain way of being for you. This bodily response helps to reset your neurology, facilitating operation within the parasympathetic nervous system, which allows for an open and adaptable state of being.

When you think back on the qualities you exhibited in your moments of success, you probably remember the feeling of being able to accomplish anything you set your mind to within the capabilities that you had available. This memory is flooding your mind with new possibilities and providing confidence that you can do great things. This is the basis of the *Green State*: knowing what it is like for you when you are at your best. You become organized to recognize possibilities and begin to link strategies to outcome possibilities. You start to think through what would have to be happening for you to realize the outcome you are thinking.

Anchors for the *Green State*

You can also utilize anchors for access to the *Green State*. For many people, a particular piece of music can serve as an anchor and trigger. Knowing what it is for you, you can utilize that music to ensure you are in the *Green State*, for example, before entering a meeting with a customer.

Another anchor to help you access and maintain the *Green State* might be your unique specific word or phrase you use to describe the *Green State*. When you use that word or phrase, you recognize that physical representation - a way that you feel in your body - that is linked to that word or phrase. One way to identify that word is to imagine that if you saw somebody walking down the street, and you knew that in that moment they were experiencing what you feel when you are at your best.

"What would you call that person?"

"What would be a word or a phrase that you are able to reference and know that they are having that experience?"

They could be in their "power," "balance," or something else. So, think about your unique word or phrase because that will be one of your access points to this *Green State*.

When you are accessing the *Green State*, your body typically does certain things the same way every time. You can also utilize a physical movement as a deliberate anchor to access the *Green State*. It could be where specifically you look in the space with your eyes. You could also lift your shoulder the same way every time or tip with your toe. When you know yourself well enough to recognize these anchors, they become compelling ways to access a good state.

Exercise to Access GDS – Your Generalized Desired State

This short exercise can help you access the *Green State*. You can also use it as a quick daily meditation routine, for example, in the morning.

1. Think about the last time when you had an experience where you were successful in sales or creating value for the customer. What happened? Where did it happen? Who was there? When you are thinking about your entire experience over again, find the exact moment in the experience where your experience of being successful was best.

2. Replicate your body position exactly as it was at that exact moment.

3. See the picture of the situation in your mind, notice the sensations in your body, and hear the sounds. Notice where you look with your eyes.

4. Continue noticing the sensations and how you feel. What do you call this feeling you have in this situation? (e.g., enthusiastic, engaged, happy)

5. What do you call yourself when you have this feeling? (e.g., strong, flexible, creative, balanced, unstoppable)

6. Ask yourself what is possible for you now!

Reset With Breathing Exercises

Short breathing exercises are one quick way to influence the vagus nerve and reset the system to the *Green State*. You can check your breathing rate by counting how many times you breathe per minute. During a stress response, we typically have shallow and fast breathing. When our system is neurologically at rest, we breathe only a few times per minute.

One effective exercise is the 4-4-4-4 box breathing, which involves inhaling for a slow count of 4, holding the breath for four counts, exhaling for four counts, and holding the breath for four counts before the next inhale. Continuing this for 2-5 minutes is typically enough, and there are benefits in doing this exercise regularly.

Another exercise involves breathing four times a minute, with one inhale and exhale taking 15 seconds. There are also many other breathing exercises, but the essence of all of them is to do steady and rhythmic breathing.

Essential Self-Care

The fundamental basis for any human performance is physiology. When you are hungry and tired, it can be challenging to remain open and positive. Ensuring exquisite sales performance, therefore, begins with taking good care of yourself. Influencing physiology in the body positively makes it much easier to access and maintain the *Green State* at all times. The basic recipe for maintaining good physiology is well-known: sleep well and enough - minimum 8 hours - eat healthily and engage daily in physical activities.

Henrik has developed the *Acuity Performance Model*, shown in Figure 9.1, which illustrates how our physiology affects our emotions at the preconscious level. This, in turn, affects our feelings, our thinking, our behavior, and ultimately our performance. This, in turn, creates a feedback loop back to the preconscious behavior that affects our basic physiology.

Acuity Performance Model

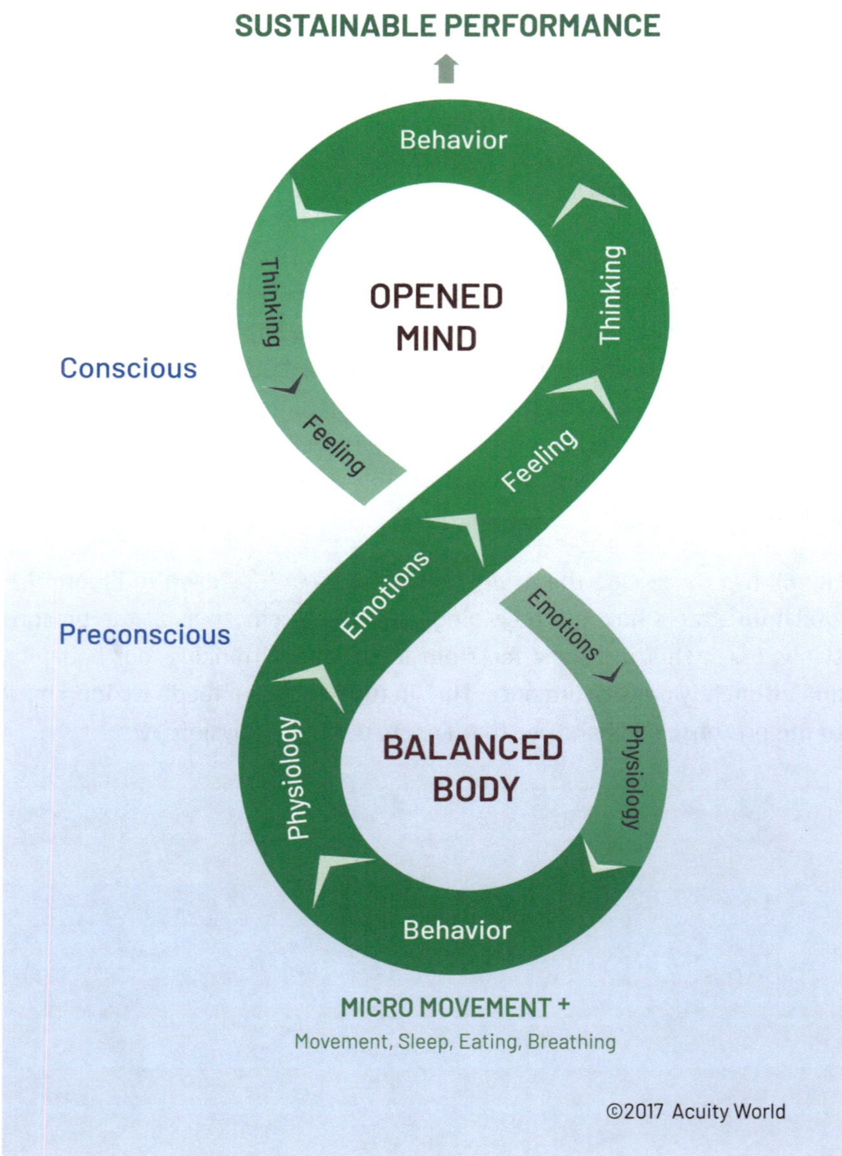

Figure 9.1 The Acuity Performance Model

The *Acuity Performance Model* is based on the idea that to create better performance, you most often need to change your behavior. If you seek continuous improvement of your performance - referred to as sustainable performance in the *Acuity Performance Model* - there will be situations where it is enough to say to yourself:

"Now is the time to do something new, instead of what I have done so far,"

And then it happens. But why isn't this always so easy? In fact, why is it generally difficult? Why is it not sufficient to focus solely on behavior? The *Acuity Performance Model* answers these questions by going a few steps further. It shows what needs to be in place for you to think right. It is important that you make sure that your feelings and emotions are in the right place - that you are in the *Green State*. If you are in the *Red State*, burdened by pressure and stress, it is harder for you to imagine that your venture will succeed, and then it becomes more difficult to get started.

But the *Acuity Performance Model* goes even deeper than that. It goes all the way down to the "bedrock" - our physiology. Our physiology is the source of our emotions and, consequently, our feelings. It begins with how you can physiologically position yourself to be in a state of well-being and practice essential self-care. From there, you can create the emotions that make you have the feelings that encourage you to think and believe that you can succeed.

It is therefore not enough to look at external behavior and the course of actions; these are only the top and the visible part of the "iceberg." We need to dive into the interior of the individual human being, seeing what is beneath the surface, to what we call the "preconscious", as indicated in Figure 9.1. Following the flow in Figure 9.1. we notice that:

Our behavior is affected by your thinking!

As mentioned above, the preconscious has a huge influence on behavior. The top layer of the preconscious consists of our thoughts. The quality of our thoughts is determined by the quality of our inner representations, values, and beliefs. The first step in influencing our thoughts is to become aware of what and how we are thinking. But this is not enough; it is only when we can also guide our thoughts that we become better able to change and sustain our behavior over time and thus create sustainable performance. However, it is not always enough to focus simply on changing our thinking to change our behavior and thus our results, because...

Our thinking is affected by your feelings!

What we think and how we think it are greatly influenced by our feelings. Thoughts and feelings mutually influence each other. However, feelings affect and control our thoughts to a greater degree than vice versa. Therefore, the ability to lead our feelings is important if we want to manage our thinking effectively. To become adept at managing our feelings, we need to delve deeper and acknowledge that ...

Our feelings are created by our emotions!

What creates our feelings are our emotions, understood as "energy in motion" (e-motions). Our emotions are the electrical and chemical signals constantly coursing throughout our bodies. Feelings represent our mind's awareness of these emotions. However, it is not sufficient to focus solely on our emotions and feelings if we aim to influence our emotions and thus our feelings. We must delve even deeper! We need to be able to manage our physiology because ...

Our emotions are created by our physiology!

As described in the Acuity Performance Model, the foundation of the human system is our physiology. Our physiology serves as the conduit for the data flowing from our heart, stomach, and entire bodies, which generate our emotions, influence our feelings, thoughts, and behavior, and ultimately shape our performance.

Persuasive Communication

Adaptive communication is an essential skill for top-performing sales professionals and the key to utilizing the *Satisfaction Cycle*. Of course, gaining technical knowledge about the products or services you sell and developing strong business acumen will allows you to understand not only your customers' businesses but also their financial drivers. However, as discussed in Chapter 8, to truly excel in sales, you must also possess exceptional interpersonal skills, including building rapport, curious listening, establishing relationships, and effective communication skills, such as using persuasive language, framing, and questioning.

Ultimately, persuasive communication is about the ability to speak the customer's language. To apply the *Satisfaction Cycle* successfully, you must have situational awareness and adapt communication in real-time. Self-awareness and sensing rapport with others are the foundation for success. Speaking in the customers' preferred communication style and matching their thought processes ensure smooth and frictionless communication.

Gathering information successfully requires knowing what, when, and how to ask questions, and while these skills and tools aren't part of the *Satisfaction Cycle* model *per se*, they are essential for applying *Satisfaction Selling* in practice. Thus, the communication tools presented here will enable you to have a conversation and deliver things in the customers' conceptual frame.

Rapport

Creating rapport involves establishing positive and harmonious connections with one or more individuals. People tend to gravitate towards those who exhibit similarities to themselves. When you encounter someone who reminds you of yourself, a sense of relaxation and security envelops you. This feeling intensifies as you continue to experience the sameness, all thanks to mirror neurons. These neurons enable us to sense other people's emotions, a pivotal aspect of human empathetic abilities. We instinctively mimic both verbal and non-verbal cues emitted by others, which can also be consciously employed to create a connection. In NLP (see Chapter 2), this process is known as building rapport.

When you are in rapport with someone, you both consciously and unconsciously experience that you respect each other. Rapport can be created by matching or mirroring the other person. In NLP, the word "pacing" is typically used as a synonym for matching and mirroring. When influencing someone else, you want first to match to create rapport, and then it is also possible to lead while maintaining rapport.

Matching entails stepping into another person's world without imposing your own perspective. It doesn't necessarily require agreement but rather the flexibility to acknowledge the other person as who they are. Matching is a potent yet delicate skill, as excessive use or not doing it right can elicit negative responses and resistance.

The ways you can match include:

1. **Body matching:** You can replicate the other person's physical cues with your body in various ways. You can mirror the entire body position as their mirror image, or alternatively, you can match the body position without creating an exact duplicate of the other person. A simple way is reverse mirroring. If the other person has their left leg crossed over the right, and you have your left leg crossed over the right, you are matching the position, but you don't create a mirror image of the other person.

2. **Matching breathing:** Another method to match another person is to synchronize your breathing with the other person – both the depth and the rate of breathing.

3. **Matching eye access and movements:** A more subtle way of matching involves aligning your eye movements with another person's eye movements and, for instance, focusing your eyes on the same spot in space where the other person is regularly looking.

4. **Matching tone of voice:** You can align the rhythm, volume, and speed of your speech with those of the other person, as well as their tone of voice.

5. **Matching vocabulary:** You can also match another person by using the exact words and phrases they are using instead of your own. This will immediately convey the impression that you have heard the other person which will lead the other person to experience that you understand him or her.

Verbally Matching with a *Yes Set*

In persuasive and influential communication, one of the techniques to match the other person and create rapport is using what is known as the *Yes Set*. This involves eliciting a series of "yes" responses from the customer to the things you say. To use the *Yes Set* technique effectively, you must identify what is absolutely true for the person. By framing your statements in a way that entirely matches their perceived reality and worldview, the person you are talking with cannot do anything other than agree with you. One way of using the *Yes Set* is to talk vaguely and unspecifically. Another way is to backtrack what the customer has said.

The *Yes Set* can also serve as an effective way to kick off your meetings. By doing so, you can achieve several objectives - you can quickly establish rapport, get the customer into a mindset of agreement by thinking "yes, yes, yes," which increases the likelihood of them continuing to say "yes" to what you will propose later. Additionally, you can use the *Yes Set* to communicate the purpose of the meeting, thereby setting a clear and explicit framework for the session. All these elements contribute to ensuring that you get off to a good start in your customer meetings. You will find three specific examples of *Yes Set*s in Chapter 11.

The *Satisfaction Cycle* has an in-built and natural *Yes Set* in its structure. When you backtrack and feed the information you have gathered from the customers, you naturally get a string of "yes" responses. For example, when you say to them:

"So, what's working for you now is ......, right?

You will get a "yes" as an answer because they already told you it is true. Because it is a positive experience for them, they will not be frustrated to hear it again. In this way, you gradually enter the customers' world with them. You are also strengthening the positive state experience and ensuring everything happens in the *Green State*.

When someone begins to say "yes" in their mind or out loud to your statements or questions, it means they are committing to a position that makes them more likely to follow through with that commitment in the future. Once you have established a pattern of agreement with several "yes" responses, they will be more likely to agree to your main request or proposition.

Channels of Communication: *Representational Systems* (VAKOG)

Sometimes, you might have experienced conversations where you have a feeling that something isn't connecting. It can seem that the other person might not get what you're saying or appear uninterested. One reason for this response could be that you're not communicating in a way that works for them. People have their preferred ways of understanding and taking in information. If your way of communicating does not match their way, they might not even be able to hear what you say.

We all create our own representation of the world in our minds. We gather data using our senses: we see, hear, feel, smell, and taste. How we filter and process the data creates our internal representation of what we experience and perceive. We call this perception a *Model of the World*. Each individual has their own *Model of the World*, and to successfully communicate throughout the sales process, it is helpful to understand how the other person is creating their representation of the world.

Our five senses are our only way to gather data. Every person has their unique way of filtering the data and eventually processing them into information and meaning. Most people tend to prefer a particular sensory system or systems over others. This choice is not conscious. You can for example notice that a person you are communicating with might prefer receiving information in a visual, auditory, or kinesthetic form, as discussed below.

In NLP, the term *Representational System* refers to the sensory system a person uses to represent the world via their senses. These preferences create preferred communication channels, and people who are good at communicating can adjust their communication to the right channel with that person. People who are good at communicating and establishing good connection and rapport with others can use all of the *Representational Systems* in their communication.

People use all of their *Representational Systems* all the time. The preference in the *Representational System* means that one system usually has the primary significance on how the person perceives the situation. Even though everyone has *Representational Systems* that they typically prefer more than others, the preferred sensory channel is also situationally dependent.

People who prefer receiving visual data generally think in pictures and imagery; up to 45% of people use visual *Representational Systems* as their primary. Auditory preference is characterized by the focus on hearing sounds and words. Only 15% of people have an auditory channel as the preference for receiving data and processing their internal representations. The typical third preference is the kinesthetic representational system, which 40% of people use as their primary preference. This preference is based on using the sense of feeling as the preferred sensory system for receiving data and creating internal representations.

There are several ways to identify the *Representational System* that you and others use. Because the various sensory-based data are processed and stored in different parts of the brain, you can notice the active *Representational System*, for example, by noticing the direction in which the eyes are looking, the tempo of speech, and where the breathing is located in the body. The person's language and choice of words can also reveal the active system. Someone might use the visual term "show," another an auditory word "tell," and a third a kinesthetic phrase "go through." Visually oriented people often speak fast, whereas kinesthetically oriented people speak quite slowly, and auditory-oriented people talk moderately. All these tools and techniques are basic NLP techniques modeled by Richard Bandler and John Grinder.

Eye movements and eye accessing cues are helpful ways to determine how a person represents the world in their internal system. Bandler and Grinder discovered the correlation between the *Representational System* and how people preferred to look up, straight, down, or to the side, as shown in Figure 9.2.

Eye Accessing

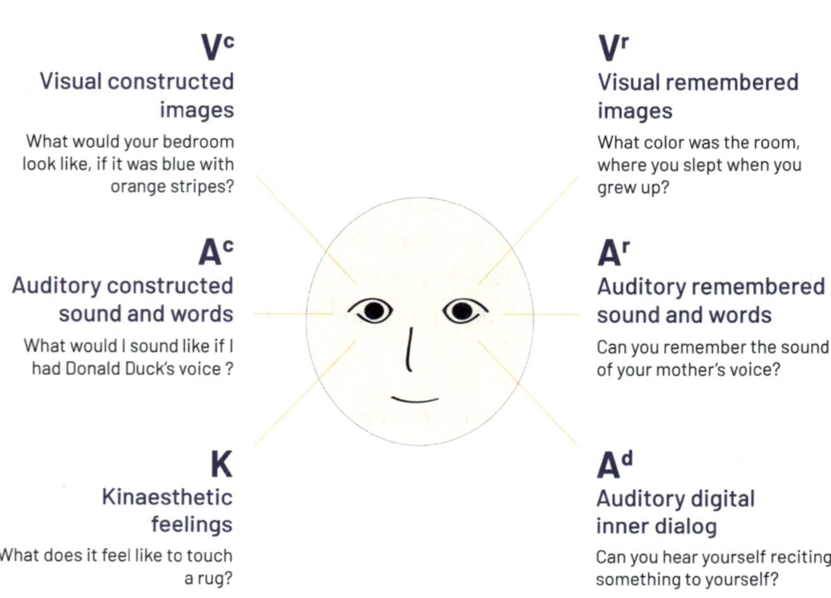

Figure 9.2 Eye Accessing Cues to Representational Systems

Noticing the eye-accessing points can inform whether the other person you are communicating with has internal images, hears sounds, has an inner dialogue, or is in contact with his or her feelings. You can use this information to understand how people represent their thoughts. Naturally, this information does not provide any insight into *what* they think when they move their eyes to certain positions, only *how* they think.

For every person, all *Representational Systems* are in use all the time. That being said, each person tends to have specific patterns in how they use them. Therefore, knowing these distinctions can help to adapt communication further. According to Joseph and his approach to applying the *Representational Systems* model from NLP, there are four main ways individuals use their representational systems:

1. **Lead system:** This is the system where the person begins. For example, a person whose lead system is visual might start by

saying, *"I see that this topic is interesting,"* while looking up. The lead system helps make a connection with the person.

2. **Processing system:** Another system usually becomes active when people are processing an idea. This could be, for example, that they are talking to themselves auditorily. The processing system is essential for the *Solution Experience* in the *Satisfaction Cycle* because it is helpful to provide presentations in another person's processing system.

3. **Integration system:** This is the system through which people primarily express themselves. This could be, for example, kinesthetic after the lead system is visual and the processing system auditory. Every person is unique, however.

4. **Latent system:** Often, a person has a representational system that they use very little, and which is often out of their awareness. This system is important in enhancing their full sensory experience. So, the latent system is often either olfactory or gustator (smell or taste).

You can adapt your communication by identifying the other person's preferred *Representational Systems*. This will help people better process their thinking and make it easy for them to interact with you. Using the eye-accessing cues, you can help people to communicate with you by leading their eyes towards the spot they tend to focus. You can point to the location with your hand or use your eyes to indicate the spot in space. When done well, this guidance remains unnoticed by the other person and makes interaction with you smoother.

Another way to adapt your communication to match the preferred communication channel of others is by using sensory-based words and language. Examples of such words are provided in Table 9.3. You can become fluent in saying the same thing for each representational system with some practice. This can help people experience that you understand what they are saying and find it easy to engage with you.

Sensory-based Words

Visual	Auditory	Auditory Digital	Kinaesthetic
Perspective	Comment	Attitude	Stance
See through	Talk through	Process	Chew over
Show	Explain	Demonstrate	Discover
Radiate	Echo	Transmit	Vibrate
Keep an eye on	Listen for	Aware	Feel for
Oversee	Shut off	Ignore	Bypass
Take a look around	Discuss	Examine	Review
Review	Unheard of	Identify	Go through
Point out	Tell	Think about	Feel
Look like someone	Talk about	Rationalize	Touch
Unseen	Speak	Evaluate	Grasp
Illustrate	Articulate	Assess	Handle
Imagine	Clarify	Strategize	Navigate
Visualize	Debate	Interpret	Explore
Display	Announce	Prioritize	Haul
Project	Declare	Analyze	Fumble
Survey	Enunciate	Decide	Adjust
Examine	Express	Categorize	Palpable
Highlight	Elucidate	Plan	Get a feel for
Illustrate	Verbalize	Remember	Hands-on

©2005 Acuity World

Figure 9.3 The Sensory-based Words

Motivational Structures and Thought Processing (*Metaprograms*)

In addition to sensory system preferences, each individual has unique underlying thought structures and motivational strategies. Richard Bandler and Leslie Cameron-Bandler investigated the structure of the way people talked and found that these structures were linked to their unique mental filters and ways of thinking. They eventually modeled and decoded what are known as *Metaprograms*.

Metaprograms are mental patterns or filters that govern how an individual perceives and processes information. They are considered deep-seated and largely unconscious, shaping people's motivation and decision-making style. Understanding people's *Metaprograms* can be helpful in communication, persuasion, and negotiation, as it allows you to tailor your message and approach to their specific way of thinking and perceiving the world.

Metaprograms are typically described as opposites, and most people tend towards one pole or another on the scale between them. However, it's important to note that there is no right or wrong position, and any position may have advantages in some situations and disadvantages in others.

Context plays a significant role in the way we think and perceive things. A person may exhibit different *Metaprograms* in different settings; for example, they may be one way in a work environment while having other kinds of mental filters at home. Additionally, *Metaprograms* are state-dependent, meaning our neurological state can affect our thinking patterns and information processing. When in the *Green State*, a person may have a different *Metaprogram* than when being in the *Red State*, feeling stressed or tired.

Metaprograms are situational and can change in seconds as a person shifts from one context or state to another. Therefore, it's crucial to identify them in the moment to adapt your communication style to another person and establish a deep level of trust. When addressing a larger group, it is helpful to incorporate both poles of each metaprogram to ensure everyone receives the message effectively. By designing your language this way, you can increase the likelihood that people will understand your message and also be motivated to do what you want them to do.

An example of what to notice with potential customers is their preference for details. Do they prefer a lot of details or rather a general overview? This information is practical during the conversation. If you talk to someone who prefers low detail in a detailed way, you'll quickly lose his or her attention. Understanding whether someone prefers information presented in a detailed or general way is also essential when delivering your *Solution Experience*.

While there are over a hundred identified *Metaprograms*, it is impossible to observe and apply all of them during a real-time interaction. In Table 9.4, we provide eight relevant metaprograms for the sales context. Even eight can be overwhelming, so start by learning and using a few. As you become more skilled in their application, you can gradually incorporate more.

Meta Programs

Internal Reference
- Have their own standards. They hear an order as information
- Evaluate their results themselves and consult their own feelings
- May find it difficult to receive feedback and accept the evaluation of others

Internal Reference —— External Reference
Indicates the place from which a person retrieves information about whether something is right or wrong.

Q: "How do you know that you have done an excellent job?"

External Reference
- Are motivated by feedback from others
- Hear information they are given as decisions or "orders"
- Depend on the opinions and evaluations of others

Sort By Self
- Make decisions based on their own values and criteria
- Do what they themselves feel is right
- Hold fast to their own opinions in discussions

Sort By Self ———————— Sort By Others
Indicates whether people are doing something they feel right (using their own criteria) or whether they are doing something others feel is right (applying criteria of others).

Q: "Will you do whatever you find important/right, or what others find important/right?"

Sort By Others
- Lsten to other people's opinions before they make their own decision
- Ask others what they think, and act based on what others believe to be right

Away From
- Problem-oriented
- Talk about what they would like to avoid (and not what they want)

Away From ——————— Towards
It tells what motivates a person most - something they want to avoid or achieve.

Q: "What is important to you in your work? Why is it important to you?"

Towards
- Goal oriented
- Are motivated by what they want to achieve
- Use positive expressions about what is possible and what can be achieved

Options
- Focus on choices and options
- The structure is not their strong point
- They will answer a "Why" question precisely

Options ——————— Procedure
It tells whether people are motivated by the options they have in a given situation or whether they are motivated by procedures they can follow.

Q: "Why did you choose your present job? (Procedure will reply how - not why)"

Procedure
- Focus on routines and procedures and are motivated by clear guidelines
- Appreciate order and structure
- Will answer a "Why" question with a "How" to describe a process

Specific
- Prefer specific and small sequences at a time
- Talk with lots of specifics about who, what and where

Specific ——————— General
Describes whether people are motivated by information that is very specific and others by information that is more general in nature.

Q: "How would you prefer to get information? Overview first or details first?"

General
- Prefers a general overview and large portions of knowledge and information but can go into specifics if required
- Talks with short sentences and deletes a lot of specifics

In Time
- Are very oriented towards here and now
- Are wrapped up in what they do in the moment and take a very relaxed view of meeting times
- Allow the activity to take control rather than the clock

In Time ——————— Through Time
Describes how people perceive themselves in terms of time.

Q: "When you're working, how do you experience time – do you lose your sense of time passing, or are you always aware of time moving? How do you respond to deadlines?"

Through Time
- Are far-sighted and very precise when it comes to time
- Are good at planning and knowing how long things will take
- Don't like to be late

Sameness
- Focus on things that are the same and what comparable things have in common
- See similarities but can point out differences afterward
- Don't like change

Sameness ——————— Difference
Describes how people are motivated by everything remaining the same or by having a constant change.

Q: "What is your job like this year compared with last year?"

Difference
- Focus on differences and what is new
- See differences first, and only then might point out similarities
- Like change and variation

Match
- React to presented information in agreement with what others think

Match ——————— Mismatch
Indicates whether people tend to agree or disagree with things to which they are introduced.

Q: "What is your first reaction when someone suggests something? Do you agree to the idea or not?"

Mismatch
- React to the information with a response that the world could be different or that things could be done differently

Figure 9.4 The eight Metaprograms most relevant to sales

The Art of Asking High-Quality Questions

In sales, asking questions is an essential tool for gathering information and understanding the wants and preferences of potential customers. By asking questions, you can collect what is commonly called "content" - the details, facts, and specifics relevant to a particular customer. The quality of the questions we ask can significantly affect the amount and quality of information we gather from a customer.

Firstly, the quality of the questions determines the depth of the information we receive. Open-ended questions that allow for free expression and elaboration are more likely to yield more detailed and insightful responses from customers. Closed-ended questions, on the other hand, often limit the amount of information we receive as they require only a "yes" or "no" answer.

Secondly, the quality of the questions can affect the accuracy of the information gathered. Asking leading questions or questions that are unclear can result in inaccurate information being provided. For instance, if you ask a customer a question that is too general or ambiguous, the response may not accurately reflect the customer's wants and needs or preferences.

Thirdly, the quality of the questions significantly influences the customer's engagement level in the sales process. Asking relevant and personalized questions can keep the customer engaged, making them feel valued and understood. This differs markedly from an interview, interrogation, or cross-examination approach, where the objective is to extract information, the other party might not be willing to share, through a series of targeted and direct questions. In *Satisfaction Selling*, a sales meeting should always maintain a conversational feel and tone and never feel like an interview or interrogation.

In conversational questioning, the questions may occasionally be closed-ended but are more often open-ended, typically starting with *"What,"* *"How,"* or *"Why."* However, the key point is that it feels like a dialogue where both you and the customer share knowledge and viewpoints. This encourages the other person to disclose more information and their personal perspective.

Asking high-quality questions naturally and conversationally facilitates a free-flowing dialog, which also contains information sharing and not only asking questions. In free-flowing conversations, it's a give-and-take process. As a sales professional and *Trusted Advisor* to the customer, you ask questions while also offering insights, information, and examples.

It takes skill to know what to ask, how to ask, and when to ask. One straightforward principle is that the customer's previous statement should guide your following response and question. However, when you're practicing the art of asking high-quality questions, it can also be beneficial to prepare some customer-specific questions before the meeting.

In asking high-quality questions, we consider it from four dimensions:

1. First dimension: Artfully using open and closed questions.

2. Second dimension: Framing questions positively in the *Green State*.

3. Third dimension: Questions guiding to a specific point in time.

4. Fourth dimension: Questions matching how the customer think (*Metaprograms* and *Representational Systems*)

1. First Dimension: Open vs. Closed Questions

Mastering the art of asking open-ended questions is a critical skill for any salesperson, as it prompts the customer to provide a detailed and thoughtful response. These open-ended questions often begin with words like "*What*," "*How*," "*Who*," "*When*," or "*Why*," leading to more than just a simple "yes" or "no" answer. Instead, they encourage the respondent to offer more detailed information or share their thoughts and feelings on a subject.

Most professionals we have worked with over the years are well aware of the difference between open and closed questions. However, merely knowing the difference is not sufficient if you aim to excel in *Satisfaction Selling*. You must also be fully conscious of which type of question you're asking so that you can make an informed choice when speaking with your customers.

Through our trainings, we have worked with thousands of salespeople, and initially, very few were capable of consciously deciding whether to ask a closed or an open question, which often led to an overuse of closed questions. Therefore, it is worthwhile to practice this skill if you want your customers to share more information with you, rather than simply saying "yes" or "no."

Examples of open-ended questions include:

"What are your goals for the coming year?"

"How did you create your success?"

"How would you define a successful outcome?"

"Why did you choose that option?"

In a sales context, closed questions are often used to confirm information that has already been gathered or to move the conversation in a particular direction. However, using too many closed questions can make the conversation less engaging and limit the information the customer provides. A closed question is a type of question that can typically be answered with a simple "yes" or "no" response. These questions usually start with words like "Do," "Are," or "Is." For example,

"Do you like your current solution?"

"Is the price within your budget?"

"Are you available to meet on Friday?"

However, an example of a closed question that effectively encourages the customer, with whom you already have a good rapport, to provide further details about their current topic of discussion would be:

"Can you tell me more about...?"

Overall, good questioning skills require using all kinds of question types purposefully. A well-rounded questioning approach that includes both open and closed questions can help you gather valuable information and guide the conversation in a productive direction.

2. Second Dimension: Positively Framed Questions

We ask questions to listen to our customers and understand their context while paying attention to the content of their answers. High-quality questions can also help salespeople establish rapport and the right frame with their customers.

You can ask questions in either a positive or negative frame - within the realm of possibilities or focusing on potential problems. When framing questions, be aware of which frame to use, as it can significantly affect the conversation's outcome. With the *Satisfaction Cycle* approach, we prefer to use the positive frame and ask *"Green"* questions.

Positive framing is about phrasing questions to emphasize positive outcomes and available opportunities, staying in the *Green State*. This approach can create a more optimistic and open-minded conversation, leading to a better understanding of the other person's perspective and more creative outcomes. For example, instead of asking,

"What problems do you have?"

"What keeps you up at night?"

"What's the worst thing that could happen?"

you could ask,

"What do you like about your current situation?"

"What have created the successes you have seen the last few years?"

"What's the best possible outcome in this situation?"

This encourages the other person to focus on the positive aspects of the situation and envision a successful outcome.

Your questions will either lead your customers to the *Red State* or to the *Green State*, and within *Satisfaction Selling*, as discussed in Part 1 of the book, we aim for you to work with your customers in the *Green State*.

3. Third Dimension: Questions Guiding to a Specific Point in Time

When we discuss the third dimension of asking effective questions in *Satisfaction Selling*, we focus on where in time your questions mentally lead the customer. We also touched upon this in Part 1 of the book, where we introduced *Time Sliding*, highlighting the value of being able to navigate your customers back and forth in time to access useful and valuable information that can aid in designing an optimal solution for you and your customer.

You can prompt your customer to reflect on the past by asking questions like:

"When you last purchased a new IT system, who was involved in deciding what to buy?"

"What are your best experiences with training your employees, and what benefits did it bring?"

For focusing your customer on the present, you might ask questions such as:

"What are you doing today that works well?"

"Which of your salespeople do you think is performing the best currently, and what are they doing that seems to work well in your industry?"

To guide your customer to consider the future, you could ask questions like:

"Where do you want your company to be in a year?"

"What experiences do you wish for your customers to have in the future when they purchase your products?"

As you can see, it works well when you build upon what you've already learned from the first two dimensions. Thus, you might have noticed that the examples in this section are both open-ended and targeted towards the *Green State*.

4. Fourth Dimension: Questions Matching How the Customer Thinks

Another crucial aspect of asking high-quality questions is ensuring they align with how the customer thinks and constructs their language. Tailoring questions in this manner simplifies the process for the customer to respond. In other words, it's not enough to just ask the right questions (open, positive, and with the correct temporal focus); it's equally essential to pose them correctly relative to the person you're engaging with. You can, after all, ask the right question in the wrong way, making it difficult and, in some cases nearly impossible for your customer to answer because it doesn't match their thought process.

One method of customizing questions for individuals is by considering their *Metaprograms*. Below are some examples of how to tailor questions according to some of the *Metaprograms* that we discussed previously:

INTERNAL VS. EXTERNAL REFERENCE

People who are more internal in their thinking tend to process information subjectively and based on their own experiences. In contrast, people who are more external tend to focus on external factors and objective data.

To tailor questions for individuals who are more internal, you can ask questions that focus on their personal experiences and feelings, such as

"How did you feel about your success?"

or

"What has been your experience with this success?"

For individuals who are more external, you can ask questions that focus on objective data, such as

"What are the facts and figures that support your success?"

or

"What do your colleagues say about what has contributed to your current success?"

OPTIONS VS. PROCEDURE

People who are more focused on options tend to be more creative and open-minded, while people who are more focused on procedures tend to be more organized and structured.

To tailor questions for individuals who are more focused on options, you can ask questions that encourage brainstorming and exploration, such as:

"What are some different approaches we could take to achieve this outcome?"

or

"What are some out-of-the-box ideas we could consider?"

For individuals who are more focused on procedure, you can ask questions that focus on structure and process, such as:

"What steps do we need to take to get this outcome?"

or

"What is the first step for handling this type of decision?"

SPECIFIC VS. GENERAL

People who are more specific in their thinking tend to focus on details and specifics, while people who are more general tend to focus on the big picture and broader concepts.

To tailor questions for individuals who are more specific, you can ask questions that focus on details and specifics, such as:

"What is a concrete example of how this works in practice?"

or

"What specific factors do we need to consider when making this decision?"

For individuals who are more general, you can ask questions that focus on the bigger picture, such as:

"How does this work in practice?"

or

"How can you make this decision?"

SAMENESS VS. DIFFERENCE

People who are more focused on sameness tend to look for similarities and commonalities, while people who are more focused on differences tend to look for distinctions and differences.

To tailor questions for individuals who are more focused on sameness, you can ask questions that focus on similarities and commonalities, such as:

"What are some similar successes you have encountered in the past?"

or

"How does this opportunity compare to others you have faced?"

For individuals who are more focused on difference, you can ask questions that focus on distinctions and differences, such as:

"What sets this success case apart from others we have encountered?"

or

"What are the key differences between this opportunity and others we have considered?"

MATCH VS. MISMATCH

Another important way to tailor questions is to consider whether the customer tends to agree or disagree with what they are presented with. Some people instinctively agree and look for commonalities, while others tend to disagree and look for differences or alternatives. Understanding this preference can help formulate questions that make it easier for the customer to respond.

To tailor questions for individuals who tend to match (agree), you can ask questions that focus on agreement and common understanding, such as:

"Would you be able to meet with us again as early as next Thursday?"

or

"Do you need more time and information before taking the first step today, so that we can get started?"

For individuals who tend to mismatch (disagree), you can ask questions that give them something to disagree with, making it easier for them to do what you and they actually want, such as:

"Would it be too soon for you to meet with us again as early as next Thursday?"

or

"Do you need more time and information before taking the first step today, so that we can get started?"

You have now been introduced to the four dimensions that can help you craft effective questions for your customers, which will enable you to understand your customers better and more quickly. Furthermore, these techniques often help your customers gain a better understanding of their own situation and what they truly desire for the future.

We have conducted training sessions for companies that deal with customers who are very cautious about what they say and to whom. More than once, we've received comments like:

"We understand it would be beneficial to know more about what works for our customers today, what they desire for the future, and why they want these things, but in our industry, it's not customary for them to share this information with their suppliers, as they're afraid the information might end up in the wrong places, such as with their competitors."

Several times, a year later, when we've met the same clients, we've heard repeatedly,

"Something interesting has happened in our industry - the customers have become much more open - now we're learning much more about them, something we could never get them to share before."

Could it be that it was just that they had become better at asking open, engaging questions at the right times and in ways that truly matched each stakeholder at their customer's end?

I think you know what we would answer to this.

The tools presented in this Chapter provide ways to lead yourself and track the verbal and non-verbal signals of the person or people you interact with during the sales engagement. The more you know yourself and the more you know about the mindset of the person or people you are trying to persuade or influence, the more likely you are to succeed. Knowing others involves noticing and tracking real-time information as it unfolds, including sensing rapport and connection with others.

In the following seven chapters, we will incorporate these tools when showing you the *"How"* - how to practically apply the *Satisfaction Cycle* in your sales world. We will build the guidance around the seven stages - the seven Cs - of *Satisfaction Selling*, presented in Chapter 8.

10

CENTERING

How to Become Ready

In the *Centering* stage you prepare for the meetings with the customer. You prepare yourself to enter the *Green State*, gaining access to understanding your own PS^+ and DS^{++} so that you can create a clear intention for the upcoming meeting. This preparation will allow you to enter the meeting in the *Green State*, fully present and with a clear and focused *INTENT*.

Preparing for a sales interaction, whether with a potential or existing customer, involves researching and understanding both what you *know* and what you *don't know* about the customer's wants and needs and situation. The more informed you are, the clearer and more confident you become. This confidence strengthens your *Green State*, allowing you to remain open to exploring various possibilities instead of solely focusing on selling a specific product.

Moreover, it's essential before the meeting to define your *INTENT* and the purpose behind investing time with this customer. Being clear about your desired outcome of the sales interaction and maintaining positive expectations are crucial steps. Once these are established, you're better prepared to enter the actual meeting process, ready to engage effectively.

Are You Ready to Be the *Trusted Advisor?*

Successful salespeople possess a variety of skills and traits, such as the ability to identify the right customers for their offering and understand the benefits their customers can receive. They know exactly where they can succeed and focus their actions accordingly. They approach potential customers with a sincere desire to help while being transparent about their goals. Rather than trying to force or control the sales process, they remain open and curious, letting go of the need to control and staying in a state of confidence and *Curiosity*.

The key to adopting the *Satisfaction Cycle* is to believe in this *Trusted Advisor* mindset, which holds that your role is to help customers get what they want. As discussed in Chapter 3, this involves viewing your role as a salesperson as not simply to "sell" something to the customer but to serve and assist them in obtaining what they genuinely want and need for themselves and their organization. As a *Trusted Advisor* you help the customer make informed and effective decisions, guiding them toward purchasing precisely what they want and need to achieve their desired outcome.

During the buying process, you have two primary responsibilities with the customer, instead of focusing on making sales. Firstly, you must help the customer get into operating from the *Green State*, where they are open, capable, and willing to share information about their desires and make well-informed decisions. Secondly, you must gather information to determine whether you can provide value and assist the customer in achieving their goals.

As discussed in Part 1 of the book, these expectations for salespeople in *Satisfaction Selling* differ significantly from traditional sales models. This approach alleviates the stress and pressure on salespeople, allowing you to let go of the feeling of being forced to sell and shift to genuinely assisting customers. Engaging with customers to gather information establishes a more sustainable foundation for long-term success.

Do Your Research Well

To be an effective *Trusted Advisor*, you must act like a consultant, analyzing each customer's unique situation before providing recommendations to improve their business. This involves gathering and analyzing extensive data about the customer's business and their environment. Before meeting with the customer, it's crucial to do your homework and prepare thoroughly. By researching the customer's business and key stakeholders comprehensively, you can enter a meeting equipped with valuable insights.

One key aspect of preparation is gathering as much information as possible about the customer's company, industry, and market situation. You may have developed routines to collect details about their business, customers, recent developments, and other relevant factors. This research provides a comprehensive view of the customer's potential business drivers, including what is working well in their business (PS^+), what could make their situation better (DS^{++}), and how they would like to get it (*Process*).

Understanding the key stakeholders is another critical part of your research. On the customer side, the entire *Buying Center* includes *Influencers*, *Users*, *Decision-makers*, *Buyers*, and *Gatekeepers*, as discussed in Part 1 of the book. Spending time to know as much as possible about the individuals and their roles within the *Buying Center* is invaluable. However, as discussed previously, high-value complex sales involve multiple people on both sides. Thus, mapping out the stakeholders within your own company who might be needed throughout the sales process is also essential.

Researching potential customers is vital to ensure that you can focus on areas where success is achievable. In high-value complex selling, where sales processes can be lengthy and demanding, thorough preparation and research are invaluable. Knowing where to invest your time is crucial. The ultimate goal of this research is to understand the potential match and identify opportunities where your offerings could significantly benefit the customer.

Is There a Potential Fit?

The research in the preparation phase provides clarity about where success is possible. By connecting the customer's business drivers with your company's drivers, you can begin to identify opportunities to create a profitable business case for both the customer and you. This clarity extends to understanding the value and benefits your offerings can provide, specifically addressing the customer's wants and needs. The benefit of your offering is not just about the product or service itself but rather about the impact of your solution: how will things be different after the customer has implemented it?

In preparing for sales and meeting with the customer, you need to have an answer to critical questions such as:

"What benefit or advantage can I bring to the potential customer to improve their situation?"

"What possible value can I provide?"

"Why would the customer want what I have to offer?"

With a clear understanding of whom your offering is intended for, you can determine whether a meeting with a potential customer is worth pursuing. It's important to remember that not everything in your portfolio may be suitable for everyone. Ultimately, conducting thorough research before engaging with potential customers can help you identify areas where you can create value and increase your chances of success.

What Do You Want?

Adopting a customer-centric view is crucial in *Satisfaction Selling,* and simultaneously, it's essential to approach potential customers with a clear *INTENT.* As a salesperson, your goal is to conduct business beneficially for yourself. Engaging with a customer without a clear purpose is unproductive. Both elements - understanding what the customer wants and knowing what you aim to achieve - are vital for a successful outcome.

Having a clear vision of what constitutes a successful outcome gives direction and purpose to the sales process. If you identify a potential match and a way to serve the customer, ask yourself:

"What do I want to achieve with the customer?"

"What kind of reward am I expecting for myself?"

"How will I know I've achieved what I want?"

"What concrete indicators will show that I've met my objectives?"

When interacting with a potential or existing customer, having a clear understanding of your personal objectives is crucial. Your unique desired outcome may range from financial gains to personal satisfaction, such as enjoying collaborative work with a customer or supporting your family. After defining your desired outcome, delve into why it matters to you by considering:

"What does achieving this outcome provide me?"

"Why is striving for this outcome important to me?"

For instance, securing a sale with a specific customer could help you meet a financial target, enabling personal rewards like a vacation or a special purchase. Understanding the motivation behind your goals is key to maintaining focus and motivation throughout the sales process. Always reflect on:

"What will achieving this outcome offer me?"

Knowing your own *"Why"* is crucial for staying dedicated to your sales goals and ensuring success. This understanding forms the foundation of your *INTENT*, preparing you for effective selling. You're not just there to meet the customer; you have a purpose and a personal stake in the interaction. Embracing the *Trusted Advisor* mindset means you're there for your customer, ready to pursue paths where success is achievable.

Establish Positive Expectations

When considering your desired outcome with a potential customer, being aware of your expectations is crucial. Even if you're confident in your skills and resources, it's essential to question whether you truly expect to achieve what you desire. It's not uncommon for initial desires and expectations to be misaligned, making it important to distinguish between the two. Thus, ask yourself:

"What are my expectations regarding my desired outcome?

Imagine you have a new lead, and your desire is to have this customer buy your entire portfolio offering. Check if your expectations align with this desire! For example, you might realistically expect to start with just one product group rather than the full portfolio. In such cases, your expectations will guide your actions, not merely your desires, leading you to focus on identifying the most suitable product group.

Establishing positive expectations is crucial for high sales performance. A gap between desire and expectation can create hidden limitations and inhibitions. To achieve exceptional performance, aligning your desires with your expectations is necessary. This alignment process, referred to by

Joseph as "collapsing" desire and expectation, naturally motivate action, driving you closer to achieving your goals.

However, it's important to recognize that achieving your desired outcome will result in consequences, both positive and negative. What will happen once you've achieved your outcome? While some consequences may be beneficial, others might not be as desirable. Therefore, when setting positive expectations, choosing outcomes that maximize positive consequences and minimize negative ones is essential.

Every action (and inaction) has consequences, and there's always a trade-off to consider. For instance, choosing to invest time in visiting Customer X means forgoing the opportunity to use that time elsewhere. For salespeople, managing the critical asset of time effectively is paramount. Ultimately, high-quality performance is about setting positive expectations to produce the desired outcome, maximizing the positive while minimizing the negative consequences.

Be Clear About the Purpose of the Meeting

After completing your initial preparation, it's time to gear up for meeting the customer. High-value complex sales processes can extend over long periods, sometimes spanning up to a couple of years, and involve several meetings. Although it's possible to cycle through the *Satisfaction Cycle* in as little as half an hour, a typical high-value complex sale usually requires multiple meetings, often many more.

Defining the meeting's purpose is crucial for a successful outcome. By clearly outlining the goals and objectives, you can set a positive tone and build trust with the customer. To start the meeting positively, it's essential to clarify and set the meeting's purpose by addressing key questions:

"Why is this meeting happening?"

"What are we aiming to accomplish?"

"What outcome is expected from this meeting?"

"What does the customer hope to gain?"

"What do I want to achieve?""How would I know that has happened?"

The clearer the purpose and expected outcomes are defined, the more likely the meeting will result in a positive outcome.

The meetings' purposes throughout the sales process may differ, depending on the stage of engagement. Although it might seem inefficient, sometimes a meeting's sole purpose is to schedule another meeting with additional stakeholders. In the initial stages - *Curiosity, Clarity*, and *Compulsion* - the main focus is on identifying the customer's PS^+, DS^{++}, and *Process*. It's crucial to remember that these meetings are not about making a sale; instead, they're focused on gathering information to help you understand if there is a match and to help the customer achieve the right outcomes.

While the first meeting always starts from the PS^+ in *Satisfaction Selling*, subsequent meetings may be necessary to collect all required information. Gathering information about PS^+, DS^{++}, and *Process* can take several meetings. In the *Commitment* stage, meetings revolve around delivering a tailored *Solution Experience* that meets the customer's wants and needs. Once the buying decision is made, the *Compliance* stage meeting(s) focus on facilitating the customer's *Actions* to turn their dreams and plans into reality.

Preparing the Meeting (With a Positive Frame)

Starting from and maintaining a positive frame during a meeting necessitates preparation. Based on your research and other sources, understanding all the positive aspects of the customer enables you to prepare for and initiate the meeting from a positive perspective, as discussed above.

You may discover that the customer is facing challenges, and their business is under strain. These difficulties could lead them to approach the meeting with a negative mindset. However, your role is still to guide them into and maintain them in the *Green State* during the meeting. Achieving this can be challenging and requires deliberate effort to ensure it happens. We will discuss this more in the next Chapter.

For instance, if the customer has experienced financial difficulties but possesses the most innovative technology in the market, you can leverage this information. Even before the meeting starts, engage the customer in a conversation about their technology to set a positive tone. This approach helps maintain a positive frame throughout the meeting.

In another scenario, if a potential customer is struggling to maintain competitive pricing but has exceptional warehouse and logistics systems, you could propose meeting at their warehouse to highlight this success. You might say,

"I've heard great things about your warehouse system and would love to see it in action. Can we meet there before our formal discussion?"

Physically situating the meeting in a place of success can positively pre-frame the conversation. Alternatively, meeting outside the customer's offices or in a setting that naturally encourages a positive outlook can be effective. By leveraging all available information, you can pre-frame the meeting from a standpoint that encourages the customer to adopt the *Green State*, at least initially.

Remain Open

After all the preparation, when you finally meet with the customer, you already have a substantial understanding of their potential wants and needs and how your product or service might offer value. While you believe in your ability to assist the customer, the exact means of doing so remain unknown until you engage directly with them to determine if there's a match.

Embracing this initial uncertainty is crucial for success in *Satisfaction Selling*. Being comfortable with *Not Knowing* – yet being open to discovery – provides a significant advantage. As discussed in Chapter 3, this stance allows you to explore how best to serve the customer effectively.

Similarly, customers may also be uncertain about the potential fit with your offerings. It's not uncommon for customers to exhibit resistance or skepticism. In these instances, it's your role as a salesperson to maintain the *Green State* and remain calm even in the face of uncertainty. Remaining open and staying in the *Green State* is the way a successful *Trusted Advisor* stays flexible and curious to explore what would make things better for their customer, whether related to their organization, processes, or other areas of need.

Moreover, as highlighted in Chapter 3, discernment in choosing whom to work with is a hallmark of an excellent salesperson. Not every potential sale should be pursued. At times, you may recognize that, despite being able to help, the challenges and potential hassles involved may render the effort unprofitable. In such scenarios, a *Trusted Advisor* understands the value of stepping back. This discernment allows you to allocate your time, energy, and resources toward engagements where you can establish successful, mutually beneficial relationships, thereby focusing on the most rewarding business opportunities.

Centering

Initial Preparation

"What do I know about the customer's needs and situation?"

"What information is still needed?"

Preparing for customer meetings by entering the Green State, understanding your PS+ and DS++, and setting a clear intention.

- Research thoroughly
- Understand your own state of mind and intentions

Understanding Your INTENT

"What is my desired outcome?"

"What is the purpose of my investing time with this customer?"

Defining your INTENT and purpose is crucial before meeting with a customer. It involves being clear about your desired outcome.

- Set clear, positive intentions and expectations
- Reflect on the desired outcomes

Trusted Advisor Mindset

"How can I help the customer achieve their goals?"

"What benefits can my offerings bring to the customer?"

Adopting the Trusted Advisor mindset means focusing on helping the customer achieve what they want and need, rather than focusing on making a sale.

- Focus on serving the customer's needs
- Prepare to act as a consultant rather than just a salesperson

Research and Analysis

"What are the customer's business drivers?"

"Who are the key stakeholders?"

Thorough research on the customer's company, industry, and key stakeholders is essential. This includes understanding where your offering can provide value.

- Gather and analyze comprehensive data about the customer's business environment

Setting Expectations

"What are my expectations?"

"Do my desires and expectations align?"

It's important to have a clear understanding of your own expectations and to align them with your desires.

- Align desires with realistic expectations
- Understand the consequences of achieving your goals

Meeting Preparation

"What is the purpose of this meeting?"

"What do we aim to accomplish?"

Preparing for the meeting involves defining its purpose, setting goals, and establishing the expected outcomes.

- Clearly define the meeting's objectives
- Understand the customer's and your own goals for the meeting

Maintaining a Positive Frame

"How can we start this meeting on a positive note?"

Starting the meeting from a positive frame is essential. This might involve highlighting the customer's successes.

- Highlight positive aspects and successes
- Choose a conducive setting for the meeting

Openness and Flexibility

"Am I open to discovering new ways to assist the customer?"

"Can I remain flexible and curious throughout the process?"

Being open to discovery and comfortable with not knowing the exact ways to assist the customer until engaging with them is vital.

- Embrace uncertainty and stay open to discovery
- Maintain curiosity to explore various possibilities

Discernment in Engagement

"Is this opportunity aligning with our goals?"

"Should we pursue this sale or focus elsewhere?"

Recognizing when an effort may not be profitable and stepping back allows for focusing on more rewarding business opportunities.

- Identify mutually beneficial opportunities
- Focus efforts on engagements with the highest potential for success.

Figure 10.1 Summary - Centering

11

CONNECTION

How to Establish Rapport and Build a Relationship

In the *Connection* stage, the priority is to establish rapport and build a trustworthy relationship with the customer while setting a clear framework for the meeting. Effective connection is achieved when both you and the customer are in the *Green State*, fostering a sense of familiarity and certainty. This psychological alignment minimizes resistance, friction, and feelings of threat, creating a solid foundation for the next phases of the process where you aim for a smooth elicitation of the customer's desires without resistance, and setting the stage for positive future expectations.

Recognizing and Maintaining the *Green State*

Understanding people's verbal and non-verbal cues to gauge their state of mind is essential when working with the *Satisfaction Cycle*. Sensory acuity is key to identifying signals that indicate whether someone is in the *Green State* or the *Red State*, as people always communicate their state non-verbally through non-verbal language and physiology.

For example, you might observe whether someone's body appears relaxed or tense, if their voice sounds resonant or strained, and how they are breathing. A relaxed individual may show physical signs such as lowered shoulders, softened facial muscles, and slower, deeper breathing. Their posture might also become more upright and open instead of hunched or closed off. These changes influence the voice's tone, making it more resonant due to the relaxation of the body and the shift in breathing patterns.

In the *Green State*, individuals often exhibit physical expressions unique to them, such as specific gestures, muscle relaxation patterns, or focusing on a certain point in space, as mentioned in Chapter 9. The physical signs of the *Red State* typically differ. Language also reflects the individual's state; for instance, someone in the *Red State* might use limiting phrases like

"The problem is..."

or

"Yes, but...".

In contrast, the language used in the *Green State* expresses possibilities.

Detecting these verbal and non-verbal cues with acute sensory perception enables mirroring them back to the customer, assisting in maintaining the *Green State* during interactions. To achieve this, the salesperson must also be able to sustain their own *Green State*, recognizing their unique physical expressions and language cues that indicate a positive state.

Build Rapport First

Building rapport with the customer even before the meeting officially starts is an excellent strategy for establishing a positive frame. You might encounter the individuals you're about to meet in the reception area, waiting in line for coffee, or even in the elevator. These initial interactions are crucial as they set the tone for the entire meeting. The goal during these informal moments is to create a positive frame and foster a state of receptiveness before formally beginning the meeting.

In these pre-meeting conversations, you have the opportunity to leverage the information gathered from your research about the customer's business. Likely, you've identified areas where their business has been successful, which can serve as talking points. An existing relationship with the individual further enhances the potential to cultivate a positive mindset. The depth of the relationship matters; shared history and past successes can be powerful tools for building rapport. There are countless ways to generate a positive atmosphere, from sharing exciting news about your company to exploring common interests. These efforts can disrupt any potential negative sentiments and set a positive tone for the meeting.

The process of establishing a *Connection* between you and the customer starts when both of you are in the *Green State*. This *Connection* goes beyond merely being in a positive state; it is rooted in finding common ground, as people naturally gravitate towards those they perceive as similar to themselves. Rapport is about creating a positive, harmonious, and favorable *Connection* with others. Mirror neurons play a crucial role in this dynamic; the more you identify with the person you're communicating with, the more relaxed both of you become. This mutual relaxation fosters effective communication and creates an environment where the customer feels open to engaging with you, as detailed in Chapter 9.

Positive Framing With a *Yes Set*

A compelling method to strengthen the customer's *Green State* and initiate the meeting positively is to use the *Yes Set* technique we discussed in Chapter 9. For example, at the beginning of the meeting, you can verbally match what the customer has said about why they wanted to meet, so they can only think or say "yes". You might say,

"In your initial email, you mentioned wanting to discuss strategies to increase your sales pipeline and grow your business."

To effectively use the *Yes Set* technique, it's essential to focus on indisputable truths about the person's situation. Therefore, avoid descriptive language, especially adjectives like "great" or "outstanding." Until you become more proficient with the *Yes Set*, practice by preparing 5-7 sentences before your meetings. These sentences should frame the meeting positively and be crafted to elicit affirmative responses. Consider statements that reflect undeniable truths about ...

- your shared history with the people in the room.

- recent events in your business environment.

- the circumstances under which the meeting was established.

- the participants in the meeting.

- the purpose of your meeting.

- the timing and location of your meeting.

Some examples of *Yes Set* openings could be:

Example 1:

"Last week, you requested this meeting, noting your company's recent growth and decision to expand operations. Having utilized our offerings for the past two years, you expressed interest in exploring how we might support your expansion during this meeting."

Example 2:

We spoke over the phone three weeks ago. You mentioned that over the past year, you've been considering upgrading your IT systems. We agreed to have a non-committal meeting today to explore how we might assist you with this. We've agreed to spend up to 90 minutes in our meeting today, and if it makes sense, to schedule a follow-up meeting where we can delve into more details. I've brought our specialist, Mark, to our meeting today - he has more than 10 years of experience with systems similar to yours. He will start by asking you some clarifying questions, so we can understand what you like about your current system and what you desire for your future system. Let's get started with the meeting.

Example 3:

"You wrote to me last Thursday requesting a quick meeting this week. In your email, you expressed the desire to review the allocations for your investments and your stock portfolio with us. You also mentioned that you wanted to evaluate whether it would be advantageous to refinance your home loan now or whether it would be better to wait for more clarity on the interest rate development. How about we start by looking at your investments?"

Setting a Positive Outcome and Expectations for the Meeting

After establishing a positive frame for the meeting, it's crucial to develop a shared purpose with the customer. This alignment ensures that both parties remain on the same page throughout the meeting. A mutual understanding of the meeting's purpose and desired outcomes increases the chance that both parties will feel accomplished and satisfied by the end of the meeting.

Since you've agreed on the meeting's purpose upfront, begin by outlining the key outcomes you both aim to achieve. Consider what these concrete results are, how the customer will recognize their achievement, why these outcomes are significant, and what they enable the customer to accomplish with you. If your customer aligns with this perspective, then your summary effectively acts as a *Yes Set*.

Should the meeting's purpose remain unclear, define it together with the customer before proceeding. Ask questions such as:

"What do you hope to achieve by the end of this meeting?"

"What will you have gained once the meeting concludes?"

"How will you know you've achieved these outcomes?"

"Why are these outcomes important?"

"What does achieving these outcomes enable you to do?"

Once you've clarified the meeting outcomes, guide the customer through the meeting's agenda and the questions you'll address, helping them "slide through time" and already realize what they have gotten out of the meeting. This involves discussing the meeting before it actually happens.

Consider asking:

"What needs to happen during the meeting to achieve the agreed-upon outcomes?"

By mentally walking your customer through the meeting beforehand, you create a safe space, making it easier for them to engage with the forthcoming questions. For example, you might say:

"During our meeting, we'll explore what's currently working in your sales pipeline and identify areas for improvement, including the specific growth targets you're aiming for."

This approach emphasizes focusing on PS^+ and DS^{++}, preparing the customer for the questions ahead and mentally equipping them to respond.

To summarize, the goal of the *Connection* stage is to create an ideal environment for conversation and dialogue, setting you up as a *Trusted Advisor*. After establishing deep rapport and *Connection*, you'll be ready to move into the *Curiosity* stage and elicit the customer's *PS*$^{+}$ which we will delve into in the next chapter.

Connection

Initial Preparation

"How can I ensure both of us are in the Green State?"

"What can I do to foster a sense of familiarity and certainty?"

The goal is to build rapport and establish a open relationship with the customer, setting a clear framework for the meeting.

- Prioritize psychological alignment to minimize resistance and friction
- Ensure that both parties are in the Green State to create an open dialogue

Recognizing and Maintaining the Green State

"What signs indicate the customer is in the Green State?"

"How can I adjust my behavior to maintain or encourage a Green State?"

Sensory acuity is crucial for identifying verbal and non-verbal cues that indicate whether the customer's is in the Green or Red State.

- Develop the ability to read and mirror verbal and non-verbal cues to maintain the Green State
- Recognize and sustain your own Green State

Building Rapport First

"What opportunities exist to build rapport before the meeting begins?"

"How can shared interests or successes be leveraged to establish rapport?"

By matching the customers verbal and non-verbal signals you will establish rapport with the customers.

- Use pre-meeting interactions to foster a positive atmosphere
- Leverage information from research about the customer's business and shared history

Positive Framing with a Yes Set

"How can I frame my initial statements to ensure a positive, affirmative response?"

"What truths about the customer's situation can I highlight?"

Starting the meeting with the Yes Set technique involves making statements that elicit affirmative responses from the customer, thereby strengthening their Green State.

- Prepare statements that reflect undeniable truths about the meeting's context to create a positive frame
- Avoid descriptive language that might lead to disagreement

Setting Positive Outcomes and Expectations

"What outcomes do we aim to achieve by the end of this meeting?"

"Why are these outcomes important to the customer?"

"How will we know we've achieved these outcomes?"

Developing a shared purpose with the customer is crucial for alignment and helps ensure that all feel satisfied by the end of the interaction.

- Clearly outline the key outcomes both parties aim to achieve
- Discuss the meeting's agenda beforehand to mentally prepare the customer

Preparation for the Curiosity Stage

"How can we smoothly transition to discussing your current successes and desires?"

After establishing a deep rapport and Connection, and setting a positive frame for the meeting, you are ready for the Curiosity stage.

- Guide the customer through the meeting's agenda
- Focus on preparing the customer mentally for the questions ahead

Figure 11.1 Summary - Connection

12

CURIOSITY

What's Working?

O nce *Connection* and a clear frame are established, you are ready to proceed to the *Curiosity* stage and elicit the customer's *Present State Positive* - the *PS⁺*.

The *Curiosity* stage begins with the question,

"What's working?"

or more specifically,

"What is already working well for you today?"

As stated boldly in Chapter 5, this question is strategically positioned to be the first you ask in a sales meeting. However, the right approach, as discussed in Chapter 8, is crucial. This question is potent but nuanced; it is most effective when the potential customer feels positive and secure, being in the *Green State*. Asking this of someone in the *Red State* could inadvertently lead to resistance, confusion, frustration, or annoyance - a situation you want to avoid.

The significance of initiating conversations from the *Green State*, fostering *Connection*, and building rapport cannot be overstated. These elements are crucial for a fruitful engagement, as they set the tone for the entire interaction. Therefore, it is a good idea to start out by ensuring that this is the case.

Positive Framing by Asking About Past Successes

A powerful way to start a conversation, one that can shift even the most skeptical customer into a positive state of mind, is to remind them of their past successes. As a salesperson, it's your role to help the customer recall and relive those moments of triumph and accomplishment, bringing to the forefront of their minds all the ways they achieved that success and how it felt. You can engage them with questions that transport them back to those successful times:

"When was the last time you had a success that stood out, something that's relevant to our discussion today?"

It could be anything, such as winning a large new project or successfully launching a new offering to the market.

"What was it like to achieve and experience that outcome?"

"How did you do it?"

"What else can you tell me?"

To fortify the customer's experience of their past success, you can further ask about a specific moment when their experience of success was at its peak.

By focusing on their past successes and the positive feelings associated with them, the customer automatically shifts into the *Green State*, becoming more open and receptive to what you have to say. This technique is not only powerful for establishing a positive frame for the conversation but also builds rapport and trust with the customer, strengthening the *Connection* between you and solidifying your role as a *Trusted Advisor*. By helping the customer relive their past successes, you demonstrate that they have been capable of making good decisions and that you are there to help them achieve even greater success in the future.

Preframing PS⁺ Questions

Even now, when the customer is in the *Green State*, and you have established the right *Connection* and set a positive frame, diving straight into discussions about what is working well might not always yield the desired openness and can sometimes lead to resistance. It's common for customers to dwell on challenges or aspects that aren't working. Hence, directly posing a *PS⁺* question without context may be challenging for them to engage with.

To navigate this, it's beneficial to preframe *PS⁺* questions in a way that acknowledges the customer's current focus while gently steering the conversation towards their strengths and achievements. Here are a some of examples of how you could preframe *PS⁺* questions:

Example 1:

Meeting with a Sales Director contemplating sales training:

"I understand you're looking into a training program for your sales team to accelerate growth. Often, the focus might be on the gaps and shortcomings. In your situation, it can be easy to focus on what's missing and what's not working. However, to maximize the effectiveness of our training, it would be insightful to know what your team excels at currently. This way, we can concentrate our efforts on areas that truly need development. What are your salespeople doing well right now?"

Example 2:

Meeting with a Hospital Administrator considering a major medical device purchase.

"I'm really pleased that we are meeting to expand your imaging department's capabilities. As someone who lives in this area and knowing what I know about the importance of high quality imaging in health care, I'm personally pleased to know that new cutting edge care will be available here locally. Of course, I would love to see you working with us to supply the equipment for the new center you're building, and I will do everything I can to share with you what we've found in working on the major installations we delivered in the past year or two. I also respect that you need to make a decision that balances initial investment, quality of outcomes, and long-term maintenance and reliability too. I'll understand if we cannot demonstrate that our solution is the best one for you that you'd be obligated to go elsewhere, but it's my intention to give you everything you need to see why we've been the supplier of choice for some of the most significant imaging centers on the East Coast for the past decade.

Given your experience with past installations, what aspects of those projects went particularly well that you would like to replicate with this new center?"

Example 3:

Major Retail Purchase of Home Kitchen Renovation

"We know that making a decision to invest in a major home renovation project like designing and installing a new kitchen can feel a bit overwhelming, but it's our task to make every step of the process as easy and clear for you as possible, and to insure you that our experience and expertise will get you what you need and want the way you expect it to happen. Typically, the greatest frustration we've seen is that projects go over budget and over time, but our expertise allows us to insure you that once we agree on a budget that's what it will be, without change orders, in fact we'll guarantee it. We'll also let you know before we begin the actual construction the precise time we'll need to get in and get out of your home, with your new kitchen installed, all appliances working, and the cabinets cleaned and your floors spotless, so you can enjoy your new kitchen without any stress or delays. Thinking back to your previous home improvement projects, what aspects of those experiences worked well and contributed to your satisfaction?"

Ways to Ask: "What's Working?"

The question,

"What's working?"

can be asked in a thousand ways. It often makes sense to start with more open questions about what works:

"What is working well in your business/ company/ department?"

"What is your company's most recent success in the area we're discussing?"

"What have been the most significant factors in driving your recent success?"

"What have been the key drivers of growth in your business over the past year?"

"What is an example of a particular strategy or approach that worked excep-tionally well for you?"

"What do you feel has contributed most to your recent successes?"

Then, you can delve more into how things work to understand the current solution in detail:

"How is your current solution working well?"

"How have you been able to achieve the results you've seen so far?"

"What steps did you take to achieve your most recent success?"

"How have you been able to stay ahead of the competition in this area?"

"What aspects of your current solution are delivering the most value for your organization?"

"What benefits have you seen from your current solution that you didn't expect?"

"What is it about your current solution that makes it an effective tool for your team?"

Exploring further into people and resources that are working well:

"Who is working well?"

"What resources have been the most valuable in achieving your goals?"

The *Curiosity* stage is also an excellent stage to inquire how the customer employed their current solution, as discussed in Chapter 5 and Chapter 8. Their process and what worked about it will also reveal how they made their decision and who was involved in the process.

"How did you make the decision about your current solution?"

"Who was involved in decision-making?"

"What specific strategies have you employed that have been successful?"

What Else Can You Tell Me?

The previous examples of how to ask *PS*$^+$ questions should provide you with some inspiration. Initially, it may be challenging to see the value in this step because it doesn't reveal much about what the customer wants. Engaging in this type of conversation might even feel like a lack of progress, as the customer may discuss things that have already happened, including their successes with your competitors. Many salespeople feel the urge to rush through this conversation, but there are several reasons why you should not.

Firstly, showing sincere curiosity towards the customer will make them feel that you are there to help them succeed, rather than just trying to sell your product. You become their *Trusted Advisor*. Imagine a scenario where a customer needs to switch from a competitor's solution to yours. They might initially be uncomfortable with this idea, fearing a mere sales pitch. Instead, demonstrate genuine interest in their current solution by saying something like,

"That's great. I am sure that's a powerful solution."

"What do you like about it?"

"What worked well for you?"

"How did you implement it?"

This approach helps the customer see your curiosity as genuine, trusting you are truly interested.

Secondly, understanding what works for the customer in their current situation and with their current supplier will also help you present your offering more successfully. You are naturally gathering all the minimum criteria your solution must fulfill.

Therefore, in the *Curiosity* stage, always take your time and ask,

"What else can you tell me?"

Once you embrace the idea of listening to everything competitors have done well, you can use that information to enhance your solution.

Case: Shipping Goods Across the Atlantic

As an example of how to elicit the customers' PS^+, consider the following sales encounter between John, a sales representative from a shipping company, and Lisa, the procurement manager for a major apparel manufacturer:

John: *"Hi Lisa, thanks for taking the time to meet with me today. I know you've been shipping your products from Vietnam to the U.S. for a while now. To get started, could you tell me a bit about what's working well with your current shipping process?"*

Lisa: *"Sure, John. We've been using our current supplier for the past few years, and overall, things have been quite smooth. They're reliable, and our shipments usually arrive on time."*

John: *"That's great to hear. Reliability is certainly key. Besides timeliness, what other aspects of their service have you found particularly satisfying?"*

Lisa: *"Well, their customer service is quite responsive. If there are any issues, they get addressed quickly. Plus, they offer competitive rates, which is always a bonus."*

John: *"Responsive customer service can really make a difference, especially when dealing with international logistics. Can you tell me about a recent situation where their customer service stood out to you?"*

Lisa: *"Yes, actually. There was a delay due to a storm a few months back, and they kept us updated constantly and managed to reroute our shipment to minimize the impact. That kind of communication is invaluable."*

John: *"That sounds impressive. It's clear that communication and problem-solving are high priorities for you. Are there any other specific features or services from your current supplier that you find particularly beneficial?"*

Lisa: *"I also appreciate their flexibility. We sometimes need to make last-minute changes, and they've been very accommodating in those situations."*

John: *"Flexibility is certainly crucial in your industry. It's good to know that's a priority for you. Is there anything else you'd like to highlight about your current shipping experiences that have been particularly positive?"*

Lisa: *"Overall, I think those are the main points. Reliability, good customer service, competitive pricing, and flexibility. These aspects really make our operations smoother."*

In this dialogue, John effectively initiates the *Curiosity* stage and elicits Lisa's *PS⁺* by focusing on what is currently working well for her. He starts by asking about the positive aspects of her current shipping process, which helps to create an excitatory bias. Lisa is clearly in the *Green State*, and her responses reveal valuable information about her priorities: reliability, responsive customer service, competitive rates, effective communication, and flexibility.

John's questions are designed to keep the conversation positive and focused on what Lisa values in her current supplier. This approach not only builds rapport but also allows John to gather critical insights that will be useful in the subsequent steps of the *Satisfaction Cycle*. By understanding what Lisa appreciates and expects, John can tailor his future presentations and solutions to align with her needs and preferences, as discussed below.

Let the Customer Lead!

Now is the time to gather information, but how can you know in advance what information to collect? Which questions should you ask, and in what order? The truth is you don't. During a customer meeting, your role is to gather information that the customer considers important.

There isn't a predefined list of questions or specific pieces of information you need to uncover. Forcing the customer to share information that you deem essential might lead you to overlook details the customer finds significant. While certain information is undoubtedly valuable, it's crucial to take your time. Letting go of the belief that you must uncover specific things allows you to be open to potentially useful information. The customer's responses should guide your next questions, serving as your principle for inquiry.

This approach is critical - you must allow the customer to lead. Customers know their business best, and it's unwise for salespeople to dominate the meeting when the customer has much to contribute. It's easy, and regrettably common, to become so focused on our agenda that we miss valuable insights. We tend to see and hear only what matches our expectations, ignoring everything else.

Instead, a skilled Trusted Advisor is fully present, listening attentively and with curiosity to what is being said and observing the dynamics at play. *Trusted Advisors* who engage with genuine attention seek to understand the customer's perspective, desires, and needs. They ask questions and strive to learn more, setting aside their own agenda and intentions to remain patient and open-minded.

On the other hand, "intention" refers to the salesperson's personal goals and desires, including the drive to persuade the customer toward a specific solution. While intention can motivate and help maintain focus, as discussed in Chapter 10, it's crucial not to impose your own wants and offerings prematurely but to understand and appreciate the customer's viewpoints and values. High-performing *Trusted Advisors* masterfully balance a focus on their objectives with openness and empathy towards the customer's wants and needs.

What Information to Gather

As discussed above, the customer's wants and needs and preferences should always guide the conversation. Although there isn't a specific checklist for the type of information a salesperson should gather, it's crucial to map the entire structure of how the customer achieved their previous successes. Depending on what is important to the customer, you should dive deeper to find out more. Typically, you will gather information about the following areas:

The customer's criteria for what is a significant result

- Typical information to gather includes what specifically worked for the customer in the past and the results they achieved. Understanding how they define a significant result is relevant, as this can vary significantly between individuals and organizations. It will be an important aspect of how they will evaluate your offering

Market environment and business model

- By listening to the customer's perspectives on how they created their successes, you can identify various contributing factors, ranging from market position, customer segments, channels to market, and offerings, to company policies and operational strengths. The ultimate value for any company is profitability. So, all aspects of how their existing solution contributes to increasing revenue, reducing costs, or reducing mental friction in work processes might be relevant for you to know.

Stakeholders and decision-making process

- Additionally, it's beneficial to understand who has been involved in purchasing and implementing existing solutions and their roles in decision-making and implementation.

Available resourcesIt's important to note what resources the customer has utilized to create their past success. Relevant resources on the customer's side can include:

- Financial resources, including their previous budgets for similar purchases.

- Human resources, including skills, knowledge, and experience, as well as the number of people.

- Physical resources, including assets and IT systems.

- Intellectual resources, including proprietary knowledge, partnerships, etc.

Missing resources

- Noting what the customer identifies as missing from their past successes is equally important. They may mention that specific resources were absent, which could have resulted in much larger success, or they may have faced challenges getting started due to budget limitations.

Why Information from PS⁺ is Valuable

As the customer speaks, you gather valuable information, as discussed above. You learn about their past purchasing experiences, budget allocation strategies, and the results they consider significant. Additionally, you gain insight into the decision-making and purchasing processes, allowing you to understand the factors contributing to the customer's success, as illustrated by the example with the sales encounter between John and Lisa above.

This information will be invaluable later when figuring out how to help the customer address any gaps and achieve their desired outcomes. The conversation also enables you to tailor and present your *Solution Experience* in the *Commitment* stage in a way that makes the customer inclined to agree with your proposal and say "yes" to you. By doing so, you create a self-referencing case, utilizing the customer's own examples to bolster your argument.

How to Deal With Problems

When asking the question

"What is working?"

it's crucial to ensure the customer is in the *Green State*, as we have emphasized throughout our discussions. However, if you find the customer in the *Red State* during the *Curiosity* stage, you might be unsure of how to proceed.

First and foremost, it's essential to meet the customer where they are mentally - even if that's in the *Red State*. That said, transitioning the customer back to the *Green State* and asking the relevant variant of the question,

"What is working?"

should involve the shortest and most direct route possible. The longer they dwell on negative thoughts, the more challenging it will be to steer their perspective towards positivity.

For instance, you could acknowledge their concern and reframe the conversation by saying,

"I understand you have some concerns that you want to address, and we can tackle those together. However, let's focus first on how you've created your successes. Afterward, we can revisit these concerns and strategize on overcoming them for even greater success."

While you might not completely sidestep the customer's inclination to discuss their problems, initiating the conversation with positive aspects is preferable. Once you have established cognitive inertia within the positive frame, you can better address issues and concerns without mentally entering the *Red State*. The key is to always stay in the *Green State*, working within the positive frame, and applying your sensory acuity to maintaining deep rapport with the customer.

Curiosity (PS+)

After establishing a connection and a clear frame, the Curiosity stage aims to understand what is currently working well for the customer.

Starting conversations from the Green State is crucial for fostering openness and minimizing resistance.

Positive framing involves reminding the customer of their past successes, making them more open in the conversation.

Preframing PS+ questions help acknowledge the customer's current focus while gently steering the conversation towards their strengths and achievements.

Explore various aspects of what's working in the customer's business, aiming to uncover specific strategies or approaches that have led to success.

The Curiosity stage is critical for gathering information about the customer's criteria for success, stakeholders, decision-making process, available resources, and missing resources.

Showing sincere curiosity about the customer's current solutions and successes establishes you as a Trusted Advisor.

Understanding the customer's past successes, decision-making processes, and resources used is crucial for designing your solution.

If the customer is in the Red State, it's essential to acknowledge their concerns and quickly refocus the conversation to help them back to the Green State.

Transition to the Curiosity Stage
"What is already working well for you today?"

- First ensuring both parties are in the Green State
- Focus on positive aspects to foster an open dialogue

Importance of the Green State
"Can you share a recent success that stood out to you?"

- Encourage the customer to recall and relive past successes to bring them into the Green State

Positive Framing
"What was it like to achieve that outcome?"
"How did you do it?"

- Engage customers with questions about past successes to foster a positive frame and build deeper rapport

Preframing PS+ Questions
"In preparing for growth, what strengths do you see within your team?"

- Acknowledge existing concerns but focus the conversation on capabilities and what's working

Asking What's Working
"What has been the most significant factor in driving your recent success?"
"What do you feel has contributed most to your recent successes?"

- Use open-ended green questions to understand customer's recent successes, strategies, and benefits from current solutions

Gathering Valuable Information
"How did you achieve your most recent success?"
"Who was involved in the decision-making process?"

- Let the customer lead the conversation
- Be present and listen with curiosity to understand the customer's perspective thoroughly

Engaging with Genuine Curiosity
"What worked well for you with this solution?"
"What do you like about your current solution?"

- Demonstrate genuine interest in their current solutions

What Information to Gather
"What specific strategies have you employed that have been successful?"
"What resources have been most valuable in achieving your goals?"

- Map the entire structure of how the customer achieved their previous successes

Dealing with Problems
"I understand you have some concerns; let's first focus on your successes. Can you share a recent achievement?"

- Acknowledge concerns, then redirect to focus on successes before addressing problems
- Always aim to keep the conversation in the Green State

Figure 11.1 Summary - Curiosity (PS+)

13

CLARITY

What Do You Want?

T he natural progression from the *Curiosity* stage is to the *Clarity* stage, where you elicit the customer's *Desired State Positive, DS^{++}*. After gathering sufficient information about the customer's current state through PS^+, you can transition into DS^{++} by asking a simple and straightforward question:

"What do you want?"

or

"What would make the current situation even better for you?"

Your goal is to encourage the customer to envision the ideal outcome they desire without any limitations. In simpler terms, the DS^{++} is an amplified version of the existing PS^+. It encompasses what is already working well for them and what their current solution has not yet delivered. This is a crucial point.

As we enter the *Clarity* stage, the customer starts to harbor positive expectations and enthusiasm for elevating their situation beyond the present. By steering yet allowing the customer to lead the dialogue, their vision feels completely self-derived. In this stage, you're eliciting not just their immediate desired outcomes but also their ultimate aspirations - the *Outcome of the Outcome* - which is the DS^{++} that the *Future Memory* should be based on.

As you guide the customer from PS^+ to DS^{++}, they maintain a positive emotional tone. They continue to discuss what is working and what will work even better for them once they have achieved DS^{++}. This journey fosters an ongoing sense of satisfaction, now amplified and intensified, with the customer associating this enhanced satisfaction directly with the sales process and the facilitating salesperson.

Is the Current Situation as Good as it Gets?

At this stage of the Satisfaction Cycle, your potential customer has highlighted their successes, such as high-quality products, customer engagement, and profitability. These positive indicators are a good starting point, but it's crucial to explore if they've reached their full potential.

Directly answering the DS^{++} question,

"What do you want?"

or

"What would make the current situation even better for you?"

might not always be straightforward. To encourage the customer to think beyond their current achievements, consider asking one of the following questions, tailored to whether the person exhibits a match or mis-match *Metaprogram* (as discussed in Chapter 9):

"Can the current situation improve?" (A matcher will say yes to this)

"Is the current situation the best it can be?" (A mis-matcher will say no to this)

This approach facilitates the shift from the PS^+ phase, where you identify what's already working, to the exploration of the DS^{++} for the customer, focusing on potential enhancements.

Ways to Ask, "What Would Make it Even Better?"

The DS^{++} question,

"What would make it (what's working) even better?"

prompts the customer to envision future possibilities. Depending on the context of your conversation, the future possibilities can be on a higher business level, such as attracting new customer segments, increasing profit margins, or finding other ways to improve their current success, or the desired outcome can be more tangible.

Always use what the customer gives as information to guide you forward. Your customer knows what is important to them, and your task as a *Trusted Advisor* is to hear what is being said. In the context of your conversation, start eliciting the customer's DS^{++} with open questions about what would make what works today better:

"What would make your current situation even better in your business/ company/ department?"

"Regarding X, what enhancements would make the current situation even better for you?"

In DS^{++} like in PS^{+}, demonstrating curiosity is key. Don't hesitate to ask,

"What else can you tell me?"

Based on their responses, you can ask more detailed questions to clarify their DS^{++}:

"What do you want more specifically about (what would get better)?"

"When would you like to have this (what would get better) in place?"

"Where would you like this (what would get better) to happen?"

"Why would you like to have this?"

By asking these questions, you facilitate a detailed exploration of the customer's DS^{++}, building a foundation for proposing solutions that align with their aspirations.

Maintain the Context for Safety and Positivity

The DS^{++} process centers on identifying a positive dream and igniting a *Burning Desire* in the customer by focusing on what they most desire. A true dream involves envisioning new possibilities, not merely fixating on current issues. It's about imagining what can be achieved without being constrained by past or present barriers. This distinction is critical when framing questions to aim for high-quality outcomes.

Often, when customers are asked how their current situation could be improved with the question,

"What would make it better?"

they initially point to a specific issue or challenge they believe is holding them back, suggesting everything would be better without it. This response indicates a shift back to a problem-focused mindset. In such cases, it's crucial for the salesperson to recognize that the customer might see resolving the issue as the sole path forward.

Many customers come into meetings prepared to outline a problem, expecting the salesperson to propose a solution, a dynamic discussed in Part 1 of this book. While articulating problems is commonplace, discussing dreams isn't as familiar for many. Society often makes it more acceptable to share problems, even with strangers, whereas dreams and desires are typically reserved for close, personal relationships.

Sharing true dreams in a sales context can make individuals feel vulnerable. Consider a customer sharing their aspirations with a salesperson; they face two potential outcomes. The first is hearing that their dreams are unattainable, leaving them disheartened. The second is being told their dreams are achievable, which, while encouraging, also opens them up to potential manipulation. This puts their dreams - and by extension, their trust - in the salesperson's hands, creating a sense of vulnerability that many find uncomfortable in a business setting.

Feeling vulnerable can trigger the amygdala, leading to resistance. As explained in Chapter 4, the amygdala governs our fear response and is designed to protect us. Consequently, its activation can dominate our decision-making processes, pushing us into the defensive, *Red State*. In sales, if a potential customer enters this state, it complicates forming a positive relationship. Should this occur, the salesperson must then work to return the customer to the *Green State*, where they feel secure and open to discussion.

Recognize Dreams from Mere Expectations

When you ask,

"What would make the current situation even better?"

you may receive a positive response, but that answer isn't necessarily reflective of a true dream. Often, the reply may merely be an expectation shaped by the current circumstances, with the customer potentially rehashing familiar ideas in a slightly different context.

It's crucial to distinguish between what someone considers achievable based on their current reality and what they genuinely aspire to achieve. Your conversations with the customer should focus on uncovering their dreams, not just their immediate expectations. Desired outcomes represent the specific goals that an individual or organization aims to realize, usually envisioned without the constraints of past experiences. In contrast, expected outcomes are often predictions grounded in previous experiences or existing knowledge.

What if Anything Would be Possible?

By focusing on what people genuinely desire, you, as a salesperson, can deliver greater value. However, skillful communication is key to helping customers explore new and emerging possibilities. One effective strategy is to frame the conversation in a specific way that encourages imagination. You might invite the customer to enter a

"What if...?"

scenario where anything is possible without limitations. This approach, while challenging for some, makes it easier to inspire creativity and help them envision their true desires without constraints.

To pose the DS^{++} question within this framework, you can start with,

"What if anything were possible? What would make it (what works today) even better?"

This phrasing sets the stage for limitless possibilities, nudging the customer to think beyond the present.

You can further motivate the customer to elaborate on their visions by reflecting on their responses and encouraging deeper exploration. For example,

"If X were possible, what would that look like for you?"

Such questions prompt customers to move past their current expectations and limitations, allowing them to freely explore their desires and dreams.

The *Outcome of the Outcome*

We have now started to elicit the DS^{++} by asking,

"What would make it even better?"

The purpose of this initial question is to set the stage for the subsequent inquiry, which aims to identify the changes the customer anticipates after achieving their desired outcome - the *Outcome of the Outcome.* As we've discussed, this represents the ultimate benefit the customer is seeking and distinguishes the *Satisfaction Cycle* from other sales models.

Identifying this pivotal shift for the customer is essential. Thus, we don't stop at simply asking,

"What would make the situation even better?"

We aim to project the customer further into the future, to a point where their desires have been realized, by posing questions like:

"Why do you want to achieve the desired outcome?"

"When you say you want X, what will having that achieve for you?"

"When this has happened for you, what has become different?"

By delving into the *Outcome of the Outcome,* we uncover the genuine motivations behind the customer's decision-making process. This term refers to the ultimate impact or change the customer seeks, whether on a personal or business level. The question,

"What does it get you?"

serves as a potent tool for understanding and clarifying the customer's true aspirations.

As their *Trusted Advisor*, it is your role to unearth this information, assisting the customer in more vividly envisioning their ultimate goal and, ultimately, helping them to realize it.

Outcome Criteria

Trusted Advisors dedicate time to truly understanding their customer's desires, steering clear of imposing their own agendas. In the first two steps of the *Satisfaction Cycle*, *PS+* and *DS++*, you have been gathering information about what your customer wants in terms of the desired outcome. Through successful information collection, you'll start pinpointing specific criteria that need to be satisfied to achieve these outcomes. These are referred to as *Outcome Criteria* in the *Satisfaction Cycle*, as described in Chapter 8.

Outcome Criteria consist of the specific benchmarks or standards that confirm the customer's values have been honored and their objectives attained. They represent the concrete evidence customers look for to be assured that the outcome aligns with their expectations. To ascertain the most critical *Outcome Criteria* for your customer, one effective question is,

"How do you know that you have achieved your desired outcome?"

The *Outcome Criteria* have a hierarchy in terms of their importance, and it's essential to pay attention to the most critical criteria by asking the question,

"How do you know?"

While it may not be feasible to meet every criterion with your offerings, acknowledging all identified criteria is vital. Understanding the most important ones enables you to discern what aspects of your solution can meet these needs and which cannot. This understanding of *Outcome Criteria* is pivotal in crafting a successful *Solution Experience,* a topic we will revisit in Chapter 15, *Commitment.*

Case: High-end Luxury Beds

As an example of how to elicit the customers' DS^{++}, consider the following sales encounter between Mark, a sales representative from a high-end luxury bed company, renowned for its premium products, and Sarah and David, a married couple looking for a new king-sized bed for their second home in a mountain ski resort.

Mark: *"Hi Sarah, David. It's great to have you here today. I understand you're looking for a new bed for your mountain home. Could you tell me what you currently like about your sleeping setup there?"*

David: *"Well, our current bed is comfortable enough, and we sleep pretty well on it. It's a queen size, and the mattress is medium firmness, which suits us."*

Sarah: *"Yes, it's been good, but we're thinking of upgrading to a king size for more space and a bit more luxury since it's our retreat home."*

Mark: *"That sounds wonderful. Since things are working well for you now, what would make your sleep experience even better in your mountain home?"*

Sarah: *"I think having a bit more room would definitely improve our sleep quality. We've been wanting to get a king-size bed for a while."*

David: *"And maybe something with more support. Sometimes after a day on the slopes, I feel like a firmer mattress might help with recovery."*

Mark: *"So, having a king-size bed with more support would make a difference for you. Can you imagine what it would be like to come back from a long day of skiing and sink into a bed that gives you the perfect amount of space and support?"*

Sarah: *"That sounds amazing. We'd feel so relaxed and refreshed every morning, ready to hit the slopes again."*

Mark: *"And how about three to five years down the line? What would it mean for you to have that kind of experience consistently in your mountain home?"*

David: *"It would mean a lot. We'd probably spend more time there, inviting friends and family to join us, knowing we have a luxurious, comfortable bed to offer them as well."*

Sarah: *"Yes, and it would make our retreat even more special, a true sanctuary for us and our loved ones."*

Mark: *"Knowing that this would be your experience, how do you feel about making this purchase now?"*

Sarah: *"I feel excited about it. It's a big investment, but it feels like the right choice for enhancing our time at the mountain home."*

David: *"I agree. It feels like a step towards making our retreat even more enjoyable and comfortable."*

Mark: *"That's great to hear. We can certainly help you with that. Now, let's talk about the specifics. You mentioned you prefer a firmer mattress for support. Would a firm option work best for both of you?"*

Sarah: *"Yes, I think so. A firm mattress would be ideal for us."*

David: *"Definitely. We need something that offers solid support after a day of activities."*

Mark: *"Excellent. And for coordinating with your home decor, are there any particular colors or styles you're looking to match?"*

Sarah: *"Our mountain home has a lot of natural wood and earthy tones. Something that complements that aesthetic would be perfect."*

David: *"Yes, maybe something in a neutral or warm color palette to keep the cozy, inviting feel."*

Mark: *"Wonderful. We have a range of options that will fit perfectly with your decor. Let's explore those together so you can find the perfect match."*

In this dialogue, Mark effectively transitions from the *PS+* step to the *DS++*step -from the *Curiosity* stage to the *Clarity* stage - by building on the couple's positive experiences with their current bed. He asks about what would make their experience even better, leading Sarah and David to envision a future where they have a king-size bed with more support, enhancing their comfort and relaxation.

Mark extends the conversation to explore the couple's desired outcome three to five years from now highlighting the benefits of increased comfort and the joy of sharing their luxurious retreat with friends and family. This creates a *Future Memory*, where Sarah and David imagine the long-term positive impact of their purchase - the *Outcome of the Outcome*.

Finally, Mark connects this *Future Memory* to their present feelings, deepening their emotional connection to the decision to purchase a luxury bed from his company, and by addressing specific preferences for firmness and color coordination, he gathers comprehensive *Outcome Criteria*, setting the stage for the next steps in the *Satisfaction Cycle*. This approach not only clarifies the couple's values and desires but also creates motivation and excitement about the purchase, ensuring a successful sales outcome.

Sensory-Based Experience

Identifying the customer's DS^{++} and creating the *Future Memory*, as we explored in Chapter 6 and in the case-story above, involves eliciting both verbal and non-verbal indicators of their desired outcome, especially those related to the *Outcome of the Outcome*.

Non-verbal markers, such as somatic sensations or physical reactions within the body, are triggered by specific stimuli or experiences. When the customer envisions their desired *Outcome of the Outcome*, their body will manifest certain sensations or reactions observable by the salesperson. These body-based somatic markers, unique to each customer, offer invaluable insights into their emotions and motivations. Salespeople should keenly observe the customer's non-verbal language, eye movements, and other physical cues to pinpoint these markers, as discussed in Chapter 9:

"What is it that they do with their bodies?"

"Where is it that they are looking?"

"Are they still, or do they express movement – and which movements?"

Conversely, semantic markers involve mental associations or connections the brain forms between various pieces of information or experiences. Rooted in meaning and context, these markers are often conveyed verbally. Salespeople should listen attentively to the customer's language, noting specific words or phrases that resonate deeply with them concerning their desired outcome.

By identifying both somatic and semantic markers, salespeople can gain a deeper understanding of the customer's desires and motivations, allowing them to tailor their approach to meet their desires even better.

Can You Possibly Serve the Customer?

Conversations about the customer's DS^{++} have now provided information about what they desire. However, you may not yet have all the information needed to assess whether your solution can fulfill their DS^{++}. What is certain is that if you already know you cannot help the customer, this realization won't change in the later stages.

Determining early in the sales process whether you have a viable solution for the customer is crucial. As previously discussed in Part 1 of the book, if you cannot serve the customer's wants and needs, it's unproductive to continue the engagement. It's more respectful to both parties to politely decline and move on to prospects you can assist.

This approach empowers you. By focusing on customers with whom you can establish a valuable relationship, you pave the way for long-term success. You're no longer solely dependent on the customer's decision; you hold equal influence in the relationship. Adopting this perspective on sales can significantly enhance your performance.

Learning to decline opportunities gracefully is an important skill in sales. It's not just the act of saying no, but how you communicate it. A respectful and empathetic rejection can leave the door open for future collaboration. Considering the customer's perspective ensures that your response is thoughtful and aligns with their needs and concerns.

Remember that customers have the power to choose whether or not to buy from you. If your solution doesn't meet their needs, they will look elsewhere. It's crucial to recognize when there's a mismatch between what they want and what you can offer. Chances are, they've already noticed it, too. By acknowledging this, you can avoid wasting time on a deal that won't happen and move on to more promising opportunities.

Pointing out the gap when saying "no" makes it clear and obvious. Rather than simply saying "no," it's helpful to acknowledge the gap and be clear about why you can't fulfill the customer's DS^{++}. For example, you might say something like,

"I understand that you have a specific outcome in mind. However, based on what we can offer, it seems that we won't be able to provide exactly what you are looking for. I understand that you may not want to compromise on your desired outcome, and I respect that."

Your offers might simply not be the right ones for them. Or maybe the customer's budget won't allow for the desired outcome, or perhaps the time frame is unfeasible. In these cases, being upfront and honest with the customer is essential. Let them know that while you can't help them now, you're open to revisiting the conversation in the future if circumstances change.

This honesty, coupled with an openness to future discussions, builds trust and maintains the potential for a future relationship. Being transparent about your reasons for declining and keeping communication channels open for the future demonstrates integrity and respect. Remember, saying no isn't necessarily the end of the conversation - it can be the beginning of a new dialogue.

Clarity (DS++)

	Transition to the Clarity Stage	
Transitioning from acknowledging what's currently working (PS+) to exploring the customer's ideal outcomes (DS++).	"What do you want?" "What would make the current situation even better for you?"	• Guide the conversation from the customer's current state to their desired future state • Encourage envisioning the ideal outcome without constraints
	Exploring Beyond the Present	
Determining if the customer believes they've reached their full potential and encouraging them to envision further improvements.	"Can the current situation improve?" "Is the current situation the best it can be?"	• Use questions tailored to the customer's mindset to facilitate the transition from current successes to their dreams
	Eliciting the DS++	
Asking open-ended questions to help the customer to think about future possibilities that could elevate their current success to the DS++.	"What would make your current situation even better in your business / company / department?"	• Utilize information shared by the customer to delve deeper into their DS++
	Maintaining a Positive Context	
Keeping the conversation focused on positive dreams and aspirations, enabling the customer to imagine their ideal future.	"What if anything were possible?" "What would make it even better?"	• Frame the conversation in a way that encourages the customer to dream big and think beyond the present limitations
	Recognizing True Dreams	
Differentiating genuine aspirations from mere expectations shaped by current circumstances.	Follow-up probing questions to distinguish true dreams from mere expectations: "What would make the current situation even better?"	• Focus on uncovering the customer's genuine aspirations, to envision what they truly desire for the future
	The Outcome of the Outcome	
Identifying the ultimate benefit the customer seeks by achieving their desired future state (DS++).	"Why do you want to achieve the desired outcome?" "What will having that achieve for you?" "When this has happened for you, what has become different?"	• Understand the reasons behind the customer's desired outcomes to see the deeper motivations and the impact they seek
	Outcome Criteria	
These criteria are crucial for ensuring the solution aligns with their expectations and values.	"How do you know that you have achieved your desired outcome?"	• Identify and prioritize the most important Outcome Criteria for the customer
	Assessing the Ability to Serve	
If a match isn't feasible, it's more respectful to both parties to acknowledge this and potentially end the engagement.		• If you cannot meet the customer's DS++, respectfully decline further engagement, focusing instead on other prospects
	Handling Declines	
This involves declining in a way that maintains respect, and leaves the door open for future collaboration.	"Based on what we can offer, it seems we won't be able to provide exactly what you are looking for. I understand you may not want to compromise on your desired outcome, and I respect that."	• Approach declines with empathy and clarity, ensuring the customer understands the reasons

Figure 13.1 Summary - Clarity

14

COMPULSION

What Needs to Happen?

F ollowing the *Clarity* stage we enter the *Compulsion* stage. After eliciting the customer's DS^{++}, the next step is to understand how the customers want to achieve their DS^{++}. A gap exists between the PS^+ and DS^{++}, within which the customer holds ideas and preferences about what needs to happen to bridge that gap and achieve DS^{++}. The *Process* refers to the specific method by which the customer wants to attain their outcome, focusing on gathering the "*How*" information.

Pull From the Future

After discovering the DS^{++} for your customer and allowing them to vividly experience the *Future Memory* of already having achieved their outcome, the focus shifts to transforming DS^{++} into a new PS^+. It is essential throughout the sales process to hold the future for the customer as if it were already present.

Considering the entire *Process* from the future back towards PS^+ provides a historical perspective on what needs to happen to transition from PS^+ to DS^{++}. This shift from present to future is the focus of your enquiry. You are eliciting what the customer believes about how the transition had to occur for them to achieve their DS^{++}. Because you are already familiar with the mechanisms, they have used to create past successes and have made these visible in their present, you enable the customer to naturally link their past and present to the new desired future. Skillfully done, this bridge begins to feel like a natural continuation and strengthens the motivation to realize DS^{++}.

The mind of the customer is now in a clear trajectory. The customer already feels confident that they will get what they want even though they have not heard about the actual solution yet. For them, the DS^{++} begins to feel so certain, as if it has already happened. This is how the *Compulsion* is created.

Customer's View on Bridging the Gap

The *Process* step is primarily about gathering information on what the customer wants and, more specifically, how the customer envisions moving from PS^+ to DS^{++}. Many salespeople go wrong in assuming that customers are primarily concerned with the specifics of the product or service and its delivery. However, in reality, customers are mainly focused on achieving their DS^{++}, and they are interested in your product or service to the extent that they believe it will deliver the desired outcome.

The *Process* stage is exclusively about understanding the customer's perspective on transitioning from PS^+ to DS^{++}. It involves asking questions to identify what is missing and what needs to occur for the customer to reach their desired state. Bridging this gap requires considering necessary resources in the *Process,* such as time, finances, skills, and knowledge, to move the customer from PS^+ to DS^{++}.

The goal of the *Process* stage is to collect all remaining information needed to design and deliver a satisfying *Solution Experience*. The way a customer wants to achieve their DS^{++} is just as critical as the DS^{++} itself. Therefore, your solution should address both the *"What"* and the *"How,"* This means that a solution encompasses more than just the product or service offered; how the solution is delivered and implemented on the customer's side is equally vital in meeting the customer's rational and logical expectations and providing an emotionally satisfying experience.

Ways to Ask: "What Would Have to Happen?"

When asking questions about the *Process* and how the customer aims to achieve their DS^{++}, you can start with a broad question like,

"What is the primary difference between what you have now and what you want?"

This question will offer initial insights into how you can bridge the gap and provide the missing pieces for the customer to achieve their DS^{++}. Additionally, asking such questions continues to reinforce the customer's perception of you and your solution as the optimal path to their goals. To delve into the specifics of how the customer wishes to reach their desired outcome, consider asking:

"What specific steps or actions would have to happen for you to achieve the DS^{++}?"

"How would you like it to happen?"

"How would you prefer these steps or actions to be carried out?"

Understanding the resources the customer currently possesses and their willingness to allocate those resources toward achieving DS^{++} is crucial. Dive deeper by asking specific questions such as:

"What can you do?"

"What areas do you need assistance with?"

Depending on your business context, you might have very specific questions regarding your customer's desired *Process* that you need answers to.

Operating Criteria

The conversations during the *Process* step will provide you with the *Operating Criteria* in the *Satisfaction Cycle*, as discussed in Chapter 8. The *Operating Criteria* encapsulate all aspects that the customer considers in achieving their desired outcome, DS^{++}. Essentially, while the *Process* represents the overarching method of reaching the desired outcome, the *Operating Criteria* detail the specific elements within that process. Typical criteria can include:

- The overall approach of how the customer wants to work with you

- Main process steps and milestones

- The anticipated timeline

- The available budget

- Details related to the resources the customer has available

- Expectations regarding the resources the customer requires from the seller

The specifics and details of the *Process* will vary depending on the case, so there isn't a one-size-fits-all checklist. As a salesperson, you need to ask your customer targeted questions based on their specific situation. For instance, following the initial question about

"What would have to happen for you to achieve the DS^{++}?"

you may inquire about their budget, available resources, and timeframe with questions like:

"What kind of budget do you have in mind?"

"What resources are available to you?"

"What is your timeframe?"

Together, the *Outcome Criteria* - the *"What"* - and the *Operating Criteria* - the *"How"* - form a hierarchy of importance concerning what the customer wants to achieve and how they want to achieve it. Determining what is most important to the customer and then prioritizing the criteria you can actually fulfill is crucial. Therefore, in addition to collecting the *Criteria* through targeted questions, it's also necessary to understand the priority of their *Criteria*. A simple method to identify priorities is to ask,

"What is more important for you: X or Y?"

Case: Wealth Management

As an example of how to elicit the customers' desired *Process,* consider the following sales encounter between Anna, a wealth management advisor in a private banking company, and Jens, a high-net-worth client considering an investment for retirement.

Anna: *"Hi Jens, thank you for meeting with me today. From our previous conversations, I understand that you're looking to invest 5,000,000 DKK towards*

a secure retirement fund. Can we discuss how you envision the process of making this investment?"

Jens: *"Sure, Anna. My main concern is ensuring that my principal is not at risk. I want a safe investment that guarantees at least a 3.5% return."*

Anna: *"Absolutely, Jens. We can certainly structure the investment to prioritize safety and meet your return goals. Can you tell me more about the time frame you have in mind for making this investment?"*

Jens: *"I'm planning to make the full investment within the next three months. I'd like to do it in two increments to ensure everything is set up correctly."*

Anna: *"That sounds like a solid plan. Would you prefer to transfer the funds electronically, or is there another method you're comfortable with?"*

Jens: *"Electronic transfer works best for me. It's quick and convenient."*

Anna: *"Great. And how would you prefer we communicate throughout this process? Do you prefer email updates, phone calls, or in-person meetings?"*

Jens: *"I prefer email for most updates, but I'd like to have a monthly phone call to discuss progress and any adjustments that might be needed."*

Anna: *"Understood. Now, regarding withdrawals, how long do you plan to keep the investment with us before making any withdrawals?"*

Jens: *"I'd like to keep the investment for at least 10 years before making any withdrawals. After that, I'd prefer to withdraw in annual increments to supplement my pension."*

Anna: *"That sounds like a prudent approach. We can arrange for the withdrawals to be processed annually. Are there any specific tax implications you're concerned about when you start making withdrawals?"*

Jens: *"Yes, I'd like to minimize my tax liability as much as possible. I'd appreciate it if you could provide advice on the best way to structure the withdrawals to achieve that."*

Anna: *"Certainly, Jens. We can work with our tax advisors to ensure your withdrawals are structured in the most tax-efficient way possible. Is there anything else that's important to you regarding how we manage this investment?"*

Jens: *"Just that the investment remains low-risk and that I receive regular updates on its performance. Peace of mind is really important to me."*

Anna: *"We can definitely ensure that. We'll provide regular performance reports and keep the investment strategy aligned with your risk tolerance and return expectations. Thank you for sharing all this information. It helps us tailor the investment process to suit your needs perfectly."*

In this dialogue, Anna successfully elicits the *Process* step by focusing on Jens's preferred method for making the investment. She gathers detailed information on the time frame for the investment, preferred fund transfer method, communication preferences, withdrawal plans, and tax implications. By doing so, Anna ensures that Jens's investment process is aligned with his needs and expectations.

This step is critical as it transitions from understanding what Jens wants - the *Outcome Criteria* - to how he wants to achieve it - the *Operating Criteria*. By addressing Jens's concerns about safety, communication, and tax efficiency, Anna builds a clear and tailored path for Jens's investment, setting the stage for the next steps in the *Satisfaction Cycle*, the *Solution Experience*. This approach not only clarifies the logistics of the investment but also strengthens Jens's confidence and motivation to proceed with private banking company that Anna represents.

Resources to Bridge the Gap

Through inquiries about the customer's desired *Process*, you not only identify the resources the customer already possesses for implementing the solution but also gain clarity on the additional resources needed and the extent of the customer's willingness to invest in them.

When listening to the customer, it's essential to consider the range of resources that have to be in place for the customer to bridge the gap from PS^+ to DS^{++}. These resources include budgetary considerations, which involve determining the amount the customer is willing or able to invest. Time considerations pertain to when the customer expects the solution to be implemented. Additionally, factors such as the skillset, knowledge, and availability of personnel to carry out the solution are also relevant.

Time Versus Required Resources

In terms of time, your customer likely has specific desires regrading when they want to have reached their DS^{++}. Time is a critical component of the *Operating Criteria*, and during the conversation, you might want and need to adjust the customer's expectations about timeliness. In some instances, you may find that the process can be expedited by adding specific resources or by altering your approach to the work. In other cases, you might want to slow down and shift the anticipated timeline further into the future.

Within your specific sales context, you are uniquely positioned to understand how different timelines can influence the required resources, including the budget that the customer must be willing to allocate. During the *Process* discussion, you can proactively inform the customer about the potential impacts and consequences of their time-related preferences.

Budget and Finance

Discussing the budget is a crucial part of identifying the customer's available resources. Salespeople often feel uncomfortable asking about money, but being in the *Green State* changes the dynamics of the conversation about finances. Once a trusted connection is established, customers are more open to discussing their budget.

When it comes to the customer's budget, you typically want to find out:

"Who can make the decision regarding the budget?"

"What is your budget? How much are you willing to invest?"

"Do you have the funds available, or do you need to explore financing options?"

Initiating the budget conversation early primes the customer to understand that, eventually, you will present your price. It's important to remember that the customer's budget does not necessarily match your sales price. Your price may be higher or lower than their budget. At this stage, you're only collecting information and there's no need to discuss your price yet.

People, Knowledge, and Skills

In high-value complex sales, people are often the most complex resource, making it crucial to clarify early on:

"Who needs to be involved in the decision-making?"

"Who is required for the implementation?"

The journey for the customer from PS^+ to DS^{++} might also necessitate specific knowledge, experience, and skills for the customer to fulfill their needs and implement the solution the seller provides. It is essential to identify:

"Does the customer have people with the required knowledge, expertise, and skills?"

"Where can the customer acquire the required knowledge, expertise, and skills?"

"What knowledge, expertise, and skills does the customer expect the seller to provide?"

"For potential Process activities, who will be responsible for specific tasks?"

"Who will do what?"

Other Existing and Missing Resources

For your customer to transition from PS^+ to DS^{++}, they might need additional resources such as certain materials, physical assets, IT systems, or even intellectual resources like proprietary knowledge and partnerships. Therefore, the critical questions are:

"What does the customer need?"

"What do they currently have?"

"How can they acquire the resources they lack?"

For any new resources that need to be purchased, consider the lead times involved, as these might influence how you support the customer's *Process.*

Building Commitment

As a *Trusted Advisor*, you assist the customer in making informed decisions about their DS^{++} and *Process*. It's essential to ensure that the customer is prepared to take the necessary steps and invest appropriately to reach their DS^{++}. If not, you should guide them in revisiting the details of their DS^{++} and *Process*.

In guiding the customer, you can help them re-evaluate their *Outcome Criteria* and *Operating Criteria*, focusing on three key elements:

- **The level or quality of outcome** which refers to the excellence or superiority of an offering. This excellence facilitates the customer's ability to achieve what they want and can be reflected in workman-ship, materials, and design standards for creating a specific item, or in the breadth of the scope delivered.

- **Time** which relates to the speed or efficiency of the offering's delivery. This can encompass turnaround time, delivery time, and response time.

- **Financial resources** which concerns the amount of money the cus-tomer has available or is willing to spend.

Customers must understand that it is not possible to prioritize all three elements simultaneously; trade-offs are necessary. As a rule of thumb, they can focus on only two of these elements at any given time. When you are helping the customer make a buying decision, they must decide which two factors are most important to them. Do they prioritize the level of outcome/quality and time, even if it means paying a higher price? Or do they prioritize price and time, sacrificing some level of outcome to stay within budget? Ultimately, their decision depends on the desired outcome. Discussing these trade-offs naturally minimizes potential price objections later on.

Leading With Language

Once the customer believes they can achieve their desired outcome, pos-sibly with your help, the *Future Memory* creates a strong attraction. When a person mentally commits to the outcome, letting go becomes challenging.

The *Compulsion* has been created. In the customer's mind, they have already committed to achieving the outcome, making the idea of remaining in their current situation difficult. This consistency of thought and behavior exemplifies the cognitive inertia we discussed in Chapter 5. Once we start thinking in a certain direction, it requires significant effort to change our thought process.

One way to reinforce cognitive inertia in this case is by regularly backtracking on what the customer has articulated. Backtracking involves summarizing what has been said and agreed upon, while matching the other person's words, phrases, and even non-verbal cues and vocal tones. It ensures the listener's understanding matches what was communicated and intended by the speaker. Backtracking naturally creates a *Yes Set* and is an effective method for maintaining and deepening rapport.

In addition to asking questions and backtracking, introducing ideas and examples into the conversation can be beneficial. While backtracking repeats what the customer has expressed using their manner of speech and presumptive language, introducing new ideas offers fresh perspectives. Logical chaining of ideas, using structures like

"If... then"

or

"Because of x...this"

introduces new viewpoints for the customer to consider. This technique, known as causal linking, uses presumptive language to connect one point explicitly to another. By linking a new idea to something the customer has specifically mentioned, you engage in "if...then" causal linking, a form of cognitive priming that eases the customer into discussing specific topics comfortably.

Give-and-Take Conversations

As a *Trusted Advisor*, you help customers achieve what they want. You can begin to guide customers towards their desired outcome even while asking questions. The *Satisfaction Cycle* offers a framework for engaging customers' minds, enabling them to make decisions effortlessly.

The crucial point is that the conversation is conducted for the customer's benefit - not yours. As the *Trusted Advisor* your approach is not merely inquisitive but involves conversational elicitation. This type of dialogue isn't about bombarding the customer with questions; it also involves providing valuable information in return. It's based on the principle of give-and-take, where both parties exchange valuable insights.

One way a salesperson can add value to the conversation is by discussing examples of relevant, similar cases. Especially during the *Process* phase, sharing your experiences and how you've helped similar customers can introduce resources to bridge the gap.

Check That You Know All You Need to Know!

During the PS^+, DS^{++}, and *Process* phases, you've listened to and gathered information about your customer's desires. Through collaborative conversations, you've identified their *Outcome Criteria* and *Operating Criteria*, as well as their priorities. To ensure that you've collected all necessary information, it may be beneficial to ask the customer if there's anything else they believe you should know:

"What is it that I haven't asked you that I need to know?"

"What needs to be in place that we haven't discussed yet?"

Once you are confident that all of the customer's *Outcome Criteria* and *Operating Criteria* have been identified, you can proceed to the *Commitment* stage and begin to design a *Solution Experience*.

Mutually Rewarding Outcome or Walk-Away

Before moving on to providing the *Solution Experience,* take a final moment to assess if you can genuinely help the customer achieve their desired outcome. *Satisfaction Selling* emphasizes ethical selling, ensuring a transaction is beneficial for both the customer and the seller. Ethical sales focus on establishing mutually beneficial outcomes. It becomes unethical if either party must make overly significant compromises. It would be considered unethical to proceed in the sales process unless a solution exists that benefits the salesperson, their company, and the customer. Even if you clearly understand the customer's *Criteria* and how they want it, and they trust you enough to buy from you, if your offer does not fully meet their *Criteria*, you need to step back.

You might identify a mismatch early on, during the PS^+ step, by realizing there is no fit between the customer and your company, or that your solution cannot outperform their existing one. Understanding the customer's DS^{++}, a salesperson will know whether their solution can effectively bridge from PS^+ to DS^{++}. If the solution falls short of achieving the customer's goals, there is no justification to continue. This mismatch may also become evident during the *Process* step if the customer's delivery expectations cannot be met. In situations where continuing would be unethical, it is right for you to respectfully withdraw, suggesting:

"You know, I don't really have the right solution for you. It might not be the best fit for your needs. Perhaps in future projects, but not this one. Maybe you should consider talking to XYZ instead of us."

Conversely, if a strong alignment between the customer's needs and your capabilities becomes apparent, indicating a mutually rewarding outcome is possible, then it's time to proceed with providing the *Solution Experience* and taking *Action*.

Compulsion (Process)

This stage collects "How" information, detailing the customer's vision for bridging the gap between PS+ and DS++.

Understanding the Process

"What is the primary difference between what you have now and what you want?"

"What specific steps or actions would have to happen for you to achieve the DS++?"

- Encourage the customer to articulate their preferred steps and actions, focusing on collecting detailed Process information

Encourage the customer to envision their DS++ as if it has already been achieved, using this future perspective to identify necessary steps back to the present PS+.

Pull from the Future

"How did the transition from your current state to achieving your DS++ occur?"

- Maintain a future-focused dialogue that helps the customer to think retrospectively about the steps for achieving DS++

The Process step is about understanding the customer's view on moving from PS+ to DS++, focusing what needs to happen. Considering resources like time, finances, skills, and knowledge.

Bridging the Gap

"What would have to happen for you to achieve the DS++?"

"What resources are available to you?"

"What areas do you need assistance with?"

- Uncover any gaps and the necessary resources to bridge them, ensuring your solution aligns with both the "What" and the "How" of the customer's aspirations

These criteria include the overall approach, main process steps, anticipated timeline, budget, and resource expectations.

Operating Criteria

"What kind of budget do you have in mind?"

"What is your timeframe?"

"What resources are available to you?"

"What is more important for you: X or Y?"

- Collect and prioritize Operating Criteria based on the customer's specific situation. Get information about budget, timeline, resources, and preferences

Identifying both existing and additional resources needed to implement the solution is key. Understanding the customer's budget, time constraints, skillset, knowledge for achieving DS++.

Resources to Bridge the Gap

"Who needs to be involved in the decision-making?"

"Does the customer have people with the required knowledge and skills?"

"What does the customer need?"

"What do they currently have?"

"How can they acquire what they lack?"

- Understand resources required for bridging the gap from PS+ to DS++
- Pay attention to budgetary considerations, timelines, and the availability of personnel

Assisting the customer in making informed decisions about their DS++ and the desired Process involves ensuring they are ready to invest in the necessary steps.

Building Commitment

"Are you prepared to take the necessary steps and invest appropriately to reach your DS++?"

- Discuss necessary trade-offs to prioritize & addressing potential price objections and aligning expectations with the desired outcome

If a mutually rewarding outcome is possible, proceed with designing the Solution Experience.

Mutually Rewarding Outcome

"Is a mutually rewarding outcome achievable with the information and resources discussed?"

- Ethically evaluate whether your solution aligns with the customer's needs and capabilities

Figure 14.1 Summary - Compulsion (Process)

15

COMMITMENT

Moving the Customer to Saying: "Yes"

N ow that you have progressed through the PS^+, DS^{++}, and *Process steps*, you've collected all the essential information, including the *Outcome Criteria*, the *Operating Criteria*, and the customer's decision-making strategy, to formulate and deliver a successful *Solution Experience*. As discussed in Chapter 8, this phase in *Satisfaction Selling* is known as the *Commitment* stage, as its primary aim is to secure the customer's *Commitment* to the solution with a definitive "yes."

By building on the customer's sense of satisfaction, you design the *Solution Experience* to further enhance their positive perception. Begin by reiterating what they have identified as already working well for them (PS^+). From there, swiftly move to describing their desired outcome (DS^{++}). Additionally, reaffirm the essential components of their *Operating Criteria*.

This process serves two crucial purposes. First, it reinforces how effectively you have listened and gathered relevant information, demonstrating your attentiveness to what is important to them. Second, it provides an opportunity to clarify any potential oversights. When delivering your presentation, address any new information to ensure alignment with the customer.

The final step in presenting the *Solution Experience* is to guide the customer through the journey they have undertaken with you, step-by-step, to achieve their DS^{++}. To facilitate this process, consider starting from DS^{++} and presenting the main events in reverse order until reaching the pivotal initial step. Instead of delving into the specifics of how the process will unfold, focus on communicating what you will do for them and the results it will yield.

At this stage, your goal is to lead the customer to a point where they have only one decision to make: a *Commitment* to take *Action* and implement the *Solution Experience* you have presented. This decision should be relatively straightforward if you have executed the process correctly. Taking *Action* propels the customer to realize their DS^{++} in a way that aligns with their *Criteria*. At this point, you have essentially made a sale in principle. While negotiations on terms and conditions may still be required, the customer has already made the actual purchase decision.

Solution Experience vs. Solution

Decision-making, particularly in commercial settings, intertwines emotion with logic, a dynamic central to the *Commitment* stage in *Satisfaction Selling*. Here, the *Solution Experience* unfolds not just as a presentation of rational benefits but as a deep, emotionally engaging journey. This journey artfully guides customers from their current reality to a vividly imagined future where their goals are realized, leveraging both their *Outcome Criteria* and *Operating Criteria*.

While traditional solutions focus on addressing immediate needs or problems, emphasizing tangible benefits, the *Solution Experience* enriches this approach by immersing the customer in a narrative that spans time - hence the term "Experience". This narrative doesn't simply outline the steps towards achieving desired outcomes; it updates the customer's *Future Memory*, creating a vivid experience of the future they want to have achieved, including now how you have helped them get there. This memory includes your supportive role, painting a picture of success that feels both attainable and inevitable.

The power of the *Solution Experience* lies in its ability to merge the customer's specific criteria into a singular, impactful experience. It transforms abstract goals into a tangible, emotionally resonant reality that the customer not only envisions but feels deeply. This is achieved through a careful orchestration of dialogue, where every resource and strategy introduced is tailored to reinforce the customer's path to success. When executed correctly, the *Solution Experience* feels natural and effortless for the customer, creating an emotional connection with the process. Therefore, we call it a *Solution Experience* rather than just a solution.

What Do You Know by Now?

Before designing and presenting the Solution Experience, it's crucial to review your understanding of the customer's *Outcome Criteria* and *Operating Criteria* and how you can fulfill them.

To deeply understand a customer's *Criteria*, prioritize the most critical factors and assess their relative importance. This process, called rank-scale ordering, uncovers the customer's priorities by evaluating *Criteria* on a scale of importance. For instance, in financial product assessments, the weight given to risk versus return depends on the customer's financial objectives. Understanding these priorities lays the groundwork for customizing your offering effectively.

In the initial *Satisfaction Selling* stages, you'll delve into the customer's thought patterns, discerning their preferred *Representational Systems* (VAKOG), Metaprograms and decision-making strategies, collectively referred to as their *Evidence Strategy*, as discussed in Chapter 8. This comprehensive insight enables you to devise a *Solution Experience* that resonates with the customer's desires and emotional considerations.

Mapping the *Solution Experience* isn't prescriptive; approaches vary from note-taking to elaborate PowerPoint presentations. The key is crafting an experience that embodies the customer's aspirations and emotional landscape. Tailoring the *Solution Experience* to align with the customer's *Criteria* and their unique *Evidence Strategy* facilitates clarity and accelerates decision-making.

The most important thing to remember is that you're not just providing a solution; you're creating a *Solution Experience* that includes all the customer's desires and emotional aspects.

When delivering the *Solution Experience* to obtain continuous agreement from the customer, you must adjust your way of communicating. The better you can design the *Solution Experience* that not only meets the customer's criteria but also matches their *Evidence Strategy* and way of thinking, the easier it is for the customer to understand what you are presenting and make a decision quickly.

Case: Wealth Management - Continued

As an example of how to deliver the *Solution Experience,* let's consider the next stage in the sales encounter between Anna, the wealth management advisor from the private banking company, and Jens, the high-net-worth client considering an investment for retirement that we introduced in the previous chapter.

Anna: *"Hi Jens, thank you for taking the time to meet again. I've gathered all the information from our previous discussions and would like to present a tailored investment plan that aligns with your goals and preferences."*

Jens: *"Great, I'm eager to hear it."*

Anna: *"To start, let's recap what we've discussed. You currently have a solid foundation with your pension plan, which has served you well, providing a stable and predictable retirement income. You're looking to enhance this by investing 5,000,000 DKK in a way that guarantees safety and a minimum return of 3.5%. Correct?"*

Jens: *"Yes, that's right."*

Anna: *"You also mentioned your experience with your pension plan, noting its reliability and the peace of mind it gives you. Given your desire to protect your principal while ensuring steady returns, we've designed a plan that builds on these positives. Does that still sound good?"*

Jens: *"Absolutely, peace of mind is paramount for me."*

Anna: *"Great. Now, let's look forward. You shared that you envision a future where your retirement is not just secure, but abundant enough to enjoy extended time with your family and pursue your passion for travel. You want to be able to visit new places without financial worries and spend quality time with your grandchildren. How does that sound?"*

Jens: *"That's exactly what I'm hoping for. Financial freedom to enjoy life without constraints."*

Anna: *"To achieve this, we've structured an investment plan that meets your criteria. We'll invest your 5,000,000 DKK in a combination of blue-chip equity stocks and bonds. This mix ensures that your principal remains safe while achieving the desired return. The equity stocks provide steady growth, while the bonds add a layer of security and fixed income. You'll be able to count on this investment just as you have with your pension plan."*

Jens: *"That sounds like a good balance."*

Anna: *"For the first increment, we'll allocate 2,500,000 DKK, investing in high-quality blue-chip stocks and government bonds. This initial setup will immediately start generating returns, giving us a solid foundation. Three months later, we'll invest the remaining 2,500,000 DKK in a similar mix, optimizing the portfolio based on market conditions at that time."*

Jens: *"I appreciate the thoughtful approach."*

Anna: *"As for withdrawals, you mentioned wanting to supplement your pension with this investment. We'll structure them to begin after a minimum of 10 years, allowing your investment to grow substantially. You prefer annual withdrawals, so we'll arrange for these to be processed in a tax-efficient manner, minimizing your tax liability. You'll have the financial flexibility to support your lifestyle and pursue your passions without worry."*

Jens: *"That's perfect. I want to make sure I'm getting the most out of my investment without unnecessary tax burdens."*

Anna: *"Absolutely, Jens. With this plan, you'll have the peace of mind knowing your principal is secure and your returns are optimized. Imagine this plan as a well-tended garden. Right now, you have a beautiful, sturdy oak tree with your pension. Our investment plan will be like planting a variety of flowers around it—each contributing to the beauty and abundance of your garden. In 10 years, you'll be able to pick the flowers, enjoying their beauty and fragrance, just like you'll enjoy the returns from your investment. How does that future look to you?"*

Jens: *"It looks very promising and secure. I feel excited and relieved at the thought of having such a solid plan in place."*

Anna: *"Wonderful. This is precisely the future we aim to create for you. Let's finalize the details and get everything in place. We'll start with the first transfer and set up our communication schedule. I'm excited to help you achieve your retirement goals."*

Jens: *"Thank you, Anna. I appreciate your thoroughness and dedication. Let's move forward with this plan."*

In this dialogue, Anna effectively presents the *Solution Experience* by crafting a narrative that ties together Jens's current PS^+, DS^{++}, and preferred *Process*. She recaps Jens's goals and preferences, ensuring clarity and alignment. The proposed investment plan, which includes specific details about the allocation of funds, the time frame, and the withdrawal strategy, vividly illustrates how it meets Jens's needs and aspirations.

Anna integrates information from the PS^+ (Jens' satisfaction with his pension plan), the DS^{++} (Jens' vision of a financially secure and enjoyable retirement), and the *Process* (investment increments, communication preferences, and withdrawal strategy) to create a compelling story. The analogy of a well-tended garden emphasizes the value of making the *Commitment* to take *Action,* illustrating how the investment plan will enhance and beautify Jens's financial future.

This narrative not only clarifies the logistics of the investment but also strengthens Jens' confidence and motivation to proceed, setting the stage for the final step in the Satisfaction Cycle: *Action!* By doing so, Anna creates a strong emotional connection and builds Jens's confidence and motivation to proceed, leading to his commitment to the plan.

Evidence Strategy

As discussed previously, the *Evidence Strategy* comprises two components: *Evidence Criteria* and *Evidence Procedure*, each critical for understanding the customer's decision-making process. While *Evidence Criteria* delineate the type of proof needed to assure the customer of your solution's efficacy, the *Evidence Procedure* involves the nuances of duration, frequency, and intensity of evidence presentation. Recognizing these subtleties allows for a tailored approach, enhancing the likelihood of a successful sale.

During your conversation with the customer, it's important to ask enough questions to gain a clear understanding of the aspects of the *Evidence Strategy*. One effective method of eliciting the customer's *Evidence Strategy* is by listening to how they have made similar decisions in the past, which could be done already in the *Curiosity* phase (See also Chapter 12). Relying on just one example of how they have made decisions may not provide enough information to understand their decision-making process fully. Ideally, it would be best to ask for multiple instances, preferably about similar cases you are discussing with the customer. For example, you might ask,

"Have you ever made a decision like this before?"

"If so, how did you decide to choose that specific supplier?"

"Why did you choose them, and with whom did you decide?"

By asking these types of questions, you can listen carefully both to what they say and how they say it to understand their buying strategy and decision-making process more thoroughly.

Evidence Criteria

The first part of the *Evidence Strategy* is the *Evidence Criteria*. It refers to the specific type of evidence that is most meaningful to the person making the decision. The *Evidence Criteria* specify what evidence the customer needs to have delivered to be convinced that your solution will meet their *Outcome* and *Operating Criteria*.

Two main categories define how the customer prefers things to be presented: social proof and information-rich data:

Social proof

Social proof is a testimonial or reference from someone else who can substantiate your claims or verify the information you provide. It is about whom the customer needs to get the information and the evidence from to believe it. To identify if the customer is looking for social proof, you can ask about their decision-making process and see if they rely on external references or use their internal judgment. If they value social proof, you can provide examples of how your solution has helped other similar companies and the outcomes they achieved. For instance, you can say,

"We have partnered with hundreds of companies that encountered similar challenges. Take Mark's team at ABC, for example. They were grappling with the same issue you are now; we guided them through a tailored solution

that not only resolved their problem but also led to significant improvements, exemplified by their remarkable outcomes."

Information-rich data

Information-rich data can be either historically or scientifically verifiable evidence, e.g., case studies or reports. An example of this kind of evidence might be a case study that demonstrates, with historical evidence, the point being made. The level of detail required for this kind of evidence can vary from person to person. Also, where they get the evidence determines how credible the information is for them. It is important to understand the customer's preference and provide information-rich data that meets their criteria for evidence. An effective way to present this kind of evidence is by using charts, graphs, and statistics to support the claims being made.

Evidence Procedure

The other aspect of the *Evidence Strategy* is the *Evidence Procedure*, which comprises three essential components: duration, frequency, and intensity:

Duration

Duration refers to the amount of time the evidence needs to be present for an individual to accept it. For some people, the evidence becomes true for them the moment they encounter it, while for others, it may take years of having the evidence present before they accept it. For example, the duration of time a person would require before deciding to marry someone can vary greatly. Some may say they knew they wanted to get married from the moment they first saw their partner, while others may have dated for eight years before deciding to get married. The duration, i.e., how long you need to present evidence before the customer accepts it, can vary significantly from person to person.

Frequency

Frequency refers to how many times the evidence needs to be presented before it is considered convincing. For some people, one exposure to the evidence is enough to believe it entirely. Others might require repeated exposure before accepting the evidence as valid. In the example of how someone decided to get married, one person might say,

"I was immediately attracted to him/her, and we got together every day during the first week after we met. I knew right away after that, that I wanted to marry him/her."

This is an example of a person requiring a high frequency of exposure to the evidence (i.e., spending a lot of time together repeatedly with the other person in a short period).

Intensity

Intensity refers to the level of emphasis or force that is required before the presented evidence is considered valid. For some people, hearing something once from someone may be sufficient for them to believe it. For others, a more intense or dramatic presentation of evidence may be required for them to believe it truly. For example, a simple

"I love you."

may be enough for someone to trust that their partner truly loves them. But for another person, a grand romantic gesture such as a public proposal may be necessary for them to believe that their partner truly loves them.

Each component has a minimum threshold that must be reached before a particular individual accepts the evidence. Only after the threshold is reached can the person decide and be sure that your solution meets their *Outcome Criteria* and *Operating Criteria*.

For example, if a customer requires high-intensity evidence, they may need to see the solution in action or receive a detailed demo multiple times before making a decision. On the other hand, if the customer requires low-intensity evidence, they may be satisfied with a brief overview of the solution. Similarly, some customers may need to see the evidence presented frequently over a short duration, while others may require evidence presented over a more extended period. Understanding these thresholds is crucial in presenting evidence that will satisfy the customer's needs and ultimately lead to a successful sale.

Identify the Ultimate Decision-Maker!

Throughout the selling process, you'll notice and identify who in the *Buying Center* is making the purchase decision. Often, multiple people are involved. For example, you may need approval from someone in charge of financial decisions regarding funding, while another individual decides whether to proceed with the project. Additionally, someone else might handle the timing and logistics.

This complexity raises the question of how to manage the *Solution Experience* when many stakeholders influence the purchase process. As such, you may have to satisfy multiple criteria for several people, but ultimately, one person will be responsible for making the ultimate purchase decision. The power in any situation always rests with a particular individual. While many stakeholders may be involved, the idea that there would be several decision-makers is an illusion. The actual decision-maker may consider the recommendations from others, so it is essential to work with the entire team and ensure that everyone is on board with the process.

While it's important to have the whole *Buying Center* aligned with your proposal, it's not necessary to meet every individual's specific needs. Doing so could be overwhelming and counterproductive. Instead, focus on identifying who holds the ultimate decision-making power, which isn't always the person with the highest title. Achieving this requires the ability to observe non-verbal and subtle cues among the group, as these signals indicate where the real power resides in the room.

Structure of Solution Experience

As you prepare to present the *Solution Experience* to your customer, remember you've already helped them form a positive expectation of their future success through eliciting PS^+, DS^{++}, and *Process*. The core concept of delivering the designed *Solution Experience* is to build on this positive outlook. Your primary goal is to review the information shared by the customer and then guide them through a retrospective journey, illustrating how their engagement with you led to achieving their desired outcome. Essentially, the *Solution Experience* conversation narrates how your offering seamlessly integrates into their journey towards success.

A basic *Solution Experience* involves the following steps:

1. Establish Rapport and Positive Context

Establish the positive frame and put people back in their context. Start with *Yes Set* and backtracking what the customer has shared with you. This approach will be well-received because it's based solely on what the customer has said. You'll have a powerful communication position because the customer will naturally agree with what you are saying. Begin by repeating what the customer said is already working for them in PS^+.

2. Create a *Future Memory* of their DS^{++}

Once you have established this positive foundation, provide the experience of their *Future Memory* so that it becomes evident that your solution played a vital role in delivering what they truly want. Utilize sensory-based language containing all senses (VAKOG) and speak about the future point of time in the present tense.

3. Guide the customer through the Process historically

The next step to complete the *Solution Experience* is to guide the customer through the *Process* of how they arrived at their DS^{++} from PS^+. Explain the main steps and the resources you brought to the Process from the future perspective by using the past tense. You can either start by explaining the journey from DS^{++} and work backward to their PS^+ to show how you assisted the customer. Alternatively, you can begin from PS^+ and methodically demonstrate how you provided resources and helped the customer reach their DS^{++}.

4. Bring the customer back from the future to the present

First, you check if they want and expect to get this outcome with you. After you have confirmed with the customer that they believe that with your solution, they will have achieved their DS^{++}, it is time to bring the customer back to the present. To test their compliance, invite the customer to take a first step towards realizing their desired outcome. The first step should be something that the customer perceives as a low risk so that it is easy to make a quick decision and get moving.

Build the Continuous Yes Responses!

In the *Solution Experience*, the goal is to maintain positive momentum while providing the customer with an experience of success, which includes your proposal. Although the specific approach may differ, the underlying principle remains the same: building momentum through a series of positive responses. The customer must continue to mentally agree with the proposed ideas, leading to a final affirmative answer to whether they want to work with you. By eliciting a series of "yes" responses, you can confirm that you have correctly understood the customer's perspective and identified what is most important to them. Ultimately, your aim is to keep the positive momentum until you reach a mutually beneficial agreement.

One effective way to elicit a clear "yes" response is by using backtracking to recap the information the customer has already provided. You are creating the world's easiest *Yes Set* by repeating what the customer has said about their PS^+ and DS^{++}. This technique offers two main benefits: firstly, it encourages customers to continue saying "yes" because they can only agree with things they have already stated. Secondly, it allows you to verify that you have accurately understood the customer's wants and needs. This step is crucial because if you haven't, your *Solution Experience* may not be as effective. At this point, there is still the opportunity to adapt and gather any missing information.

What If...

Backtracking confirms what we know about the customer's desires. A significant uncertainty is their response to your offer, given it's their first time hearing it. As we transition from known to unknown elements, we pave the way for their decision to collaborate with us. This journey involves continuously building towards affirmative responses. It's uncertain how the customer will react to new proposals, despite potential anticipation of a "yes".

To proceed, we introduce suggestions and pose "what if" questions, focusing on areas likely to elicit a "yes". These questions should relate to the customer's acknowledged truths or points they've previously mentioned. By framing your suggestions around what has been previously discussed, you enhance the likelihood of receiving a "yes" to your new proposal. This method creates a chain of logical connections. For instance:

"During our earlier discussion about achieving your desired outcome, you mentioned a specific budget."

"What if we allocated that budget differently?"

"What if we spread that amount over a specific period?"

At this juncture, you should have a clearer picture of assisting the customer in achieving their DS^{++}. Through building a series of affirmative responses, you guide the customer towards realizing their goals with your assistance. Starting from areas where you're most confident in the customer's agreement, you gradually work towards the ultimate decision.

Clarify the Scope!

As a *Trusted Advisor* your role is to guide the customer towards approaches that are feasible for achieving their goals and aligned with their best interests, rather than agreeing to their requests without consideration of feasibility or cost. At this stage, you understand what the customer is willing to accept. Your next step is to clarify where their desires might not be realistically met as envisioned and assist them in exploring alternatives or areas for compromise, while transparently communicating any limitations.

There will inevitably be areas where customer expectations cannot be met as desired, possibly due to budget constraints, timeframe, or the scale of the desired outcome. It's your responsibility to help the customer understand what is realistically achievable. For instance, achieving a major goal within six months might be unfeasible with their current budget. In such cases, discuss what compromises they're willing to make. Could they allocate more resources or extend their timeframe? Offering alternative strategies that still aim to achieve their goals, albeit differently, is crucial.

While ambitious goals are commendable, a balance of realism is essential. Managing customer expectations to align with what is feasible is part of your job. Always propose alternatives where direct desires cannot be met. For example, if a customer wishes for a new IT system installation and complete training within six months - a timeline you know to be unattainable - you might suggest,

"Unfortunately, installing the system and completing a full training program within six months isn't feasible. However, we could focus on training power users first and then roll out broader training over 18 months. Alternatively, we could offer a condensed online training for all users initially."

Starting with acknowledgment of the customer's request and then presenting alternatives helps in maintaining a positive momentum. It shows that you are actively working towards finding solutions. For instance, mentioning that training can be delivered in multiple languages demonstrates your commitment to meeting the customer's needs as closely as possible. This approach not only manages expectations but also keeps the dialogue focused on achievable outcomes, ensuring the customer feels supported throughout the process.

Future Pacing to Create *Future Memory*

Future pacing is a critical element to the *Satisfaction Cycle* in providing an effective *Solution Experience*. As discussed in Chapter 6, in the *Satisfaction Cycle* terminology, we are creating a *Future Memory* that captures the experience of having reached the desired outcome, which occurs after obtaining their DS^{++}. This point in time represents the customer's *Outcome of the Outcome* and allows them to fully experience the value of reaching their DS^{++}.

Future pacing operates by discussing a forthcoming event as if it's occurring in the present. Employing the present tense to depict the future allows customers to vividly conceptualize and emotionally connect with their goals. This method constructs a cognitive memory of an event yet to happen, fostering nostalgia and emotional attachment to the objective. Such a deep emotional bond encourages customers to act toward making their *Future Memory* a reality, underscoring the significance of future pacing.

Nonetheless, it's essential to exercise caution in the *Future Memories* you create. Ensuring the promises made align with your tangible offers and capabilities is critical; failure to do so risks undermining the trust and rapport established with your customers. The *Solution Experience* you propose must be realistic, benefiting both parties in a mutually rewarding outcome. This alignment between expectations and deliverables is crucial for maintaining the integrity and trustworthiness of the sales process otherwise you will not end up with at *Positive Activist*.

Bringing the Resources to the *Preferred Path*

After constructing the *Future Memory* and unifying the *Outcome Criteria* and *Operating Criteria* into a cohesive hierarchy, the *Preferred Path* becomes clear. This path not only connects the *Outcome Criteria* with the *Operating Criteria* but also delineates the customer's envisioned route towards their objective. At this juncture, you are positioned to shape your presentation, outlining how you intend to assist the customer in navigating their *Process* and *Preferred Path*. This is your opportunity to detail your role in their journey and the specific actions you'll undertake to facilitate their success.

Your role is to assist in the customer's journey from PS^+ to DS^{++}, supporting their *Process*. In gathering information about the customer's *Criteria*, timeline, budget, limitations, and available resources—including material needs and human capital—you've gained insights into how you can integrate into their process and help them achieve their goals.

You can now introduce the resources discussed earlier - such as people, materials, knowledge, skills, processes, and experience - and describe how these will be utilized to support the customer. Integrating these resources within the context of the *Preferred Path* makes the *Process* seem more natural and aligned for the customer, as though everything is falling into place.

By incorporating your solution into the customer's *Process,* you guide them through the necessary steps to reach their desired outcome. Explaining the process step-by-step clarifies what will occur once they engage with you. Phrases like,

"First, we'll tackle this, then we'll move on to that..."

help the customer visualize the journey to DS^{++}. Alternatively, you might start from DS^{++} and work backwards, detailing each step in reverse until reaching the present. There's no need to delve into the minutiae of execution; instead, focus on the actions you'll take and the results the customer can expect.

As customers begin to grasp the benefits of your solution, they connect more deeply with their desired outcome and its positive impact. They gain a deeper understanding of how your solution can help them achieve their goals. However, it's important to remember that this experience is not yet a reality. Once the customer has fully experienced your solution, you must guide them back to the present. While the customer may still long for their desired outcome, they need to take action in the present to make it a reality. By guiding customers back to the present and encouraging them to take action, you empower them to transform their dreams into tangible achievements.

Conversational Narrative

The *Solution Experience* approach for presenting your offer represents a paradigm shift in the world of sales. We are introducing an entirely new method that leverages our understanding of brain function and guides customers on a journey towards their desired outcome. Forget the boring and outdated PowerPoint presentations. Truly connecting with your customers requires flexibility and creativity.

The *Solution Experience* should unfold through a dynamic conversation rather than a static, one-way presentation. Although there's no set formula, the sales professional's role is to steer the discussion, ensuring the entire *Solution Experience* is explored. The ultimate aim is for the customer to enthusiastically agree to work with you. Employing a conversational narrative that incorporates *Time Sliding*, as discussed in Chapter 6, is a powerful means to achieve this goal.

Our unique human ability to perceive time means we are always grounded in the present, experiencing life as it unfolds, yet capable of mentally projecting ourselves into the future or into imaginary realms. We live through stories, whether reading a book or watching a movie, feeling the emotions in our bodies as though the events were genuinely happening to us.

This capacity for narrative is not just entertaining but profoundly impactful, allowing us to reframe our understanding of time within the sales context. By weaving narratives, we can position the customer's future success as a current experience, compelling them to move towards it. Narratives also enable us to reinterpret past events to support the desired present and future outcomes, emphasizing time as a critical element in the *Satisfaction Cycle*.

For a more advanced conversational narrative structure, you can consider using the following sequence to guide the person through the *Solution Experience:*

- Past - Future

- Future - Present

- Present - Past

- Past - Present

- Present - Future

- Future - Past

- Past - Future

Guiding the customer through the conversation in this manner will begin to feel natural, and it will seem as though all the time points are becoming one. However, starting with this complex approach isn't necessary. You can choose whatever order you prefer, as long as you start from the present and move towards the future. This is how you build a trajectory for success.

We provided a simple example of this sequence in Chapter 6. To make it more accessible for you as a reader, we have included another example below to illustrate how it looks when you work with these different tenses in your language. We hope this will give you a better understanding of the power of this method and provide additional clarification.

To move someone through time, we must always be clear about where we are beginning in terms of the time sense, i.e., past, present, or future, in relation to where either the customer has placed themselves in the conversation or where you want to position the conversation as the starting point.

The key is tracking the verb tenses being used, as discussed in Chapter 6. Most of them are obvious, such as references to the verb ¨to be¨ in the past tense, e.g.:

¨I was/he was/she was/we were/they were”

all reference the past. The same is true of the verb "to be" in the present tense, i.e., am/are, regardless of the pronoun reference, e.g., "it is" when referring to an object like a chair or computer. This establishes the starting point in the temporal landscape that allows movement to happen by tracking shifts in the verb tenses being used.

To illustrate how shifting temporal references can guide a conversation, consider the following dialogue between Sarah and John:

Sarah: *"I was really interested in mathematics in school before I got into computers and programming."*

The linguistic time markers here ¨was,¨ ¨before,¨ and ¨got¨ are all references to a past event.

Moving Sarah forward in time is easiest beginning from where she begins in time, i.e.: her past.

John: *"Sarah, when you first got involved in computers it was your interest in mathematics that led you there. Today, do you still have that kind of interest or fascination with math?"*

The change in language from the verbs ¨was¨ and ¨led¨ to the time reference ¨today¨ and the verb ¨have¨ move the moment in the conversation from the past to the present. Keeping the contextual reference constant, i.e., the interest in mathematics, makes it easier for Sarah to move mentally to a new point in the temporal landscape. Making the movement only about time minimizes the cognitive load versus asking a customer to make a shift in topic and time simultaneously.

John could also have gone even further in his opening reply by saying:

"Sarah, when you first got involved in computers it was your interest in mathematics that led you there. Today, you want to build a strong team of programmers. How can we help you do that?"

In this example he would be asking Sarah to simultaneously shift

1. The time from the past (¨got,¨ ¨was,¨ and ¨led¨) to the present (¨today¨ and ¨want¨) and then to the future (¨build¨ and ¨help¨ implied in the future, as these haven't happened yet),

2. The context (mathematics to programmers), and

3. The outcome ("how can we help")

However, this kind of cognitive processing is more demanding and has the potential to redirect or even shut down dialogue. Thus, using simple temporal shifts like in the first example from the past to the present keeping the contextual reference consistent then allow you to make the second level shift in context in the time frame that's intended. I.e. back to the conversation between John and Sarah:

Sarah: *"No, today my interest is really in developing excellent clean programming, using math to help that happen."*

John: *"Thanks, that helps me understand a bit better. Do you think that with our help you can build the team you want around you?"*

Here, John is using a temporal form that keeps the conversation in the present tense ("understand," "think," "can") while talking about an event that will happen in the future. This effectively forces Sarah to project the intended event as though it's already happened, i.e., building the programming team, and mentally positioning the intended event in the present. This is a very powerful and subtle way to create a *Future Memory*.

As discussed in Chapter 6, *Satisfaction Selling* uses the idea of *Future Memory* to create powerful motivation and drivers to take action in the direction of the intended outcome. The next step is therefore to place the intended outcome in the past.

Sarah: *"Yes, I think that with you helping us to identify and recruit the talent we need, would make a big difference to us. Maybe our first step could be to build a specific profile and avatar of our ideal candidate."*

John: *"I think that's a great idea too, and we can then review the candidates we get based on how well they match our profile."*

This is a very gentle way to position the intended outcome in the past, i.e.: if there is a profile that's been developed and that they are reviewing then by default it means Sarah and John are working together. In this way the future intended outcome, for Sarah to engage John and his company to assist them in recruiting programmer candidates, has been positioned in the past, as a memory. Extending this further into the future makes the memory more indelible.

Sarah: *"That sounds great John, like it's the approach I want to use."*

Sarah is now in a present where she has mentally hired John and his company to assist her.

John: *"Sarah I'd like to recommend something else, and we'll include it in our services for the same fee. Let's do a second review of the candidates you select in, say, three months, after you've hired them, focusing on the best ones in your opinion, and update our profile and avatar based on real-world experience."*

Sarah: *"John that will be really helpful, thanks!"*

John: *"It's really powerful in our experience to work with the experience you're having to update the profile and avatar we originally built for you, so over time our results just keep getting more targeted and better."*

Here, John puts the future event in the present, i.e.; the programmers that are going to be hired as though they are and have been working for Sara already with the sentence:

"... the experience you're having ..."

and the work that will happen in the future to build a profile and avatar in the past with the sentence:

"...we originally built..."

and then creates a future of the future, i.e., the results that haven't happened yet with the sentence:

"...keep getting more targeted and better..."

This moves Sarah to a point in the future mentally where she can now consider how successful it "has been" to work with John and his company.

This is the ultimate effect of Time Sliding: creating futures that haven't happened yet as if they already have, thereby fostering a future condition of success in your customer's mind. This makes the mental decision the customer has to make about giving up what they now have a sense of already having.

Time Sliding and moving customers through the temporal landscape intentionally is one of the most powerful things that can happen in the sales process. It is especially useful in building the *Solution Experience*. The advantage of beginning with the *Solution Experience* is that it is the step in the *Satisfaction Selling* process where you can plan what you will share ahead of time. This is a perfect opportunity to practice working with time sliding and using verb tense to move customers in the temporal landscape.

The Ultimate YES

You're almost at the *Action* step in the *Satisfaction Cycle*. You've guided the customer through what's currently working for them, their aspirations - where they want to go - and how they can achieve them. By crafting a *Solution Experience,* you've illustrated what collaborating with you looks like and how it can lead the customer to their desired outcome.

Now, how do you recognize when the sale is made? Interestingly, it's not marked by receiving the purchase order. Rather, the deal is essentially sealed much earlier when both you and the customer express the ultimate "yes." For the customer, this pivotal moment arises when they are convinced that your proposal will effectively deliver their sought-after outcome.

At this critical juncture in *Satisfaction Selling*, your goal is to position the customer so they face a singular decision: a *Commitment* to taking *Action* and implementing the *Solution Experience* you've outlined. This decision should be straightforward, assuming the process has been meticulously followed. At the opportune moment, seek this decisive confirmation, the "yes." This definitive agreement is sought at the conclusion of the *Solution Experience,* shifting the query from:

"Do you want to buy what I have?"

to a more consultative approach:

"Does it make sense that if we implement the discussed solutions, you will achieve your desired outcome?"

"Do you believe that you can accomplish the goals we outlined?"

These inquiries pave the way to securing the ultimate "yes," and when everything has gone well, you will get the answer.

"Well... YES!"

At this point, it's essential to pause and allow the customer to lead the conversation. This approach may challenge many salespeople but pausing after receiving the ultimate "yes" is crucial. The customer has just acknowledged their need for your assistance to achieve their DS^{++}. Now, you have the opportunity to let them elaborate on how you will collaborate to achieve this. This is your ultimate buying signal.

In *Satisfaction Selling*, our goal is for the customer to close the deal with their own "yes," rather than having the salesperson close the deal for them. This approach significantly reduces the risk of buyer's remorse, as the customer truly experiences making their own decision. The design of the *Solution Experience* ensures that objections are minimized, eliminating the need for extensive handling. We focus our time and energy on understanding the customer's wants and needs so we can present a solution that perfectly aligns with their desires.

Having essentially secured a sale in principle, the next and final stage in Satisfaction Selling awaits: *Compliance*. This stage is dedicated to mobilizing the customer towards actualizing their DS^{++} in alignment with their criteria. Though negotiations on terms and conditions may still be pending, the customer's decision to proceed signifies it's time for *Action*.

Commitment (Solution Experience)

The Commitment stage is about securing the customer's agreement to implement the proposed Solution Experience.

The Solution Experience transcends a typical solution by incorporating an emotionally engaging journey that helps the customer visualize achieving their goals.

The Evidence Strategy consists of Evidence Criteria and Evidence Procedure, detailing the type of proof the customer needs to assure the solution's efficacy.

Recognizing who in the Buying Center holds the ultimate decision-making power is crucial. Understanding who has the final say allows you to tailor your Solution Experience accordingly.

Presenting the Solution Experience involves a retrospective journey, illustrating step-by-step how the customer's engagement with you leads to achieving their DS++.

The goal is to maintain a positive momentum where the customer continuously agrees with the proposed ideas, leading to the final decision to work with you.

Guide the customer towards feasible approaches for achieving their goals. This involves clarifying where their desires might not be met and assisting them in exploring alternatives.

Future pacing creates a cognitive memory of an event yet to happen. This technique is used to construct a vivid experience of the future, encouraging customers to act towards making their Future Memory a reality.

After creating a compelling Solution Experience and eliciting the ultimate "yes," guide the customer back to the present and encourage them to take the first steps towards realizing their DS++.

Commitment Stage Overview

Solution Experience

Evidence Strategy
"Have you ever made a decision like this before?"
"How did you decide to choose that specific supplier?"
"Why did you choose them, and with whom did you decide?"

Identifying Decision-Maker
"Who needs to be involved in the decision-making?"
"Who is required for the implementation?"

Solution Experience Delivery

Building Continuous Yes Responses
"Does it make sense that if we implement the discussed solutions, you will achieve your desired outcome?"
"Do you believe that you can accomplish the goals we outlined?"

Clarifying the Scope

Future Pacing for Future Memory

Navigation to Action!

- Begin by reiterating what works well (PS+) and swiftly move to describe the desired outcome (DS++), reaffirming the Operating Criteria

- Craft a narrative that connects the customer's current situation with a vividly imagined future where their goals are realized

- Delve into the customer's past decision-making instances to uncover their Evidence Strategy
- Tailor the Solution Experience to satisfy the customer's Evidence Criteria

- Tailor the Solution Experience to satisfy the primary decision-maker's criteria while still considering the perspectives of other stakeholders

- Guide the customer through their journey to DS++, starting from the future perspective and presenting events in reverse order or vice versa

- Utilize backtracking to confirm the customer's perspective & identify what is most important to them, ensuring a natural progression towards a mutual agreement

- Manage customer expectations by discussing the feasibility of their desires and proposing alternative strategies where direct desires cannot be met

- Employ future pacing by discussing future events in the present tense, helping customers vividly conceptualize and emotionally connect with their goals

- Propose an initial, low-risk step to get a smooth transition from planning to doing, ensuring the customer feels confident in beginning their journey towards their DS++

Figure 15.1 Summary - Commitment (Solution Experience)

16

COMPLIANCE

Time for Action!

The next stage in *Satisfaction Selling* is called *Compliance* and involves the *Action* step in the *Satisfaction Cycle*. When you receive a "yes" from your customer, you have their *Commitment* that they desire the outcome your offering enables. They are ready to allocate a budget, resources, and whatever else is necessary to make it happen. What has now been agreed upon needs to be actualized to achieve the outcomes for both parties.

Commitment is about agreeing to do something, but it is not the same as executing what has been agreed upon. *Commitment* alone is not enough. The only thing that matters is that the customer follows through with what was agreed. This adherence to the agreement is called *Compliance*. The *Action* step in the *Satisfaction Cycle* is about taking *Action*, starting from the first step, and then moving on to the next, and so on.

In the *Action* step, the focus shifts to assembling the actual content of what you will deliver and what you won't. One of the initial steps is to negotiate the terms and conditions. You provide the price and your commercial terms and conditions. You also agree on time – when it is going to happen. Additionally, it becomes essential to establish a detailed execution plan that outlines specific *Actions* and their respective timelines. And then... just act!

Mutuality in Actions

In the *Action* stage, to build *Compliance*, it's time to backtrack again. This time, you want to go through all the details of how the customer will receive your solution. Along the way, you begin to request concrete actions - real and physical tasks the customer should undertake next. This could involve signing the contract, authorizing the payment, or any other relevant *Action*. You need to secure an *Action* commitment for the next step they practically have to take. This confirms the agreements you have now made and ensures you have *Compliance*.

While you allow the customer to take the first *Action*, there should also be mutuality in taking *Action*. You assign a specific *Action* to the customer, but you should accompany it with a step you will take in response to their *Action*. You communicate clearly that your *Action* depends on them completing their part first. This mutual dependency in *Actions* ensures that you have *Compliance*.

Getting into Details

In the *Compliance* stage, it's time to delve into the specifics of the agreement with your customer. At this juncture, it's essential to at least define the details of:

1. The agreed scope of what is included and what is not.

2. The actual price, along with commercial terms and conditions.

3. The timeline, outlining a specific execution plan detailing exactly what happens and when.

Maintaining some flexibility regarding pricing could prove beneficial. For instance, presenting the price within a typical range, rather than a fixed amount, allows room for adjustments should the customer decide to expand the scope by adding additional elements.

Case: Specialized Pet Diet Solutions

As an example of the *Compliance* stage, consider the sales encounter between Emma, a sales representative representing a professional pet food company and Dr. Andersen, a veterinarian considering ordering specialized pet diet food.

Emma: *"Hi Dr. Andersen, thank you for meeting with me today. I'm excited to continue our discussion about how we can enhance your practice."*

Dr. Andersen: *"Hi Emma, good to see you again. I'm looking forward to hearing more."*

Emma: *"Last time we spoke, you mentioned how important it is for you to have a reliable, single solution for treating common intestinal issues in dogs. You've been pleased with the consistency of our products and the positive outcomes you've seen with your patients. Is that right?"*

Dr. Andersen: *"Yes, that's correct. It's been very effective, and I appreciate not having to stock multiple products for different issues."*

Emma: *"Building on that success, you shared your vision of being able to confidently prescribe a single professional diet that addresses various stomach issues, from diarrhea to sensitivity caused by illness. This would simplify your processes and provide immediate relief to your patients, creating trust and satisfaction among pet owners. How does that align with your goals?"*

Dr. Andersen: *"That's spot on. I want to streamline my inventory and offer a product I know will work in multiple scenarios."*

Emma: *"Great. In terms of process, we discussed setting up an initial order of 12 cases of our basic intestinal diet dog food. This product is specifically designed to address the issues we've talked about, ensuring that you can confidently prescribe it to your patients. It's easy to store, and the bulk order will provide you with a steady supply to meet your needs without frequent reordering. Does this sound like a good plan?"*

Dr. Andersen: *"It does. I like the idea of having a consistent supply on hand."*

Emma: *"Now, imagine how this will benefit your practice. You'll be able to quickly alleviate common issues for your patients, leading to almost immediate positive effects. Pet owners will see the results and have increased confidence in your care, knowing that you have reliable solutions. Additionally, prescribing this food enhances your profit center, as it's an effective and trusted option. Just like having a dependable remedy that works across various conditions, this food simplifies your approach and builds client trust."*

Dr. Andersen: *"Yes, I can see that. It will definitely boost client satisfaction and trust in our services."*

Emma: *"Exactly. By taking this step, you're not only providing a valuable service to your patients but also strengthening the relationship with pet owners. They'll appreciate the quick resolution of their pets' issues, leading to increased loyalty and trust in your expertise."*

Dr. Andersen: *"Emma, this sounds like a perfect solution for our needs. How soon can we get an order delivered? I'd like to start with 12 cases of the basic intestinal diet dog food as we discussed."*

Emma: *"That's fantastic, Dr. Andersen! I can get the paperwork started immediately and confirm the delivery schedule for you. I'm confident this will be a great addition to your practice and look forward to hearing about the positive impact it has."*

Dr. Andersen: *"Thank you, Emma. I'm excited to see the results and continue our partnership with our organization."*

In this dialogue, Emma effectively transitions Dr. Andersen through the *Action* step by reinforcing the positive expectations established in the *Solution Experience* step. She begins by recalling the veterinarian's satisfaction with the current state (PS^+) and the envisioned future benefits (DS^{++}). Emma then recaps the process they discussed, including the specifics of the product and the logistics of the order.

Emma uses an analogy to emphasize the value of the *Commitment*, comparing the immediate relief provided by the food to a reliable and trusted remedy that simplifies Dr. Andersen's practice and builds client trust. This analogy strengthens the emotional appeal, making the benefits of the product tangible and compelling.

By maintaining the excitatory bias - the *Green State* - and connecting it to the *Action* needed - placing the order - Emma ensures that Dr. Andersen is ready to commit. The dialogue concludes on a positive high note, reinforcing the veterinarian's decision and setting the stage for a continued positive relationship. This step effectively closes the loop of the *Satisfaction Cycle*, turning the desired state (DS^{++}) into the present state (PS^+) through *Action*, and preparing for future positive interactions.

Starting Point for Negotiation

In *Satisfaction Selling*, the actual price discussion always occurs after the customer has emotionally committed. Therefore, potential negotiations of commercial terms and conditions are part of the *Compliance* stage. Negotiation serves to close the remaining gaps between the *Solution Experience* that the customer has accepted, and the actions required to realize it.

In *Satisfaction Selling*, the starting point for negotiation is unique. Both parties have already agreed on the outcome they aim to achieve through the negotiation. The customer wants to buy, and you have agreed to sell because both parties recognize the potential for a mutually rewarding outcome. This negotiation becomes feasible only after establishing a preliminary agreement:

"Let's proceed with this."

The negotiation then focuses primarily on the terms and conditions.

Our approach to negotiation within the *Satisfaction Cycle* is centered on securing the best possible outcome for all parties involved. A WIN/WIN outcome is the only truly successful option, embodying the plus-sum game mentality, as discussed in part 1 of the book. You continue to act as the *Trusted Advisor* for the customer, operating as a consultant to help them achieve what they want.

Points of Views in Negotiation

WIN/WIN negotiation requires both creativity and courage. You need creativity to find possibilities within feasible terms and conditions to achieve the best outcome for both parties. Holding your position with great courage is also essential, ensuring you don't settle for anything less than a WIN/WIN outcome. With courage, you refuse to accept compromises that typically result in a losing party, such as WIN/LOSE or LOSE/WIN scenarios. When you possess sufficient creativity and courage, you can maintain a stance where both parties achieve a positive outcome.

To communicate effectively throughout the negotiation, you must understand what is essential and valuable for all parties involved. Simply put, what benefits does the negotiation offer to the customer and to you from your respective perspectives? Achieving WIN/WIN requires holding three perceptual positions:

1. **First position**: Be mindful of your unique stance and what you aim to achieve, ensuring you don't compromise or relinquish something critical.

2. **Second position**: See the situation from the customer's viewpoint - understand what they value and their experience of the negotiation process.

3. **Third position**: Observe the situation externally, as if you were "a fly on the wall," watching the dynamics and communication between you and the customer unfold in real-time.

One strategy for creating a WIN/WIN situation is to evaluate the economic value of the negotiation subject. Remember, price is relative and only meaningful in context. Economic value concerns the worth a person attributes to the outcomes and benefits they gain from their expenditure. The *Satisfaction Cycle* facilitates the shift from price to perceived value, even during negotiations.

Prepare for Negotiation

Good negotiation starts with thorough preparation. The significance and scope of the negotiation dictate the depth and detail of your preparatory work. Consider these seven essential steps for negotiation preparation:

1. Always be in the *Green State*

Ensure that you are in the *Green State*, both during preparation and in the negotiation itself. This state ensures full access to creative ideas and possibilities.

2. Decide what you want to achieve

Clarity about your desired outcome provides a clear answer to the question, *"What will it take to achieve this?"* Creating a *Future Memory* of what it will feel like having completed the negotiation allows you to envision the path you took. Listing criteria for success enables you to measure progress along the way.

3. Know what the customer wants to achieve and what they value

Before negotiating, compile what you already know about the customer's objectives and expectations. If this information is unknown, use the negotiation process to uncover it.

4. Consider the interests and needs of all parties involved

Recognize the key stakeholders that are influencing the negotiation and who are able to make decisions. You should consider the motivations of the key people and why it would be important for them to reach an agreement.

5. Evaluate your own power and influence in the negotiation situation

The more there is a need to reach an agreement, the easier it is to get a WIN/WIN outcome. That is not always the case if the buyer has multiple options. The more you can put yourself into a unique position, the stronger you will be in the negotiation.

6. Prepare a BATNA (Best Alternative to a Negotiated Agreement)

The basic idea is to get WIN/WIN or walk away. The concept of BATNA refers to options available if you are not easily reaching a satisfactory outcome. You can prepare a Walking-In BATNA based on things you can influence and check before negotiations. During negotiation, BATNA becomes more dynamic as new information unfolds. Ultimately, you need to know how far you are willing to go before you walk away. When you are entirely confident about your boundaries in the negotiation, it becomes much easier to stand firm in the necessary areas and ensure WIN/WIN.

7. Define your negotiation strategy

Strategy involves setting a goal and devising a plan to achieve it. As an influential strategist, consider various paths to reach the ideal outcome.

With these steps, you are now prepared to negotiate successfully, aiming for a WIN/WIN outcome, or knowing when to step back and walk away.

Effective Behaviors for Negotiation

A skilled negotiator exhibits several behavioral characteristics. The principles we've discussed in the *Satisfaction Cycle* are still applicable. Effective negotiation, leading to a WIN/WIN outcome, is conducted within a positive framework. Here are some effective behaviors for successful negotiation:

- Start with assessing your own state and ensure that you are in the Green State

- Create an appropriate context that encourages all participants to adopt a highly positive mindset.

- Make sure you understand the desires and objectives of all parties involved before initiating the negotiation.

- Calibrate and track how people communicate and adapt your communication to match their communication style

- Use backtracking often to build on an agreement and clarify what is being agreed upon

- Initiate each step of the negotiation from common ground or a shared positive outcome (PS^+).

Fulfill Promises

When all the details for execution, including commercial terms and conditions, have been settled, it is time for you to deliver and fulfill the promises you have made to your customer. You should continue on the trajectory you have established and apply the principles of Satisfaction Selling to ensure satisfaction throughout the execution and implementation phases. The selling process does not end here. Sales conclude only when the customer has received what they desired.

As a *Trusted Advisor*, it is crucial to demonstrate accountability and discipline in delivering exactly what the customer expects, in the manner they anticipate. Throughout this process, your role includes consistently reassuring the customer that they will achieve their desired outcome. Selling this certainty is key to maintaining customer satisfaction.

During the sales process, you and the customer have outlined how they will recognize success. These success metrics may evolve over time. As you fulfill your promises, continue to demonstrate the impact on the customer's metrics of success.

In high-value complex sales, delivering and implementing the solution often involves many individuals. Here, exemplary leadership practices become essential, and recognizing the contributions of everyone involved in the project regularly is important. The *Satisfaction Cycle* offers a framework not only for selling but also for leading teams and managing projects effectively, as discussed in part 1 of the book.

Success as a New Beginning

When the customer has achieved their desired outcome, their DS^{++} transforms into a new PS^+. By facilitating this transition, you have proven yourself as a solution provider. The customer now recognizes all that works well for them, which may prompt them to consider further improvements that could be made in a potential new DS^{++}. The satisfaction derived from this transformation creates momentum for ongoing success.

Experiencing success presents an opportunity to reconnect with the customer and start to encourage a renewed interest in achieving a new DS^{++}, followed by *Recommitment* and, eventually, *Recompliance*. Over time, as this cycle repeats, another DS^{++} becomes the customer's new *PS*, leading to further development and ultimately turning the customer into your *Positive Activist*.

Compliance (Action)

Compliance involves taking the necessary actions after gaining the customer's commitment. It's about ensuring the agreed-upon steps are executed to achieve the desired outcomes.

Introduction to Compliance

- Focus on transitioning from commitment to action by outlining what needs to be done, negotiating terms & conditions, and setting a detailed execution plan

Establishing mutuality in actions means both you and the customer take steps towards fulfilling the agreement. This approach confirms compliance and moves the process forward.

Mutuality in Actions

What action will you take next?"

"How can we move forward together?"

- After the customer agrees to take the first step, communicate the Action you will take in response

Detailing the scope of what will be delivered, the price, commercial terms, and the execution timeline

Getting into Details

"What specific actions need to happen next?"

"What is our timeline and execution plan?"

- Define the specifics of the agreement, including what is and isn't included in the scope, the price range, and the detailed execution plan

Negotiation focuses on closing any remaining gaps between what the customer has accepted and what you want.

Starting Point for Negotiation

"How can we make this work for both of us?"

- Begin negotiations with a clear understanding of both parties' desired outcomes, focusing on achieving a WIN/WIN situation

Creativity and courage are essential for WIN/WIN negotiations, where both parties achieve a positive outcome without compromises

WIN/WIN Negotiation

- Use creativity to explore feasible terms and conditions for the best outcome and courage to hold your position for a WIN/WIN result

Understanding both your and the customer's needs and values, evaluating your power and influence, and preparing a BATNA (Best Alternative to a Negotiated Agreement).

Preparing for Negotiation

"What are our respective needs and how can we address them?"

- Ensure you're in the Green State and have a clear vision of your desired outcome
- Know the customer's goals, the stakeholders' motivations

Effective negotiation preparation involves understanding both your and the customer's needs and values, evaluating your power and influence.

Fulfilling Promises

"How will we ensure that we meet your expectations throughout the implementation process?"

- Maintain accountability and discipline in delivering what the customer expects, in the way they expect it

Once the customer achieves their DS++, this success becomes a new PS+, potentially leading to a new DS++. This creates an opportunity for ongoing engagement & more business.

Success as a new Beginning

"Now that we've achieved this goal, what's next on your horizon?"

- Use the completion of one cycle as an opportunity to identify new areas for improvement, giving a continuous cycle of success and further collaboration

Figure 16.1 Summary - Compliance (Action!)

EPILOGUE

As we draw the final curtain on our exploration of *Satisfaction Selling*, I, Henrik Wenøe, invite you to envision a future where the principles and methods we've discussed not only transform your approach to sales but also redefine the very fabric of your professional interactions.

A Legacy of Three Generations

This book stands as a testament to the dedication and innovation of three generations of *Satisfaction Cycle* enthusiasts.

First Generation: Dr. Joseph Riggio, the visionary behind the model, whose groundbreaking ideas in the 1990s laid the foundation for a sales approach that prioritizes genuine customer satisfaction and ethical engagement.

Second Generation: Myself, Henrik Wenøe, having immersed myself in the method initially as a sales and marketing leader for five years alongside my team, and subsequently dedicating the past two decades to leadership, sales training, and consulting for numerous international companies.

Third Generation: Virpi Varjonen, who seamlessly integrates the *Satisfaction Cycle* in her role as a country manager for an international company, utilizing it both in her leadership and as a sales methodology.

We hope you, dear reader, will become part of the fourth generation, championing a *Green* wave that transforms how businesses and organizations operate and engage with their customers.

The Integration of Mindset, Skills, and Ethics

Throughout this journey, you've seen that having the right mindset is crucial, but it alone is insufficient for achieving results. Similarly, focusing solely on skills can lead to unethical behavior. It's the synergy of the right mindset, effective strategies, and strong personal and social competencies that enables you to create real value for your customers, your company, and yourself.

The *Platinum Rule*

Many people advocate for the *Golden Rule* - treating others as you wish to be treated. However, we propose adopting the *Platinum Rule* - treating others as they wish to be treated. This subtle yet profound shift in perspective can significantly enhance your success in customer interactions, leading to more ultra-satisfied customers - *Positive Activists* - who advocate for your brand.

Our entire methodology is centered around taking the perspective of your customers - their situations, desires, and needs - to ensure a greater perceived value creation for them. Rather than focusing on your products and prices, it's about understanding and aligning with what truly matters to your customers. It is only when you can genuinely put yourself in your customer's place that you can create fantastic and meaningful buying experiences for them. This approach fosters deeper connections, stronger loyalty, and ultimately, a more successful and sustainable business.

Embracing Change and AI

We live in a dynamic world where change is the only constant. Since we began writing this book four years ago, another transformative force has emerged: Artificial Intelligence (AI). Experts suggest that AI will revolutionize our professional and personal lives. You have a choice: ignore AI and continue as before or embrace it and become part of the future. We believe that it won't be AI that outcompetes humans, but rather those who use AI wisely who will outcompete those who don't.

With the strategies and methods outlined in this book, you can develop the mindset and competencies to leverage AI effectively. *Satisfaction Selling,* combined with AI, can elevate your performance to unprecedented levels, benefiting your customers, yourself, and your stakeholders. AI can assist with administrative tasks such as emails, meeting notes, and proposal writing, freeing up more time for deep, meaningful dialogues with your customers to better understand their dreams and ambitions and create solutions that match them.

A Call for Action

Our ambition with this book has been to provide you with everything you need to start working with your customers in the *Green*, aiming for more enthusiastic customers (*Positive Activists*). While nothing prevents you from starting now, we are more than willing to assist you in implementing *Satisfaction Selling* and the *Satisfaction Cycle* in your organization. It would be our pleasure to help you spread our approach to more sales professionals globally. Our goal is to transform how we engage with customers and sales worldwide, believing it to be beneficial for you, your colleagues, your customers, your company, and all of us.

Let's create a *Greener* world!

Good luck with your work and your life ahead!

Henrik Wenøe

ABOUT THE AUTHORS

Dr. Joseph Riggio is the creator of the MythoSelf® Process, Soma-Semantic Modeling®, and the Satisfaction Cycle® model and the CEO and owner of ABTI | Joseph Riggio International. He holds a Ph.D. in Business Administration focused on leadership development and decision-making, and is a Master Trainer of NLP. With over three decades of experience, Joseph is renowned for his expertise in transformational change, metaphor, and storytelling. His innovative methodologies, including Persuasion Technology® and Negotiation Technology®, have been utilized by Fortune 100 companies and translated into multiple languages, underscoring his global influence. Joseph has mentored thousands of executives and professionals, recently focusing on helping entrepreneurs and small business owners become thought leaders and build successful practices. His published works, widely recognized and cited in academic and professional circles, reflect his deep expertise in applied mythology, decision-making, performance, sales, and leadership.

Virpi Varjonen, M.Sc. (Tech) in Industrial Management and Administration and B.Sc. (Eng) in Engineering (Biotechnology), is an experienced international business leader in the high-tech B2B market. She started her career 25 years ago as a development engineer, but soon moved into B2B business development and consulting before taking on roles in B2B sales, account management, and leadership. Virpi is a dynamic leader, renowned for her ability to inspire and elevate individuals, social systems, and businesses from a state of strength to one of excellence. Alongside her career, she has intensively trained in NLP and The MythoSelf® Process since 2017. She is a Certified New NLP™ Business Coach by Acuity World and a Licensed NLP Consultant by the Society of Neuro-Linguistic Programming.

Henrik Wenøe, B.Sc., with a diploma in sales and marketing, and a Master Trainer of NLP™ & NLP Consultant Trainer for Business, is the CEO and owner of Acuity World with over 30 years of experience in Sales & Marketing, Communication, and Leadership. Since 2000, he has professionally trained leaders and Sales & Marketing professionals worldwide and has co-authored several books on sales, leadership, communication, coaching, and personal development. Henrik specializes in designing and executing customized training programs for sales performance and communication and is the designer of the Personal Leadership Program – PLP™ and the Personal Selling Program - PSP™. He is also a MythoSelf™ Master Trainer and has been significantly influenced by Soma Semantic™ Modelling and The MythoSelf® Process, and he trains professionals globally in the Satisfaction Selling method and the Satisfaction Cycle®.

OUR BOOKS

We hope you have enjoyed reading *Satisfaction Selling*. To help you actively apply and implement the concepts from the book, we have compiled a list of further readings that provide additional insights and tools.

Towards a Theory of Trans-Personal Decision Making in Human Systems – Dr. Joseph Riggio

This book explores transpersonal decision-making, essential for leaders in human systems. It complements *Satisfaction Selling* by offering insights into making high-quality decisions.

The State of Perfection – Dr. Joseph Riggio

This book delves into the *MythoSelf Process*, providing a method to access and operate from the *Ready State* (the *Green State* in *Satisfaction Selling*). It offers tools for achieving extraordinary results and maintaining composure in challenging situations.

The Positive Activist – Henrik Wenøe & Jesper Lemmich

This book provides strategies to attract and develop enthusiastic customers, or *Positive Activists*, crucial for a profitable and sustainable business. It aligns with *Satisfaction Selling* by focusing on leading a sales team or global sales organization in a way that supports each salesperson in becoming a *Positive Activist*, enabling them to create value for your customers. It also offers insights into what is needed to make a funnel management system provide accurate information about future revenue.

Do What You Do Best! (Volume 1) – 4 Steps to Personal Leadership with New NLP™ – Henrik Wenøe & Jesper Lemmich

This book expands on the concept of starting from what is working, a central idea in *Satisfaction Selling*, to create long-term *Positive Activists* and loyal customers. It provides deeper insights into applying this approach in all aspects of life.

Do What You Do Best! (Volume 2) – The New NLP™ Book – Henrik Wenøe & Dr. Joseph Riggio

Building on the *Satisfaction Cycle* model introduced in *Satisfaction Selling*, this book offers a comprehensive set of communication tools to connect, engage, and move customers. It also covers applications in personal leadership, goal setting, coaching, consulting, sales, and negotiation.

Mental Fitness for Warriors – Henrik Wenøe & Erik Schwensen

Originating from a pilot project with the Danish Army, this book outlines strategies to enhance mental fitness, relevant for maintaining calm and optimal performance in stressful situations. It complements *Satisfaction Selling* by emphasizing the importance of mental resilience.

My PSP™ Meeting Book – Henrik Wenøe

A practical tool for sales professionals, this meeting book supports applying the *Satisfaction Cycle* model in daily customer interactions. It helps in preparing, conducting, and following up on meetings to create *Positive Activists* and super loyal customers.

STRENGTHENING YOUR BUSINESS WITH OUR EXPERTISE

We specialize in coaching, consulting, and training for entrepreneurs, executives, and sales and marketing professionals. With over thirty years of global training experience, we focus on large-scale sales training for SMEs and multinational corporations, empowering customers in more than ten languages to enhance their performance and success.

Our mission is to help our customers achieve high and sustainable performance by developing the right mindset and personal and social competencies. We accomplish this through leadership programs, sales training programs, and executive & personal coaching, utilizing innovative methods and *Systemic Blended Learning* to provide effective, immediately applicable tools and results.

Are you ready to implement the strategies and methods from *Satisfaction Selling* and turn your salespeople into *Trusted Advisors*, starting to build a movement of *Positive Activists*, using the *Satisfaction Cycle* in your daily life and business?

If you want and need more guidance or wish to leverage our expertise, we're here to assist you.

Visit our website (www.acuityworld.com) to learn more about how we can help you and your organization achieve your goals.

If you already know that you personally or that your team or organization wants and needs professional help with strategy and/or training and coaching, you can get in touch with us quickly and easily – just click this link, and we'll get started.

Click here for more information and resources

https://acuityworld.com/satisfactio n-selling-training/

Made in the USA
Columbia, SC
18 September 2024